THE LAST VOYAGE OF
USS PUEBLO

The
Last Voyage
of
USS Pueblo

ED BRANDT

W · W · NORTON & COMPANY · INC ·

NEW YORK

327
B73L

Author's Note

MY FIRST THOUGHT, when it became my good fortune to become involved in this project, was that it would be interesting to find out the truth of the matter. Later, it became plain that even knowing the truth in the case of the USS *Pueblo* did not answer all of the questions.

I was much impressed by the character of the men of the *Pueblo*. They are young, mostly, and like other young people live life to its fullest. But they were willing to risk death if their leader so ordered, and their remorse at their own failures was boundless. And it continues.

They have restored in me the faith that there remains in this country a great reservoir of strength. Among the crew of the *Pueblo*, honor was lost, but it was found; tradition was breached, but it prevails; and patriotism was forgotten, but it returned. In some ways the men came out stronger than they went in, and so did the country, which lost its honor and its tradition, but kept its composure and regained what it had lost.

Before you judge the country and the men in their failure and their success, please ask yourself one question: What would you have done?

Among the many who helped in the preparation of this book, my special thanks go to certain members of the crew of the *Pueblo*. They are Tim Harris, Charlie Law, Stuart Russell, Chuck Ayling, Don McClarren, Vic Escamilla, Mike O'Bannon, Don Bailey, Jimmy Layton, Angelo Strano, Jimmy Shepard, Larry Mack, Frank Ginther, Steve Woelk, and Robert Hammond.

Of special help in the preparation of the manuscript were Lawrence H. Hirsch, Robert C. Ramage, George Linyear, Carl McAfee, Charles Daniels, Marcee Rethwish, and Robert W. Ayling.

ED BRANDT

July, 1969, Virginia Beach, Va.

THE LAST VOYAGE OF
USS PUEBLO

One

I T WAS LATE ON THE COLD, clear night of January 22, 1968, in Washington, D.C., when Walt W. Rostow, special assistant for national security affairs to the President of the United States, began to dress hurriedly in his home at 3414 Lowell Street, Northwest.

As a White House car drove quickly through the quiet streets toward his home, Rostow, considered to be a hawk on foreign policy, turned over in his mind the information he had just received in an urgent call from the Situation Room in the White House.

The USS *Pueblo*, an oceanographic and research ship, had been attacked and boarded in the Sea of Japan by naval units of the North Korean People's Army. Rostow, a graduate of Yale University and a former history professor at Massachusetts Institute of Technology, had been in his present job long enough to be used to late-at-night emergencies. But this one sounded particularly bad, and he wanted to check all the available facts before notifying the President.

Upon arriving at the White House, Rostow went straight to the Situation Room, which had received word of the trouble shortly after 10 P.M. The report was sketchy but chilling. The *Pueblo* had been a few miles off the North Korean port of Wonsan when it was approached by several hostile ships about noon January 23, Korean time, which is fourteen hours ahead of Eastern Standard Time. The *Pueblo* had been fired upon and four of its crew had been wounded. Then North Korean soldiers had boarded the ship, which had offered no resistance.

The rest was silence. Abruptly, the *Pueblo* had ended radio transmission to Kamiseya, a large relay station in Japan.

The report seemed incredible, but Rostow found himself believing it. He immediately called the headquarters of the U.S.

commander in chief, Pacific, to find out what, if any, counter-moves had been made.

He jotted down the information and hung up the overseas phone. Then he assembled his notes, picked up an inside phone, and dialed the extension of President Lyndon B. Johnson.

The ringing woke the President. He listened without comment while Rostow told what he had learned. Then the President said, "Thank you," as was his custom, and hung up.

Apparently no military decisions were to be made immediately. It was too late for that. But, in a few minutes, phones began to ring all over Washington.

Two

Ensign Timothy L. Harris was just dozing off as the USS *Pueblo* backed slowly from its berth in India Basin. Harris wasn't feeling well. He had started the last night in port early and had ended it late—so late that he barely made it back to the ship in time for sailing.

He need not have hurried quite so much. Many of the *Pueblo* crew had spent the last night in Sasebo, a friendly Navy town on the west coast of the island of Kyushu in Japan. Good Japanese whiskey sold for a quarter a shot, Japanese beer went for sixty cents a quart, and there were plenty of friendly girls. Harris had encountered many of his shipmates from time to time on the streets and in the bars of Sasebo. Because of some late arrivals aboard, the *Pueblo* left its berth exactly five minutes after its scheduled starting time of 6 A.M. on January 11, 1968.

It had been an exciting last night ashore for Harris. Twice he had been challenged by the Shore Patrol after the curfew hour of 1 A.M., and twice he had talked his way out of trouble. Shortly after the second incident, he was eating a hamburger in a small restaurant when a Shore Patrol wagon pulled up in front. Harris ran out the back door, leaving his half-eaten hamburger on the plate, and stood in the alley until the two Shore Patrolmen left the restaurant. He could see through a crack in the door that they were the same two who had stopped him before.

Harris, age twenty-one, had won his commission after Naval Reserve training at Jacksonville University in Jacksonville, Florida, and had joined the *Pueblo* in Bremerton, Washington, in August, 1967, as supply officer. He had fit right in. The skipper of the *Pueblo*, Lieutenant Commander Lloyd M. Bucher, took Harris under his wing immediately, and the two spent many pleasant evenings ashore together while the *Pueblo* was being outfitted.

An ex-submarine officer, Bucher was in command of his first ship. Five feet, ten inches tall and squarely built, he was overweight at 215 pounds at the start of the cruise. He was considered not only a competent officer but also a normal man who liked to have fun ashore when the day's work was completed.

The *Pueblo*'s men for the most part followed their dark-haired, graying skipper's lead. They worked hard and they played hard. On January 10, 1968, the last night before sailing, nearly half the men were playing hard. Some drifted back to the ship early, including one who came back to borrow money. He collected some, but it took him so long that he needed it all to pay off the cabbie. Another came back, still half-scared by what had happened to him. He had gotten drunk and stepped into what he thought was a taxicab. It was a police car, but he took off before the startled Japanese policeman could recover.

Others defied the curfew and went to Saki Town, a section of small bars and savvy bar girls. The girls knew a great deal about ship movements, and a couple of the men found out they were to be back in port the first week in February. They made dates for February 5.

Although some information had leaked out on the *Pueblo*'s role, the men were cautious in discussions of the ship with outsiders. Many of the crew didn't know the *Pueblo*'s mission, but they had been warned by Bucher not to discuss the *Pueblo* at all. At the same time, Bucher had told them they would be doing nothing illegal on their mission or anything of which they would be ashamed.

The *Pueblo* had started her career as the FS 344, a light cargo ship used by the U.S. Army to carry supplies to South Pacific islands near the end of World War II and afterward. Theater fans later saw an amazing similarity between it and the USS *Reluctant*, the supply ship in the movie *Mr. Roberts*. After ten years the FS 344 was taken out of service and loaned to the South Korean government. In 1966 it was brought to the Puget Sound Naval Shipyard in Bremerton, where conversion began on July 5.

On May 13, 1967, it was brought back into service in a joint commissioning ceremony with its sister ship, the USS *Palm Beach*. The foreword in the program issued for the commissioning ceremony read:

The commissioning ceremony marks the initiation of service of a ship of the operating forces of the United States Navy. At the moment of breaking their commissioning pennants, the USS *Pueblo* (AKL 44) and USS *Palm Beach* (AKL 45) become the responsibility of their respective Commanding Officers, LCDR Lloyd M. Bucher, U.S. Navy, and LCDR Albert D. Raper, U.S. Navy, who, together with their Ship's Company, then have the duty of making and keeping their ship constantly ready for any service demanded by our country in peace or war.

The commissioning program offered other information that bore the seeds of irony. Installed aboard the *Pueblo*, it said, was the most modern equipment available for technical operations to support oceanographic, electromagnetic, and related research projects. "The *Pueblo*," it said, "joins the fleet proudly in the knowledge that the research operations that she will conduct will be an aid to the Navy and mankind toward the complete understanding of the oceans and the improvement of the Naval Communications System."

Statistically, the program noted that the 906-ton *Pueblo* was 176 feet, 6 inches long; had a beam of 32 feet; and was propelled by two 500-horsepower Gentral Motors diesels that turned twin screws for a speed of 12 knots.

Two pages in the program were devoted to Bucher. One was a full-page picture of him. The other gave a brief background. He was born on September 1, 1929, the son of the late Mr. and Mrs. A. William Bucher of Pocatello, Idaho.

He graduated from Boys Town High School, Boys Town, Nebraska. Following two years' enlisted service in the U.S. Navy, where he attained the rate of quartermaster second class, he attended and graduated from the University of Nebraska.

The program noted that Bucher had been commissioned in June, 1953; listed various assignments, including one to Submarine School in 1955 and the various submarines he served on; and said he was married to the former Rose Delores Rohling of Jefferson City, Missouri, and had two sons, Mark Stephen, fourteen, and Michael Francis, twelve.

But those who knew Pete Bucher well felt there was a good deal more to the man. And they knew there were at least one inaccuracy and several omissions in the program's account. Pete Bucher had been born to Nola and Harold Baxter, not to the Buchers. His mother had died in childbirth, and at the age of one he had been adopted by Mr. and Mrs. Austin William Bucher of Pocatello. Mrs. Bucher died about a year later;* thereafter, life became a series of orphanages for the child. Finally, in September, 1941, Bucher arrived in Boys Town as a freshman and quickly established himself as a good student and a likable personality. He played tackle in football and was considered tough and aggressive despite his size. He then weighed 165 pounds.

He joined the Navy after graduating from Boys Town in 1944, served two years, then quit and went to Lewiston, Idaho, and worked as a bartender. Later he went to Omaha, Nebraska, and became a construction worker. He enrolled in the University of Nebraska in 1949, working part time for a railroad, and during a Nebraska-Missouri football weekend that fall he met Miss Rohling. They married the following spring.

But there was even more to Pete Bucher than that, his friends knew. He loved to read and write poetry. He liked to paint. He told a joke well, and the party never really got cranked up until Pete Bucher arrived. He was a self-taught, self-made man with wide interests and an inquiring mind.

If the program notes on Bucher were incomplete, they were equally inadequate about the *Pueblo*. That phrase about aid to mankind wasn't what the Navy had in mind when it began putting into service ships like the *Pueblo, Palm Beach, Liberty*, and *Banner;* and the *Pueblo* was an excellent example of exactly what

* Mr. Bucher died in a veteran's hospital in Walla Walla, Washington, in the mid-forties.

the Navy did have in mind.

When the *Pueblo* emerged from the shipyard across Puget Sound from Seattle, most of its equipment was unsuited for environmental research, even though it was shortly designated an auxiliary general environmental research ship, or AGER 2. Eight antennas poked into the sky from its superstructure, and below the main deck, just forward of the pilot house, was a locked room full of electronic gear.

Some of the crew saw the equipment come aboard in crates that remained unopened until hidden away below decks. Specialists from Ling-Temco-Vought company in Houston, Texas, spent months installing and testing the equipment.

The gear included two $60,000 tape recorders and another piece of equipment worth more than $150,000. Altogether, the equipment jammed into the Sod Hut, the unclassified code name for the research space, and into the cryptographic center in an adjoining room cost more than $2 million.

The *Pueblo* was equipped to listen in on anything in or under the water or in the air that transmitted messages by radio, and it was able to reach far inland to pluck radio and radar emissions for its recorders. The tapes were to be forwarded to U.S. security agencies on the *Pueblo*'s return from a mission. Its own sending gear was the finest that U.S. industry and the U.S. Navy could devise.

Also aboard were "the Spooks," the communications technicians under the command of Lieutenant Stephen R. Harris, thirty, of Melrose, Massachusetts, a quiet, reserved Harvard graduate and ex-destroyerman who spoke several languages fluently, including Russian. The Spooks were communications technicians, CT's, given the slang name because they were secretive and mysterious about their work. Of the thirty CT's who eventually were to man the research space, only four had been to sea before.

Despite their lack of sea experience, the CT's were the heart of the *Pueblo*. Among their complement were some of the top men in their various electronic fields.

By the time the *Pueblo* was ready to leave Bremerton in early September 1967, all its officers had reported for duty. Besides

Bucher, Tim Harris, and Steve Harris, there were Lieutenant Carl F. Schumacher, twenty-four, of St. Louis, Missouri, the operations officer; Chief Warrant Officer Gene H. Lacy, thirty-six, of Seattle, the engineering officer; and Lieutenant Edward R. Murphy, thirty, of San Diego, California, the executive officer. They were a strange mixture. Stephen Harris, Schumacher, and Murphy had strong religious backgrounds. Schumacher planned to enter the ministry after his Navy service, and Murphy was a Christian Scientist. Lacy, a solid Navy veteran with more than twenty years of experience, was a close companion of Bucher's; he mixed his religion and his fun in unequal parts. Tim Harris hid a sharp mind behind a carefree, laughing front. He was ready to join in the fun, but he admitted he sometimes had difficulty keeping up with the indefatigable captain of the *Pueblo*, at work or play.

Finally, the *Pueblo* was ready to sail from Bremerton, and on September 12 it left for San Francisco. It had hardly departed before the crew found out something about their skipper. He was a sportsman.

Just before leaving Bremerton, he had sent James D. Layton, twenty-five, of Binghamton, New York, a CT, to the Navy Exchange with a blank check. Bucher had discovered that Layton was a hunter and fisherman and knew something about salmon fishing. Layton bought some salmon rigs from the Exchange while two other crewmen went to a bait shop near the shipyard and bought some herring. As the *Pueblo* moved south along the coast, it idled off the mouth of the Columbia River. Bucher and half a dozen crewmen fished for a couple of hours, but it was windy and the *Pueblo* drifted too fast for the bait to get down deep enough. The luck was all bad.

The *Pueblo* made up for it later when it lay to off San Diego and Layton and two other crewmen threw a big meathook over the side baited with a chunk of beef from the galley and caught a huge shark. Layton wanted to bring it aboard, take out the teeth, and give them to the crewmen as souvenirs, but Bucher didn't want it on the deck. He pumped bullets into it with a carbine until the hook tore out of its mouth.

The ship stopped for a few days in San Francisco on the way

south, long enough for Tim Harris and Bucher to take a drive through Haight-Ashbury, and for two members of the crew to risk court-martial. Bucher was interested in the hippie movement. The two crewmen were interested in seeing the sights, too, and spent a day cruising the shops and bars of Chinatown. While leaving one shop, one of the men accidentally walked smack into a girl and knocked her flat. Fortunately, she had a friend with her. After the four had had a couple of drinks together, one of the sailors invited the girls on a post-midnight tour of the *Pueblo*. One couple found their way to the flying bridge, and by 1 A.M. the two were snuggled up and making love in the captain's chair, which had a cushion and padded arms and could be put in a reclining position.

That it was a court-martial offense even to sit in the captain's chair went unmentioned. Perhaps the crewman thought it was poetic justice anyway. The chair had been stolen from a Navy building in Bremerton.

The other officers, too, were having fun. Two of them found an English racing bicycle and brought it aboard one night. They pedaled it around the quarterdeck, then detailed the watch to stand guard over it. The watch, who was serving on his first ship, thought the Navy was going to be a lot of fun, even though he had gotten seasick on the first day out from Bremerton.

Seasickness was one of several problems that began to crop up. The *Pueblo* was in fairly good working condition because it had just been converted, and it was easily maneuvered. But it rolled heavily—some said thirty-five or forty degrees in rough seas—and many became seasick.

There were problems with the electronic gear in the Sod Hut. Senior Chief Petty Officer Ralph D. Bouden, forty, of Nampa, Idaho; Angelo S. Strano, twenty-two, of Hartford, Connecticut; and Charles W. Ayling, twenty-one, of Staunton, Virginia, were charged with maintaining the cryptographic and Sod Hut equipment, and they worked long hours trying to get it straight. There was a heavy burden on Strano, in particular, since he was the only one aboard who knew how to operate all the equipment. Strano had joined the Navy in 1964 after graduating from Buckley High School in Hartford and was on his first sea duty, but he was a well-trained technician who had worked at some of the Navy's most highly classified installations. He was also well trained in destruction techniques.

In Bremerton, he had helped to rip out installed equipment after a Navy specialist came aboard and pointed out faults in the placing of the gear. Strano mourned the $150,000 alteration cost and wondered why the Navy hadn't called on the people who had to work with the equipment when it had had the research room designed.

Strano was especially concerned with the major piece of equipment in the Sod Hut; its function was to pick up radar emissions for analysis. While most of his mates were looking forward to San Diego as a good liberty town, Strano was looking forward to working with some technicians who were to meet the ship there and help him with the major piece, which was one of the few second-hand pieces in the research space.

The equipment was a constant worry to Lieutenant Stephen Harris, also. Unless it was working properly, the *Pueblo* was useless.

The *Pueblo* arrived in San Diego on September 22 and tied up at the Antisubmarine Warfare Piers. Bucher planned to stay about six weeks and spend the time training the crew. By this time the men knew a good deal more about Bucher, and while they considered him entirely competent as a skipper, they didn't like some of his methods.

The research section under Steve Harris was assigned to the *Pueblo* as a detachment—that is, the communications technicians were supposed to go about their business and leave the ship's operation to the ship's regular complement. But Bucher demanded that they help keep the *Pueblo* shipshape as well as work in the research space. Aside from disliking the manual labor involved, the CT's thought this interfered with their training. Bucher also required his senior enlisted men to work as seamen, and a petty officer shining brass is an unhappy man. Bucher overrode all objections and on several occasions told dissenters he wanted "the cleanest ship in the Navy."

But, once the ship was in port again, all this was forgotten, and the frolicsome atmosphere returned. A tape recording of

Herb Alpert's "The Lonely Bull" was played over the general announcing system whenever the *Pueblo* went out on training missions and it became the trademark of the ship. There were cruises
for the men's families, and there were the beckoning lights of
San Diego to keep the spirits up.

On one pleasant but long evening, a junior officer, egged on
by his superiors, vaulted a bar in an officers club and yanked off
the wall a four-by-five-foot picture of a nude woman. He ran outside, threw the picture in the trunk of his rented car, and took
off for the ship. His shipmates followed, laughing, in another
car, and the small cavalcade almost ran down the quartermaster
of the *Pueblo* as he went through the gate to the ASW Piers.

The stocky, broad-chested quartermaster, Charles B. Law,
Jr., twenty-six, of Chehalis, Washington, was indignant and complained to the officers when he got to the ship.

The *Pueblo* didn't get the last laugh in the picture incident,
however. A shore-based lieutenant junior grade came aboard
and somehow unscrewed the ship's plaque from a bulkhead on
an inside passageway and made off with it. The big bronze
plaque had been given to the ship by the people of Pueblo, Colo-
rado, after which the ship was named.

The inscription on the plaque wished the crew good luck and
smooth sailing.

The next day an officer from the Office of Naval Intelligence
called the ship and demanded that the picture of the nude woman
be returned. It went back to its place above the bar. A few days
later, the plaque was returned to the ship.

On November 6, 1967, the *Pueblo* left San Diego for Pearl
Harbor, Hawaii, and soon ran into trouble. The steering mechanism was old, and the contacts in its electrical system became
corroded. The system failed continually, and the ship frequently
had to be steered manually from the pilot house. This was one
more annoyance for Bucher, who also learned that the CT's were
having trouble with the equipment in the Sod Hut. Bucher could
get the steering mechanism repaired eventually, but he wondered
whether the electronic problems could ever be solved.

Practically everyone was getting seasick from the heavy roll,
and the crew's lack of sea experience began to show. Only about

half the men were career-designated. The rest were reservists
and short-termers who were merely discharging their service
obligations. They appeared to be reasonably competent, and the
crew as a whole was well above average in intelligence, mainly
because of the CT's aboard. But beneath the thin layer of talented
senior men was a depth of inexperience.

Bucher as usual found a way to lighten the burden. The
Pueblo slowed occasionally on its way across the Pacific while he
fired a .45-caliber pistol from the flying bridge at garbage thrown
overboard for target purposes. And, just before entering Pearl
Harbor, the *Pueblo* lay to while the crew took a swim in the
ocean. Brandy was passed out afterward for medicinal purposes
in case anyone had suffered overexposure in the warm waters.

The *Pueblo* arrived in Pearl Harbor on November 14 and remained four days. During this period Bucher discussed his mission with the head of the operations department on the staff of the
commander in chief, Pacific Fleet. Bucher was advised by this
officer that if the *Pueblo* was harassed and in need of assistance,
such assistance might not arrive as quickly as Bucher would like,
but that plans for retaliatory action did exist.

Bucher was promoted to commander while at Pearl Harbor,
and his friends thought that he had made remarkable progress for
a man without a Naval Academy background. He had just turned
thirty-eight.

The *Pueblo* left Pearl Harbor on November 18 for its home
port of Yokosuka, Japan; and since the brandy supply had been
replenished, there was another swimming party on the way out.
But that was the end of the fun for a while.

The *Pueblo* ran into a severe storm about four days out of
Yokosuka, and some in the crew said the ship rolled as much as
forty-five degrees. Others said that it would have capsized with
such a roll but agreed that it had been bad. It was certainly bad
for the CT's in the research space. Their chairs weren't riveted
down and the heavy rolls frequently sent them sliding away from
their equipment and, on occasion, turned them over. It was bad
for Jimmy Layton. He was transmitting a message at the height of
the storm when a Webster's dictionary fell off a shelf and conked
him on the head.

By now, the CT's were angry enough with their situation to try to do something about it. They still couldn't understand why the Navy had sent them to join the *Pueblo* in Bremerton in May in the first place. Except for a trip to San Diego in August to attend fire-fighting school, they had sat and done practically nothing until September, when the equipment in the research space was ready, and now they felt they were being worked to death for the sake of the ship's cleanliness. Between their earlier inactivity and the current work load Bucher had put on them, they felt they had lost touch with their main function, and they were rusty at it.

They went to Lieutenant Harris seeking relief, but he didn't seem to want to get involved. He said he would try to do something about the situation, but the CT's knew he wouldn't. They called a meeting and invited Bucher. Layton asked how he, as a first class petty officer, could convince seamen to remain in the Navy when the seamen could see a first class cleaning a passageway. He told Bucher it hurt incentive.

Bucher replied: "I don't care about incentive. I want the ship kept clean."

That was the end of it.

Lieutenant Harris didn't attend the meeting, and neither he nor Bucher came out of it well in the eyes of the Spooks.

The *Pueblo* arrived at Yokosuka on December 1. There was much work to be done. The *Pueblo*'s engines were old and balky. Although Chief Engineman Monroe O. Goldman, thirty-six, of Lakewood, California, and Engineman First Class Rushel J. Blansett, thirty-four, of Orange, California, did an excellent job of keeping them running, they had trouble maintaining fuel pressure because of faulty regulators. The engines had to be overhauled at a shipyard in Yokosuka.

It was a busy time for Bucher, too. While in Yokosuka he received orders to install two .50-caliber machine guns, one on the starboard bow, the other on the superstructure aft. A third mount, but no machine gun, was placed on the port bow. The machine guns had been ordered placed on all intelligence ships after the Israelis attacked the USS *Liberty*, a sister ship of the *Pueblo*, off the coast of Egypt in the summer of 1967. At least one *Pueblo* man, Ensign Tim Harris, was happy to see the guns aboard. He hadn't felt quite right serving on a Navy ship with no guns and had remarked to another officer in Bremerton that the *Pueblo* "looks just like a damn Russian fishing trawler."

Bucher ordered fifty of his crew to the Marine training range, to fire the type of gun installed on the *Pueblo*, and then discovered that his own gunner's mate, Kenneth R. Wadley, twenty-nine, of Beaverton, Oregon, was not familiar with the operation of the guns, which had been borrowed from the Army.

Bucher was not entirely pleased with the guns. He thought their presence might give the *Pueblo* a more aggressive appearance. Nor did he believe they would be of much use in case of attack.

But he was more concerned with the research equipment than he was with the guns. He wanted a destruction system installed on the equipment in case the ship was overwhelmed by hostile fire, and he sought fifty-pound cans of TNT. Thermite bombs, which when activated would burn right through the equipment, were considered too dangerous by Bucher, and the TNT cans were unavailable, so the *Pueblo* remained without a destruction system.

But, if the *Pueblo* didn't get such a system, it was to get a bit of supposedly preventive medicine in the form of a human early-warning system. On January 3, 1968, two Marine sergeants from a Navy security group at Kamiseya, thirteen miles from Yokohama reported aboard the ship still wearing their Marine uniforms. They were Robert J. Hammond, twenty-two, of Claremont, New Hampshire, and Robert J. Chicca, twenty-four, of Hyattsville, Maryland. Both were on temporary assigned duty to the *Pueblo*, and both had already complained bitterly to their superiors about the assignment. Each had a pregnant wife. Hammond's red-haired wife, Hazel, not only was suffering severely from morning sickness but was desperately concerned about their baby daughter, seriously ill in a hospital near Yokohama.

There was an even better reason for their not joining the *Pueblo*. Hammond and Chicca had been classmates at the Defense Language Institute at Monterey, California, for nine months and had graduated in 1965 after a course in the Korean language.

But they hadn't used their Korean since then. When they received the assignment to join the *Pueblo*, they told their Navy superiors they couldn't possibly help the ship since they couldn't understand the language unless it was spoken slowly, and then not well. They also told Commander Bucher, but Bucher had no choice but to take them, and the Navy wasn't worrying about it. Their service records said they spoke and could understand Korean.

Chicca and Hammond were to split the day into eight-hour shifts, monitoring North Korean radio traffic around the clock when the *Pueblo* reached its operational area. If the *Pueblo* was depending on Chicca and Hammond for warning in case of an impending attack, the *Pueblo* was out of luck.

Four other CT's joined the *Pueblo* from Kamiseya with Chicca and Hammond. They were Don E. Bailey, thirty-six, of Portland, Indiana; James F. Kell, thirty-one, of Culver City, California; Ralph McClintock, twenty-three, of Milton, Massachusetts; and David L. Ritter, twenty-three, of Union City, California.

McClintock and Kell had volunteered for the mission. McClintock's friends had told him he was crazy because the trip was dangerous. Kell volunteered to replace a chief petty officer who was due to be transferred and whose replacement had not yet arrived. Kell was just going on this one mission. McClintock replaced a man who had appendicitis.

Bailey, a veteran and a highly knowledgeable communications specialist, found himself on the *Pueblo* because he was too conscientious. The large relay station at Kamiseya had had trouble picking up the *Pueblo*'s transmissions after it left Hawaii, and Bailey thought the problem was with the crypto people on the *Pueblo*. They knew their job well when operating from land, but perhaps didn't understand that transmission at sea was different and a good deal more difficult. Bailey, from his shore post at Kamiseya, figured out what they were doing wrong and finally raised them. Then he suggested to his superiors that they send on the mission for training purposes someone who understood the problems from both sides. Bailey got the assignment.

The *Pueblo*'s crew now consisted of seventy-five enlisted men, including the two Marines; six officers; and two civilian oceanographers, Dunnie R. Tuck, thirty, of Richmond, Virginia, and Harry Iredale III, twenty-four, of Holmes, Pennsylvania.

Tuck and Iredale were assigned to the ship from the U.S. Oceanographic Office in Suitland, Maryland. They had legitimate assignments for collecting oceanographic data off the coast of North Korea. But they were, essentially, aboard the *Pueblo* as cover for the ship's real mission. (A ship of the *Pueblo*'s size on an oceanographic research mission normally would operate with a crew of less than thirty men.)

Word spread quickly through the ship that the two Marines aboard spoke Korean. To many of the crew it was the first real clue as to where the *Pueblo* was going. All the officers, as well as Quartermaster Law and Signalman Wendell G. Leach, twenty-five, of Houston, Texas, knew by now the ship's destination and mission. For ten days they were briefed each afternoon on Russian, Chinese, and North Korean ships that might be sighted. They were to identify such ships as they encountered and to report on any radar or other electronic gear visible. They were also informed of one type of shore radar of special interest to the Navy.

But even with all the work there was fun as usual aboard the *Pueblo*. Members of the engine-room crew, tied down by the balky equipment, had stocked up on liquor to keep them going. Stored behind a panel on an air conditioner in a space next to the Sod Hut were bottles of Japanese beer, a fifth of sloe gin, a pint of Seagram's 7, a fifth of Ancient Age, a fifth of Smirnoff vodka, two cans of frozen orange juice, three quarts of Japanese wine, and seven miniatures of brandy.

In a corner of the same room were stacked several guitars, including one worth $500 owned by Fireman Steven E. Woelk, nineteen, of Alta Vista, Kansas. The engine-room crew, anyway, was ready for a party.

In fact, there was at least one party aboard. On New Year's Eve some of the crewmen with duty crowded into the Boatswain's gear locker and toasted in 1969.

Yokosuka, on the west side of Kyushu, is not considered by Navymen quite as warm and friendly as Sasebo, but the men of the *Pueblo* had a knack for making a home everywhere they went, and Yokosuka was no exception.

One morning about nine o'clock, members of the crew on deck were surprised to see a Japanese woman emerge from below, stroll calmly down the length of the ship to the bow, then step across the bow onto the USS *Banner*, moored inboard, and onto the bow of the *Winnebago*, a Coast Guard cutter, and from there onto the pier. It was confirmed by the watch that she had come aboard the *Pueblo* at 3 A.M., and the *Pueblo* crew took a great deal of ribbing from the *Banner*'s crew about the incident.

The *Pueblo* crew, growing daily more savvy about the ship's mission, heard other things from the *Banner*, which had been on several intelligence missions in the general area in preceding months.

The *Banner* had undergone considerable harassment from Soviet ships, and on one occasion had been signaled: "Heave to, or I will fire on you." The *Pueblo* crew learned that the *Banner* had been lightly brushed by a Russian destroyer on one occasion, and that once it had been surrounded by Chinese fishing boats, their guns trained on the American ship. The story went that the captain of the *Banner*, Commander Charles R. Clark, got out of that predicament by pointing his ship at the nearest boat and ordering full speed ahead. If the stories worried the men of the *Pueblo*, they didn't let on, although there was some joking about the North Koreans throwing a line on the ship and towing it into Wonsan Harbor.

Late in December the *Pueblo* received a vital message from ComNavFor, Japan. It contained the ship's operational orders and the first official word, with detailed instructions, on the mission. The order was taken to Lieutenant Harris, who took it to Commander Bucher. Essentially, the order was for the *Pueblo* to proceed through Tsushima Strait to a point just off the North Korean–Russian border and about opposite the Russian port of Vladivostok, cruise thirteen to fifteen miles off the coast, then turn south and cruise at the discretion of the captain. Shortly thereafter the *Pueblo* received a message outlining its operations until June. The ship was to return to Sasebo early in February, remain in port for a couple of weeks, then return to monitor Vladivostok. Another trip in May would take the *Pueblo* farther north.

The CT's were briefed on their immediate goal, and some wondered what the point was. They were surprised that the United States would waste so much time and effort on North Korea because they didn't believe that country had much intelligence information to offer. Some decided the trip was principally a training mission, and not a very worthwhile one.

If there were similar notions in Bucher's head, he didn't voice them. Despite the strain of getting the ship ready, he was the same as always when the day's work was over. A hard driver aboard ship, he was just the opposite to his crew ashore. It was not uncommon for him to wander into the enlisted men's club wearing a wide-brimmed straw hat and a wild-colored print shirt, sit down with some of his crewmen, and buy a round of drinks. And he could frequently be seen in the nightclub, next to the piano, his arm draped over a friendly shoulder and singing an old favorite in a clear, strong voice.

He was always ready to help a shipmate in trouble. In San Diego he had gotten out of bed at 3 A.M. and gone downtown to rescue three crewmen arrested by the Shore Patrol for improper dress. Among other things, he called the patrolmen Nazis. One night in Yokosuka a crewman knocked on his door and asked to borrow money. Bucher gave him what he asked for. The next day the same crewman apologized. He complained that the captain shouldn't have given him the money. Bucher's only comment was that the crewman had left the ship too quickly. Bucher had wanted to go with him.

On January 5, 1968, the *Pueblo* left Yokosuka. It sailed around the southern end of the island of Honshu and arrived in Sasebo on the 9th. It was an eventful trip. Sergeant Hammond got seasick on the first day out, as did other members of the crew, and Bucher tried out the ship's new armament himself, taking a turn at the .50-caliber machine guns. And there was serious trouble below decks.

The *Pueblo* was equipped with two generators of one hundred kilowatts each in the main engine room for operation of the ship itself, and two sixty-kilowatt generators in the auxiliary engine room to run the equipment on the research space. There also was a twenty-five-kilowatt generator in the auxiliary engine room for emergency use. On the way to Sasebo one of the research-space generators developed trouble with its governor, and a chain on the other 60-kilowatt generator snapped and wrapped itself around a shaft, putting the generator out of action. Fireman Michael A. O'Bannon, twenty-one, of Beaverton, Oregon, a naval reservist on his first sea assignment, took the governor off the inoperative generator and put it on the other one. When the *Pueblo* arrived in Sasebo he and other members of the engine-room crew went to the U.S. Naval Shipyard for the $600 worth of parts needed to repair the broken generator, but the parts were unavailable.

Bucher told the enginemen the *Pueblo* would have to sail with the generator out. The ship had a job to do, Bucher said, and the enginemen would have to do the best they could.

Also doing the best he could while the ship lay over in Sasebo was Victor DeLeon Escamilla, twenty-six, of Amarillo, Texas. Escamilla was an inner communications specialist and a first-generation American. His father, Alfredo, was a Mexican citizen. A second class petty officer, Escamilla was one of the relatively few aboard with sea experience, having served on the destroyer *H. R. Dickson* for more than two years. Commander Bucher, concerned about the shipboard communications system, thought it ironic that despite millions of dollars' worth of communications and other electronic equipment stored in the research space, the *Pueblo* was pitifully weak in its own communications. Escamilla was set to work supplementing the sound-powered telephone system with a second, less comprehensive system. Only one party at a time could use the installed system. Escamilla, with Steve Woelk's help, was stringing wire to eight stations on the new system. In between, he was installing an intercom between the flying bridge and the pilot house that Bucher also wanted. Neither system was ever completed.

There was minor friction among the officers. Bucher rode Lieutenant Murphy on some security clearance papers, and Murphy had to stay up all one night to do the paperwork. Bucher made it plain to Steve Harris who was running the ship and everyone on it, regardless of their status. Harris withdrew from the fray early although he was unhappy when Bucher persisted in bringing his Navy friends into the research space to show them around without presenting their clearance papers to Harris. They didn't have clearance papers anyway. One day Bucher walked into the space with friends while Harris was talking to some CT's. Harris said they had some highly classified material out that they were studying. Bucher said: "Okay, put it away and I'll be back in five minutes."

Bucher ran the ship the way he pleased. If Harris and Murphy objected, they weren't strong enough to do anything about it.

While in Sasebo, the *Pueblo* was receiving reconnaissance reports on two Russian ships in Tsushima Strait, the corridor between the island of Kyushu and South Korea. One Soviet ship was a Rigel-class destroyer, the other a tanker. They were cruising between the South Korean port of Pusan and Sasebo, apparently watching ship movements in both ports. The *Pueblo* would try to slip out of Sasebo without the Soviet ships' detecting it.

For Seaman Third Class Stuart Russell, twenty-four, of Glendale, California, one of the two college graduates among the enlisted men, there was one ominous note. Russell was scrubbing down the decks the morning before the *Pueblo* left Sasebo when he overheard Commander Bucher say to Harry Iredale: "We could be lucky, or we could run into trouble."

The remark had no substance for Russell. He had no idea where the ship was going or what it was going to do.

The men were much like the *Pueblo*—a little unprepared and a little out of shape—as they came aboard on the final night in port.

Three

CHARLIE LAW WAS NAVIGATING as the *Pueblo* straightened up from its backing maneuver and headed toward the wide, clear channel and the Tsushima Strait two and a half miles away. Law, a little overweight at 205 pounds, was still somewhat bleary-eyed from his night on the town, but he was one of the best navigators in the Navy and could have handled the *Pueblo* half drunk. He had arrived aboard at 5 A.M., and after a cup of coffee he had gone to the pilot house to prepare for sailing. It was still dark, but the weather was crisp and clear on that morning of January 11, 1968, and Law could see the outlines of the Navy cargo ship *Castor*, the repair ship *Ajax*, and a destroyer at their berths in India Basin as the *Pueblo* started down the channel.

He lit off the radar, but Commander Bucher, on the flying bridge over the pilot house, noticed the antenna rotating and called down to Law to turn it off. The *Pueblo* would be under radio silence for the rest of the trip, except in an emergency, and radar emits signals. Lieutenant Murphy leaned over Law's shoulder at the chart table in the pilot house and passed information from Law to Bucher on the other end of the voice tube above. Boatswain's Mate Ronald L. Berens, twenty-one, of Russell, Kansas, was at the wheel, and three other crewmen were in the pilot house operating as bearing trackers or bearing recorders. The atmosphere was subdued.

The only immediate problem was to evade detection by the Soviet ships, then sixty miles away in Tsushima Strait. Bucher planned to hug the west coast of the island of Kyushu for a day, in the hope that the Russians would read the *Pueblo* for a fishing vessel, and then turn northwest into the Sea of Japan toward the North Korean coast. It was about 360 miles from Sasebo to Wonsan, North Korea's major seaport.

The first day's sailing was good, except that a second generator broke down. It was the No. 2 generator in the main engine room and the problem was insoluble. The block was cracked, and the engine-room crew began to tear it down. This left the *Pueblo* with one hundred-kilowatt generator in good working condition, and the remaining sixty-kilowatt generator for the research space jury-rigged with a borrowed governor. The *Pueblo* could operate, but another breakdown would mean the end of the mission.

The *Pueblo* moved along the coast using its Loran (long range navigation) system for position fixes. This would be the standard method on this trip because Loran doesn't emit signals.

There were many Japanese fishing boats in the area, and Law thought they would serve as a good cover.

On the second day out, January 12, 1968, the *Pueblo* turned toward the northwest just after passing the island of Ullung-do, which is due east of Seoul, South Korea, and headed for its operational area, which was to begin about thirty miles east of Wonsan.

The operational area itself, about 180 miles long and 60 miles wide, was divided into sub-areas with the code names Mars, Venus, and Pluto. The names may have had some significance to the Spooks, but to most of the officers and men aboard the *Pueblo* they meant nothing.

On the night of January 13 the *Pueblo* moved slowly into the area of Wonsan. The coast of North Korea here takes a sharp bend inward, and the *Pueblo* lay to about thirty miles off Wonsan while the eight technicians on duty in the Sod Hut put their equipment to its first real test. The equipment was working well now. Angelo Strano had spent most of his last night in Sasebo getting the major piece in shape. He and Don Bailey had also installed a speaker in the crypto room so the men could get some radio music.

The *Pueblo*, although it could hardly be called frisky, was like a curious puppy, moving from spot to spot, sniffing here and there, listening intently to the slightest sound and probing the area thoroughly with its eager electronic nose. And, whenever the ship stopped to sniff, the two oceanographers dutifully dropped their gear over the side and made their tests.

The weather was colder now, and cloudy. On the night of January 14, as the ship took its slow course northward, Bucher turned the crew to de-icing the ship with wooden mallets and steam hoses. Heavy seas could capsize a ship like the *Pueblo* if it got loaded with ice. It snowed and the bitter wind drove the crew from the uncovered flying bridge into the pilot house, where thick safety glass afforded protection.

On January 16 the *Pueblo* reached the northern boundary of its operational area, which was about even with the border between North Korea and the Soviet Union, and just below Vladivostok. There they turned west toward the coast to return south, and came within fourteen miles of land. Those who wanted to look could see the jagged coast of North Korea in the distance. But many in the crew were more interested in their future course than in geography. Francis Ginther, a twenty-six-year-old communications technician from Pottsville, Pennsylvania, on his first sea voyage despite eight years in the Navy, was marking the days off on his calendar with a big red crayon. He hoped to get off the ship when it returned to Sasebo. His wife, Janice, was ill, and he wanted to go back to Pottsville to see her. Charlie Law had a date lined up for the night of the *Pueblo*'s return, as did others. Chuck Ayling was looking forward to some more time off in Japan to study the country's transit system.

But the *Pueblo* was in no hurry. It wasn't picking up much information, so it moved south to the port of Chongjin and lay to there on the evening of January 16 and all the next day. It moved south about fifty miles to Songjin on the 18th and lay to about fourteen miles out. Bucher left standing orders that the ship was to remain fourteen to fifteen miles out at all times unless he was on the bridge.

North Korea claimed a twelve-mile territorial limit, but even if the *Pueblo* intruded on that limit there was no reason to expect anything but a warning. Under the concept of freedom of the seas as it has come down through the centuries, ships of all nations have the right to use the seas as they please. If there is an intrusion, it is common practice to use diplomatic channels to register a protest. Under no circumstances is it considered "legal" to board, control, or seize a warship, even in territorial waters. There is, however, no record of North Korea's ever having become a party to the international conventions on the subject. There was a discussion of the subject among several CT's one night off the coast. Someone noted that nearly every major war between the United States and a foreign power had evolved from an incident or action involving ships.

So the *Pueblo* was being careful, and by the afternoon of the 19th it was laying to fifteen miles off the port of Hungnam. There was some special interest in the area because there was information that North Korea had some obsolete Russian submarines based nearby. The *Pueblo* never found any indication of such, but it was off Hungnam that the *Pueblo* officers experienced their first slight tingle of excitement.

Two large merchantmen were sighted leaving the port, moving north parallel with the coastline about three and a half miles from the *Pueblo*. Bucher came to the bridge to take a look at them through binoculars, and discussed the sightings with Lieutenant Schumacher while Charlie Law counted masts and kingposts and noted their superstructures in an attempt to identify them. Law went through a book on merchant ships in the Communist Bloc and decided they were from one of the Balkan countries. Bucher was unconcerned. He figured that even if the *Pueblo* had been sighted no one aboard the merchantmen would be likely to identify his ship. He was under orders to break radio silence if he was certain he had been identified, but he thought there was little chance of it in this case.

On the afternoon of January 20 the bridge got word from the Sod Hut that a piece of its gear on a mast was inoperative, and Chief Petty Officer Bouden and Sergeant Chicca were to go aloft to replace it. Bucher headed the *Pueblo* northeast into the seas to keep the roll down while the two men were aloft. It took about an hour to replace the gear. When the *Pueblo* turned to go back to its original station it was 12.8 miles from the North Korean coast, the closest it would ever come during normal operations.

The *Pueblo* remained in the area for a full day, and about dusk on January 21 another little alarm bell rang. A relatively small ship was sighted headed south, apparently toward Wonsan. It passed within a thousand yards of the *Pueblo*. Bucher called for Photographer's Mate Lawrence W. Mack, thirty-four, of San Diego, to get some pictures of the ship, but the light had faded too much for a clear print. Steve Harris and Lieutenant Schumacher were called to the bridge, and between them they identified it as a North Korean subchaser. Since the subchaster didn't seem to slow down or change its course, Bucher decided the *Pueblo* hadn't been seen, or at least hadn't been identified, and he kept to his planned course. He wanted to give Wonsan another thorough probe. About midnight on the 21st, Charlie Law took the ship down to just below Wonsan and lay to about fifteen miles off the coast.

Four

DAWN OF JANUARY 22, 1968, was clear but cold. The *Pueblo* lay to just below Wonsan, about fifteen miles off the coast, after probing without much success at the installations in and around Wonsan. Lieutenant Harris complained to Bucher about the mission's lack of success so far and told Bucher he thought the quality of work from the communications technicians was low, perhaps because of their lack of sea experience. Harris was an expert in his specialty field of communications but was not considered entirely knowledgeable in the several other areas of work being done in the research space, such as intelligence gathering.

Lieutenant Schumacher was on watch about 1:30 in the afternoon when another alarm signal rang, much louder than the previous tingles. A lookout in the wing of the pilot house had sighted two large motorized fishing vessels heading from Wonsan and straight for the *Pueblo*. He pointed them out to Schumacher, who immediately called for the captain. As the vessels approached off the port bow, Bucher, Schumacher, Lieutenant Harris, Chicca, and Hammond discussed the vessels and agreed that the subchaser they had seen the evening before had probably detected the *Pueblo* and that the visit by the Korean fishing vessels was the result.

News of the approaching vessels quickly circulated, and crewmen not on duty hurried to the weather decks for a look, some bringing cameras. Jimmy Layton, fishing off the fantail, kept one eye on his bobber and one on the boats. The steel-hulled, diesel-powered trawlers, about 140 feet long, came to within 50 yards of the *Pueblo* and circled it slowly while Bucher watched through binoculars and Photographer's Mate Mack took pictures from the bridge. Chicca and Hammond read the Korean inscriptions on the trawlers and told Bucher they were named *Rice Paddy* and *Rice Paddy 1*. There was no one on the decks of the two trawlers, but Bucher could see that the pilot houses were crowded with men and women. Bucher used the 1MC, the

general announcing system, to order everyone below. He didn't
want those aboard the trawlers to get an idea of how many men
were aboard the *Pueblo*. The trawlers circled the ship for about
an hour and a half, then turned and headed back to Wonsan.

Commander Bucher didn't consider the visit any more than
routine, but his orders were to inform ComNav 4, Japan, as soon
as he was certain that the *Pueblo* had been detected, so he asked
Lieutenant Harris to prepare a message for transmission to
Kamiseya. About 4:30 Lieutenant Harris came into the crypto
center and told Don Bailey to get the circuit operable.

Under ordinary circumstances it would take about ten minutes to make contact with the big Navy relay station. Bailey called
Yokosuka first, telling the station there to call Kamiseya and acti-
vate the special secure channel to the *Pueblo*. Several minutes
later, Bailey got an acknowledging message from Kamiseya and
tried to reply. But Kamiseya couldn't pick up the signal clearly.
Bailey continued to punch out his call letters every thirty sec-
oncs, trying to make clear contact.

Meanwhile, below decks there were some excitement and
much discussion over the visit, which was considered a welcome
break in the monotony. No one took the visit seriously, although
many thought the *Pueblo* could expect some harassment now that
it had been detected. There was only one sour note. About 7 P.M.
Charlie Law came up to Stuart Russell in the crew's quarters
forward and asked Russell if he had seen anyone in the crew
"shoot the finger" at the Korean trawlers. The gesture, a good
old American custom, consisted of pointing the middle finger on
either hand straight up. Its meaning was plain to most Americans, and it was considered a vulgar gesture of defiance. Russell
had seen one crewman give it with both hands to the trawlers
and had heard that others had done the same. Law was angry
about it, so Russell told him he hadn't seen the gesture. As Law
walked away he said to Russell over his shoulder: "It was a stupid
trick. Those guys are fanatics. You never know what they're
going to do."

Russell that night asked Peter M. Langenberg, twenty-two,
of Clayton, Missouri, a communications technician, what he
thought of the trawlers. Langenberg said he didn't think it

was such a big deal. Langenberg had heard that many PT boats were around. He wanted to see them.

In the crypto center, Don Bailey and Donald R. McClarren, thirty-two, of Johnstown, Pennsylvania, an ex-Air Force man who had joined the Navy in 1965 and was on his first sea duty, continued to try to get through to Kamiseya, without success. Bailey thought there were two reasons. The *Pueblo*'s signal was relatively weak and had trouble squeezing through the stronger signals pouring into Kamiseya. There was also some atmospheric interference. Bailey stayed at the job the entire night, frustrated because he could read Kamiseya clearly but couldn't get the *Pueblo*'s signal through. The operator at Kamiseya, a friend of Bailey's, stayed right with him. Bailey could have gotten through by transmitting in the clear on another frequency but he had orders not to do so unless there was an emergency. About 8 A.M. Bailey, who had been up for twenty-four hours, went below to rest and turned the sending apparatus over to McClarren, who continued to try to reach Kamiseya.

The night of January 22 was mildly interesting to Charlie Law for another reason. He had the eight-to-midnight watch. About nine o'clock Law saw a string of lights moving out from Wonsan.

As the lights came closer, Law determined that he was seeing a fishing fleet moving out. By counting the lights he figured there were thirty to thirty-five boats in the fleet. About 10:30, Law saw a large merchantman coming toward the *Pueblo* from the direction of Wonsan. It passed within three thousand yards of the ship. There was sufficient light for Law to determine with a pair of binoculars that it carried Russian-made radar.

About 9 A.M. on January 23 McClarren went below and woke Bailey to tell him contact had been made with Kamiseya. Bailey immediately got dressed and found Lieutenant Harris, who gave him the message noting the detection, as well as an operational message listing the *Pueblo*'s position, fuel and food on hand, and other routine notes.

Bailey had left school in the ninth grade and joined the Army in January, 1949, when he was seventeen. He served for three and a half years, then quit and worked as a bus driver for five years. He joined the Navy in 1957. He had considerable sea experience and had been on at least one sensitive mission. He didn't like the feel of the *Pueblo*'s situation now and decided to stay on in the crypto center in case the ship received more attention from the Koreans.

Commander Bucher decided to move up the coast and lay to about fifteen miles off the island of Ung-do near the mouth of Wonsan harbor.

It was a perfect day for snooping. The sea was calm under a sunny sky. There were a few scattered clouds. The wind was bitter as the *Pueblo* rocked gently in the shallow water. There was little to be concerned about on board, and some happiness. The *Pueblo* would start its return trip to Sasebo in two days.

Five

CHIEF WARRANT OFFICER LACY had the 8 A.M.-to-noon watch on January 23, but Law came up to the flying bridge and relieved him about 11:30. The *Pueblo* was laying to, facing due north.

A few minutes before noon, Law sighted a boat coming at high speed toward the *Pueblo* off the port quarter and judged almost immediately that it was a North Korean subchaser. He estimated its distance at six miles. He called for Commander Bucher, who was in the wardroom eating lunch. Bucher told Law to call him again when the ship approached to within three miles, but a few minutes later Bucher, wearing a ski mask to protect his face from the cold, came to the bridge and took a look through binoculars, agreeing with Law that it was an SOG-1 class subchaser belonging to North Korea. Word spread quickly through the *Pueblo* that another North Korean vessel was approaching. As the subchaser came to within one thousand yards of the port bow, the *Pueblo* men either came on deck or crowded around portholes below to watch.

There was a stir of excitement when the crew saw that the subchaser was apparently at general quarters, with four deck guns manned and pointed at the *Pueblo*. The Korean crew was helmeted and wearing flak jackets. In the subchaser's pilot house were several officers wearing long black greatcoats and fur hats, peering at the *Pueblo* through binoculars.

Stuart Russell was in the galley looking for something to eat when he heard a call over the 1MC for Photographer's Mate Mack to come to the bridge. It was usually a sure sign that something was up. Russell walked out onto the fantail, taking time on the way to note the menu for the evening meal. It was chop suey.

The fantail was crowded, but Russell got to the rail and took a close look at the subchaser, which was circling the *Pueblo* about sixty yards away. Russell glanced over the port side and saw in the distance three more boats approaching. They were moving so fast that Russell judged that they must be torpedo boats. Beyond them, Russell could see a fourth ship throwing up a high rooster tail and heading toward the *Pueblo*. Russell was unconcerned. "Who are they kidding with those guns?" he said to a shipmate. Still, he thought it would be something to talk about when he got back to Glendale.

On the flying bridge, Bucher was not quite so unconcerned. Neither was Bailey in the crypto center. Quite on his own, Bailey requested of Kamiseya that it keep the circuit open. "We have company coming," he messaged.

Bucher also took action. He called through the voice tube to Lieutenant Murphy to have someone keep a narrative of the event and to draw diagrams of the North Korean vessels and their positions in relation to the *Pueblo*. Law lit off the radar to confirm the *Pueblo*'s position, then went to the pilot house to look at the charts. He came back to the bridge and reported to Bucher that the *Pueblo* was 15.2 miles from Ung-do. Bucher said, "Very well," and began talking into a tape recorder, giving a general description of the situation. Law was doing the same, writing in pencil a narrative in a green memo book. About then, Dunnie Tuck, the oceanographer, came to the bridge and asked Bucher if he should make a Nansen cast, which would record the water temperature at various depths. Bucher told him it was a good idea, and Tuck went to his winch on the well deck and started making his cast with the help of Harry Iredale.

Bucher also called Lacy to the bridge and told him to order everyone below. Then Bucher called for Signalman Wendell G.

Leach, twenty-five, of Houston, Texas, to come to the bridge, and asked Lieutenant Schumacher to break out previously prepared message blanks for reporting emergency situations. There was a good deal of commotion aboard the *Pueblo*, but almost everyone considered the situation as routine harassment.

There also was action in the research space below as the subchaser circled, its intentions still unknown. Sergeant Chicca, wearing headphones, was listening to the transmissions from the subchaser to a shore station. He could decipher a word or two, but he had no idea what sort of instructions the subchaser was receiving or sending. Finally he put down the earphones and ran into the crew's berthing forward and awakened Sergeant Hammond. Chicca told Hammond he needed help and ran back to the research space while Hammond dressed quickly and followed. Hammond took a turn with the earphones, but the Koreans were talking much too fast, and neither he nor Chicca could understand what they were saying. Hammond finally stepped away, feeling frustrated and useless. The *Pueblo*'s warning system had failed.

By now, Bucher and Law had been joined on the flying bridge by Signalman Leach and Steven J. Robin, twenty-one, a communications technician from Silver Spring, Maryland, who had come up to help identify the ships. In the pilot house immediately below, Ensign Harris, obeying orders from Lieutenant Murphy, was sitting in the captain's chair writing and drawing pictures on a large lined pad. No one was ever supposed to sit in the captain's chair except the captain, but it had a metal table attached to it and it was a convenient place for Harris to lay his pad to write on.

After about fifteen minutes on the scene, the subchaser raised a signal flag asking the *Pueblo*'s nationality. Bucher ordered the national colors broken out, and Law and Leach went to the signal desk on the flying bridge and hoisted the American flag.

The *Pueblo* was dead in the water with no engines running, as it had been all along, when it got its first really rude shock. The subchaser hoisted a flag which meant: "Heave to or will open fire."

Bucher turned angrily and said: "Goddamn, we're already heaved to. What the hell do they want us to do?" Then he ordered Leach to raise a signal flag meaning "I am hydrographic."

A thoughtful observer to all this was James A. Shepard, twenty-seven, of Williamstown, Massachusetts, a communications technician on his first sea duty despite nearly eight years in the Navy. A top expert in his particular electronics field, he had taken five other CT's to Fuchu near Tokyo to give them some special training while the *Pueblo* was in Yokosuka. He had been asleep when the subchaser first approached the ship and had gone to the bridge on awakening. When he saw the order from the subchaser to heave to, he went below to the research space and asked Lieutenant Harris if they should prepare for emergency destruction of the hundreds of pounds of classified material aboard, as well as the equipment. Harris called the pilot house but was told to wait a while, that the situation was still considered harassment. Shepard went back to his bunk and prayed.

While he prayed, Shepard wondered what had happened to the destruction bill he had composed and typed out before the ship reached Japan. The bill, about a page long, listed in order of priority the equipment to be destroyed. He learned later that it had been taped to the door between the research space and the crypto room at about 11 A.M., approximately an hour before the subchaser was first sighted.

Francis Ginther had just eaten a turkey sandwich for lunch when he heard about the subchaser and looked out. He saw it once as it cruised past his porthole at about three knots. Then he went into the research space. One of the CT's was holding a dictionary and was arguing with two or three crewmates. They had heard about the signal to heave to and, inexperienced sailors all, thought "heave to" meant to "move on." Although the *Pueblo* was Ginther's first ship he understood the term and told the others it meant to stop.

Ginther and Communications Technician Elton A. Wood, twenty-one, of Spokane, Washington, were scheduled to burn material at 1 P.M. in the incinerator on the starboard side of the ship next to the pilot house. It was a normal detail, involving the destruction of paper no longer in use. The paper was to be crumpled up and put inside a paper sack called a burn bag, then stuffed into the incinerator.

The incinerator was nothing unusual. One just put a match to the material and waited there while it burned. The device took five bags at a time. Each load took about twenty minutes to burn. The *Pueblo* also had two paper shredders in the forward electronics room for the destruction of material. Each shredder took three or four legal-size sheets of paper at a time and spit the shreds out into a big plastic bag, which would then be burned in the incinerator or dumped over the side.

Wood asked Ginther if they should start burning, but Ginther said they ought to wait until the subchaser left. Ginther also heard Lieutenant Harris tell someone he wished the ship would start moving and get out of there. Everyone seemed a little excited.

Six

THINGS WERE GETTING HOTTER on the flying bridge. Bucher ordered the engines started, and the subchaser responded by hoisting a signal: "Follow in my wake. I have a pilot aboard." Law, looking through binoculars, could see a man standing on top of the subchaser's pilot house waving red semaphore flags. He wasn't attempting to signal a message. He was waving the *Pueblo* toward shore. Bucher ordered another signal flag raised: "I plan to remain in this area, depart tomorrow." Again, the *Pueblo*'s signal had no visible effect, and the Korean on the pilot house kept waving the *Pueblo* toward land.

The *Pueblo*'s pilot house was now crowded with spectators anxious to lend a hand. Michael T. Barrett, thirty, of Kalamazoo, Michigan, a CT, was standing next to Ensign Harris, who was writing furiously on his pad. Barrett loaned Harris his watch, remarking as he passed it over that the Koreans wouldn't fire on them. "It would create an international incident," he said. Harris was too busy to reply.

The skipper wanted this detailed account, Harris thought, and he was going to do his damnedest to give it to him. He glanced up in time to see a PT boat pull alongside the subchaser and several soldiers carrying guns climb onto the PT boat. He noted that down.

Bucher, meanwhile, had left the bridge and run down to the research space. He told Don Bailey he was concerned about the amount of tension building up and dictated a message to CT Jerry Karnes, twenty-two, of Havana, Arkansas, for transmission by Bailey. Bailey assured Bucher that the circuit was working well, and then sent Bucher's message, which outlined briefly the general situation and said he would ignore the subchaser's signals and steam out to sea. Then Bailey sent a message on his own hook. "Sure looks like we could use some help out here," he punched.

By now the excitement had filtered down to the engine room. Fireman Woelk and Fireman Duane Hodges, twenty-one, of Cresswell, Oregon, were on duty in the auxiliary engine room. Woelk was the electrician on duty. Hodges was the watch on the evaporator, which supplied the *Pueblo* with fresh water. They were close friends, and during many watches they had been studying for an exam they were to take the next day. Hodges was going to take the exam for engineman third class, Woelk the exam for electrician third class. Back in the States, Woelk had gone on leave to Hodges' home in Cresswell for a weekend, and Hodges had fixed him up with a date and taken him to the jalopy races. During the weekend, Woelk had been impressed by how the tall, lanky, deep-voiced Hodges had helped his parents around the house.

Now the two of them were somewhat excited by the subchaser and took turns going up the ladder and looking out the hatch at the North Korean ship. But they weren't really worried.

Commander Bucher was, however. He didn't like the way the three torpedo boats had surrounded his ship, and he was deeply concerned when he saw armed soldiers transfer to one of the torpedo boats. About that time two MIG jets flew over at about four thousand feet and started circling. Bucher watched the jets, and when he looked down again he saw a torpedo boat backing down on the *Pueblo*'s starboard side, a man standing on the bow with a line to throw aboard the *Pueblo*. Law saw that the boarding party of about eight soldiers carried carbines with bayonets attached. He saw the soldiers working the actions of their guns, and thought it was time for the *Pueblo* to bug out of there.

Bucher was furious. The PT boat was within twenty feet of the *Pueblo* when he yelled into the voice tube: "Those sons of bitches are trying to board us!" He ordered the ship ahead one third; it started to move almost immediately.

Bucher asked Law to give him the course to the open sea. Law suggested 090, or a right turn. Bucher set the course at 080 and told Leach to hoist another signal flag: "Thank you for your consideration. I am departing the area." As the *Pueblo* came right he ordered full ahead and the *Pueblo* began leaving the torpedo boat behind. Then a second PT boat pulled in front of the *Pueblo* and began zigzagging across its bow.

Law turned to Bucher and said, "It looks like we're out of it. Leach must have said his prayers right." Bucher laughed and said he was saying his prayers, too.

A fourth PT boat had come up in the meantime and was off the port quarter when Bucher, uncertain as to what was going to happen next but happy that he was moving out to sea without being fired upon, went down to the pilot house and consulted with his veteran engineering officer and right-hand man, Gene Lacy. He asked Lacy how long it would take to scuttle the *Pueblo*. Lacy said too long, perhaps an hour and a half, and that the men wouldn't last five minutes in the thirty-five-degree water. The two never discussed using their machine guns or other weapons. Bucher apparently thought it would be suicide. Even if they could hold off the subchaser, Bucher had no doubt the PT boats would torpedo the *Pueblo*. Chuck Ayling earlier had asked Lacy what would happen if the *Pueblo* was torpedoed. He said a torpedo would break her back and she would sink quickly.

While Bucher was in the pilot house, the subchaser had fallen off about three thousand yards astern, but as Law looked over the stern he could see it coming up again on the port side. He called down to Bucher, who immediately returned to the bridge. Bucher ordered Leach to send a signal by semaphore: "Am in international waters. Am leaving area." He told Law to watch through binoculars for a reply. But the man on the subchaser's pilot house kept waving the *Pueblo* toward shore, and Law thought that the Korean either had a one-track mind or couldn't read signals. Bucher was obviously worried now but still composed. Law could see two men on each of the subchaser's four gun mounts, and as he scanned the ship he heard a popping noise.

Law thought it was a machine gun firing and hit the deck with Steve Robin behind the captain's chair. Bucher and Leach dived behind the metal signal desk. Law looked up and realized that the captain's chair was raised a step off the deck and he and Robin weren't hiding behind anything but canvas. Before he could move to a safer place, he heard louder booms, and realized the Koreans were shooting their 57-millimeter cannon at the *Pueblo*. He heard a crashing noise as a shell hit the stack about ten feet behind him and then heard Robin shout: "They got me!"

A second shell tore through the Plexiglas screen on the bridge and exploded on the signal desk hood about six feet from where Law and Robin were lying. Law turned over on his side, frightened, and saw Robin trying to take off his jacket. Law helped him, then called to Bucher that Robin had been hit in the arm but it didn't seem too bad. Bucher replied: "Well, they got me in the ass."

Seven

ENSIGN HARRIS had just finished drawing a diagram of the PT boat criss-crossing in front of the *Pueblo* when he heard firing. He was vaguely aware that everyone else in the pilot house had hit the deck at the first sound of shots, but he was too engrossed in his chore to move. He saw smoke but thought the North Koreans were just firing across the bow of the *Pueblo*. When he heard still another explosion, however, he dived out of the chair and onto the deck. He lay there for a moment, unaware that he was in a bed of broken safety glass, and continued to log the shots. He turned on his side to look around and saw a jagged hole in the glass directly in front of where he had been sitting, about head high. Then he saw his torn pants and blood on his knees, from where he had been cut by the glass.

Still bewildered and a little scared, he said: "What the shit is this!"

He vaguely heard general quarters ordered over the 1MC, the order modified to keep the crew off the weather decks regardless of their general-quarters stations. This modification meant the *Pueblo*'s exposed machine guns would not be manned.

On the flying bridge, Bucher scrambled from behind the signal desk and shouted into the voice tube an order to pass the word to the research space to commence emergency destruction. Then he looked over his shoulder at Law and said: "Let's get the hell out of here."

Law ran for the starboard-side ladder to the pilot house. He hit the deck again when he heard firing and saw bullets passing over the length of the ship. The subchaser was on the starboard side, but Law figured that the *Pueblo*'s whaleboat would screen him, so he went in that direction anyway. He didn't remember using the ladder but he was aware that Leach and Robin piled on top of him as he hit the landing. The three of them went through the door to the pilot house together.

For Bucher, it was no longer a question of North Korean intentions. Now it was a matter of buying time while the crew destroyed the classified material and equipment in the Sod Hut and Crypto center. The *Pueblo* carried secret codes and the key material for the codes, as well as highly classified cryptographic equipment. One without the other wasn't of great use to a foreign power. Together, they were of immense value.

But things weren't going well in the research space.

Jimmy Shepard, who had been praying at his berth, ran to the research space when he heard firing. When he arrived he found everyone lying on the deck and no one making a move to start destruction. The men had heard the firing but not the general-quarters calls, since the 1MC didn't extend into the research space.

Shepard asked Lieutenant Harris again about emergency destruction. Harris called the pilot house and got another "No," but before he put the phone down he got a loud "Yes!"

Sergeant Hammond, standing near Sergeant Chicca, who was

trying to listen in on North Korean transmissions, thought he heard Lieutenant Harris in a low voice give the order to destruct. Others in the space heard only Chief Kell and Jimmy Layton give the orders to begin destruction.

Hammond, Ginther, and Shepard picked up eight-pound sledgehammers and began hitting the equipment, packed in bays along the walls, while others began carrying armfuls of paper outside. Ginther attacked the two $60,000 tape recorders first, but they were encased in heavy metal covers and his hammer bounced off. The others were having the same trouble in the narrow space. The equipment was screwed tight to protect it from the roll of the ship. Almost all of the equipment had heavy metal covers protecting the fragile inner works. It would have taken too long to unscrew them, so the men simply tried to hammer them out of shape. When a man's arms got tired, he turned the sledgehammers over to someone else and assisted in the burning of material.

Below decks there was the same frenzied activity when general quarters sounded. Chuck Ayling, who had been running from porthole to porthole following the progress of the Korean ships, met Dunnie Tuck and asked him if he thought it was serious. Tuck told him it was very serious. Then Ayling headed for his general-quarters station with the forward damage-control party.

Victor Escamilla had been sleeping when Anthony A. Lamantia, twenty-two, a CT from Toronto, Ohio, shook him and told him North Korean ships were firing on the *Pueblo*. As he was pulling on his pants, Escamilla heard general quarters sounded. Carrying his shirt, he ran for his general-quarters station in the auxiliary engine room, passing Duane Hodges as he went through the hatch to the engine room. Hodges had been waiting for Escamilla to relieve him so he could go to his station as phone talker in damage control central in the wardroom. Escamilla asked Hodges how things were in the engine room. Hodges said they were okay, then took off. Escamilla was followed into the engine room by Richard E. Arnold, twenty-one, of Santa Rosa, California, and Stuart Russell, whose general-quarters assignment was as a messenger on the bridge.

Russell had been in the forward berthing area, spreading the word about the attention the *Pueblo* was getting, when he heard firing. He thought it was the *Pueblo*'s guns and walked back to the galley, where crewmen were buttoning down the portholes.

Russell was still not particularly impressed by the situation, and he walked forward of the galley on the port side and sat down next to the medical locker. He thought that if he was going to be hit he might as well be near the locker. But he couldn't stand the isolation with all the excitement going on, so he walked to the hatch leading to the auxiliary engine room and stood there talking to three or four crewmen. Just then, Charles R. Sterling, twenty-eight, a CT from Omaha, Nebraska, came rushing out of the research space and pushed the group to the deck, calling them "stupid bastards" for standing up.

Russell thought this was silly since he was standing behind a metal bulkhead and remembered all the gunfighters he had seen in the movies behind wooden tables and never getting hit. He was still on the deck when a shell came through the hull and exploded near the gun locker about sixteen feet forward from where Russell and the others were lying. Russell heard the shrapnel clatter against the bulkheads and smelled the smoke, and he ran down into the auxiliary engine room and sat against the bulkhead between two pieces of solid equipment. Arnold gave him an orange.

Escamilla, on the headphones, reported to damage control that the auxiliary engine room was manned and ready. Hodges, on the other end, said: "Aye, aye."

Mike O'Bannon, an expert surfer from Oregon, had eaten and gone to bed after getting off watch at noon, totally unaware then that anything was going on. About 1 P.M. Arnold woke him to tell him about the PT boats alongside, and O'Bannon got dressed and went up on the well deck. He walked back and forth with six or seven others, watching. O'Bannon was impressed by the armament of the PT boats; he thought the torpedo tubes on their decks looked especially awesome and dangerous close up. After a few minutes, Chuck Ayling came through a door to the well deck and told the group to get below, that he had heard the Koreans had threatened to fire on the *Pueblo*. "Aw, hell,"

O'Bannon said, "they're not going to fire on us."

He went to the mess deck and poured himself a cup of coffee and was searching for the sugar when Chief Goldman came in and told him to help close the portholes. O'Bannon was walking toward a porthole on the port side when he heard a machine gun firing. He ducked down and threw his coffee, cup and all, into a trash can, then peeked through the porthole. He could see a PT boat just a few yards away firing its machine guns at the bridge. He closed the porthole and ran for the main engine room, his general-quarters station. He went through the hatch, hit the ladder once about halfway down, then jumped the rest of the way. It was a bad mistake. He struck his head on an overhead pipe fitting. The blow gashed his head and caused him to fall down. Fireman Howard E. Bland, twenty, of Leggett, California, came down on top of him.

But O'Bannon, operating on instinct and training, quickly opened the fire mains and shut off the ventilation and the boiler which supplied heat to the ship. Then he took over his duty station, at the starboard throttle.

Steve Woelk reacted like most of the rest of the crew when someone told him the Koreans were going to fire on the ship: he didn't believe it. But when he heard general quarters sounded he was careful to pick up a helmet from an open rack amidships on his way to damage control central in the wardroom. When the same shell that scared Russell struck the ship, Woelk ran the rest of the way to the wardroom, passing the shell hole on the way. He joined his friend Hodges in the wardroom. They were the only two there, and Woelk told Hodges about the shell hole. Hodges had been talking to other stations and getting damage reports for relay to the pilot house. Hodges reported Woelk's observation.

Eight

WHEN CHARLIE LAW ran into the pilot house shortly after the Koreans began firing, he saw a strange sight. Boatswain's Mate

Berens was trying to steer the ship from a sitting position, and Tim Harris was sitting crosslegged amid broken glass, writing in a book as though he were working out an exam problem.

Bucher was extremely agitated. He paced from port to starboard, looking out at the North Korean ships and cursing. But Law noted that he seemed unrattled, just angry as hell, and didn't seem inclined to stop the ship. Radioman Second Class Lee R. Hayes, twenty-five, of Columbus, Ohio, was smashing his radio gear, and Law had just picked up Photographer Mack's camera and tripod and thrown them over the side when another shell struck the pilot house just below the window.

Everyone hit the deck again. As Gene Lacy got to his feet, he yelled: "Let's stop this goddamn ship before we all get killed!" Bucher said, "Okay," and ordered all stop. Lacy rang up the emergency stop himself.

Bucher wanted the *Pueblo*'s position, and Law stepped into the chart house and got it off the track on the map. He gave it to Tim Harris as 15.6 miles off the island of Ung-do, then went back into the chart house and pulled some classified material out of a safe. The material included some chart catalogues and three secret publications on charted areas. Law went to the starboard side of the pilot house and down the three steps to the next level, where Clifford C. Nolte, twenty-two, of Menlo, Iowa, a CT, and Radioman Third Class Charles H. Crandell, twenty-seven, of El Reno, Oklahoma, were starting a fire. Law threw his material into the incinerator and went back to the pilot house, where Bucher, still pacing and cursing, told him to raise a signal meaning: "You have denied my right of free passage." Law sent Leach to the bridge to hoist the signal.

Bucher, earlier, had been on the phone to the research space and was told that destruction was proceeding satisfactorily. Thus, when he received a signal from the North Koreans to follow in their wake, he ordered the ship ahead one-third and turned it in the direction of Wonsan. Despite motions from the Koreans on the deck of the subchaser to go faster, he kept the ship at one-third, trying to give the crew as much time as possible for destruction.

At about this time Bucher discussed with Lacy the possibility that the *Pueblo* might have to be surrendered, and Lacy agreed that this might be the only course of action. Bucher did not discuss the problem with anyone else.

After a slow start the destruction was well under way. The research space was full of smoke from four or five fires in the passageways set by crewmen to burn material. Bailey in the crypto center was giving Kamiseya a blow-by-blow account of events as relayed to him by Jimmy Layton, who was standing in the doorway of the research center, picking up information from anyone who happened past. Karnes was already smashing equipment not needed for transmission purposes, and Bailey turned the transmission duties over to McClarren so he could help in the destruction. He nearly fell over Lieutenant Harris, who was kneeling and praying in the middle of the ten-by-fifteen-foot space. Bailey said: "I'm going to have to get busy and destroy this gear, sir. You're going to have to get out of the way." Lieutenant Harris got to his feet and left.

By now the CT's who didn't have general-quarters stations elsewhere had arrived in the research space, and it rang with the noise of the sledgehammers. The CT's were finding it difficult to see and breathe in the thick smoke, and there were much coughing and choking, but the equipment was being battered thoroughly. Material was going in armloads into the fires, but as Shepard left the space, he had to step over large piles of material still unburned.

Shepard went into the research administration office and found Donald R. Peppard, thirty, of Phoenix, Arizona, burning material. He saw he was not needed there, and turned to leave when Lieutenant Murphy stopped him and asked him to get some material from Murphy's file cabinet and burn it. He did, and was going back for more material, walking toward a group of men including Chicca and Hodges, bent over in the passageway burning paper, when a shell exploded in front of him. Shaken, but unhurt, he fell back into Lieutenant Schumacher's stateroom. It was about 2 P.M.

The shell was the result of a delaying maneuver by Bucher, and it had fatal consequences. After fifteen minutes of sailing toward Wonsan, Bucher ordered all stop on the engines, deciding to feign a casualty and play for more time. The subchaser fired a salvo the moment it saw the *Pueblo* slow down. One shell went through the hull near Bucher's stateroom on the starboard side. It struck Duane Hodges in the right thigh and hip and blew his leg nearly off. The young man fell back, stunned and moaning, unaware that Chicca was on the deck next to him with a hole about the size of a silver dollar in his thigh and that his good friend Steve Woelk had been badly hurt by the same shell.

Woelk had left damage control in the wardroom and gone into the passageway to help with the burning since there was nothing to do in the wardroom.

Woelk remembered that Hodges was on the phone when he left, but he didn't remember seeing him again, although Hodges must have passed him to get to the area of the gun locker, where he was hit. The explosion knocked Woelk on his back from a squatting position, but he remained conscious. He felt a burning sensation on his right thigh, chest, and face. He feared he was hit badly since he couldn't move his right leg, and he began crawling backward on his elbows. He got to the door of the wardroom and collapsed, half in and half out, aware that he was bleeding badly. He could hear cries and screams. In a couple of minutes, Hospital Corpsman Herman P. Baldrige, thirty-six, of Carthage, Missouri, came up and told him to pull himself inside. "We have someone hurt worse than you," Baldridge said. Woelk's tail bone hurt, but he thought that if he just lay still he would be okay. His main fear was that he would bleed to death.

Woelk pulled himself inside the doorway. He heard footsteps in the passageway and looked up to see Baldridge, Commissaryman Ralph E. Reed, twenty-nine, of Perdix, Pennsylvania, and two others carry someone past on a stretcher and lay him in the passageway just outside the wardroom. Woelk caught a glimpse of the man's face. It was Hodges. He was conscious but motionless; there were bandages on his hip, and someone was giving him oxygen. Baldridge came in, cut off Woelk's pants, and applied a battle dressing. Woelk drank some Kool-Aid that Baldridge handed him and worried about his and Hodges' wounds, but he thought they would be in a good old Navy hospital in a couple of hours.

Nine

WHEN THE SUBCHASER FIRED the salvo that wounded Hodges and
the others, Commander Bucher immediately ordered one-third
ahead again. Gene Lacy, who had gone below to check on damage, came back to the pilot house and walked over to the helm,
where Bucher was standing. Tim Harris heard him tell Bucher
that Hodges' leg had been blown off and that Woelk, Chicca, and
Crandell were also hit. Bucher cursed the Koreans and strode to
the starboard side of the pilot house and yelled at the subchaser
that the ship needed a doctor. In his frustration, he told Leach to
hoist a signal asking for medical aid. Then he left the pilot house,
turning the conn over to Lacy, and went below.

McClarren and Bailey were taking turns sending an account
of the action to Kamiseya while at the same time trying to destroy equipment when Bucher walked into the crypto center and
asked who was running the teletype. McClarren jumped into
the seat, and Bucher told him he wanted to send a message to
Japan. When he started dictating, McClarren thought Bucher's
voice amazingly steady, considering the situation. McClarren
punched out the message as Bucher gave it to him:

"Have three wounded and one man with leg blown off. Have
not used any weapons nor uncovered .50-caliber machine guns.
Destroying all material and as much electrical equipment as possible. How about some help. These guys mean business. Do not
intend to offer any resistance."

Bucher left as abruptly as he came, and McClarren sent the
message twice. Then McClarren added on his own, repeating
three times: "How about some help out here."

The answer came back in seconds.

"Roger your last. This is Captain Pierson. Try to hold out as
long as you can. ComNavFor, Japan, talking to ComNavFor,
Korea, about getting some 105's out there. Good luck."

Law, meanwhile, had left the pilot house and gone to Lieutenant Murphy's stateroom. He wanted to be sure the charts of

the track of the *Pueblo* since it left Sasebo would be destroyed. He found them on Murphy's desk and handed them out to some CT's who were burning material in the passageway. Law searched Bucher's stateroom for classified material, didn't find any, then went to Lacy's stateroom and used his toilet. He next went to the mess deck and got a cup of black coffee. He drank it, watching some of the crewmen who were kneeling next to the ice-cream machine burning papers from their wallets. Law was feeling the need to go to the head again when he heard shouting and someone exclaimed, "Good God!" Sergeant Chicca came stumbling onto the mess deck, his pants ripped and blood running down his leg.

Law laid him on the deck and pulled his pants off. He examined the hole on the inside of Chicca's right thigh, then went to the first-aid locker for a battle dressing. Chicca was concious but bleeding badly. After applying the dressing, Law, a husky man, picked Chicca up and carried him into Murphy's stateroom, where he laid him on the deck and covered him with a blanket. He heard Baldridge yell for morphine, but it was locked in Murphy's safe. Law called the pilot house and told Murphy that morphine was needed.

Murphy, a little dazed, asked: "Where do I have it?" Law told him, and Murphy said he would be right down. Baldridge also wanted oxygen, so Law got a bottle from a rack on the bulkhead and took it to where he was kneeling over Hodges. There was a considerable amount of blood on the deck, and Law slipped and almost fell. Hodges was on his back, still conscious, but his face was very white and he was breathing heavily. Law was amazed that he was still alive.

Law thought that the whole situation was ridiculous, and that the Koreans were in a whole bunch of trouble. Then he walked into Lacy's stateroom and used his toilet again.

Tim Harris had also left the pilot house and gone below. He wanted to check his stateroom for classified material but discovered that his roommate, Schumacher, had cleaned out the lockers and had apparently destroyed everything of value.

Harris took his personal papers and letters and burned them in a trash can and threw his rings over the side. On the way back from the railing he saw Woelk in the wardroom and walked over to him. Woelk, a shock of blond hair plastered to his forehead just over his right eye, was smoking a cigarette. Despite his wounds, he grinned at Harris and told him he was okay. On the way back to the pilot house, Tim Harris passed Lieutenant Harris's stateroom and saw him sitting hunched over in a chair.

Tim Harris went to the port side of the pilot house, where Lieutenant Schumacher was standing and looking out. A few yards away a North Korean PT boat was jockeying for position alongside the still-moving *Pueblo*. Boatswain's Mate Willie C. Bussell, twenty-two, of Hopkinsville, Kentucky, one of the two Negroes aboard the *Pueblo*, and Norbert J. Klepac, thirty-four, of San Diego, California, were on the port quarter, apparently waiting to receive a line from the PT boat.

Even though he could see the Koreans coming, Tim Harris was shocked when he heard Bucher say over the 1MC: "Prepare to take on boarding party."

Seven or eight soldiers, dressed in heavy olive green quilted jackets and square fur hats each with a big red star in the middle, began jumping aboard, carrying submachine guns with bayonets attached. An officer, in a black greatcoat and fur hat, was carrying a pistol.

To Harris, the Koreans all looked slant-eyed and short. He thought they were the perfect stereotypes of Orientals as they jumped the low railing on the fantail one at a time. The officer waved his pistol at Harris and Schumacher, motioning them to come to the fantail and sit down. In a few moments they were joined by about a dozen other crewmen. Harris was too dejected to look up to see who his companions were as he sat down on the cold deck. For the first time, Harris started getting very scared. He figured that if the Koreans were going to shoot them, they would do it now. His fears increased ten minutes later when Bucher walked up, followed by a Korean officer holding a pistol.

Bucher carried blindfolds torn from a bedsheet and his face was grim as he passed them out and said in a low voice: "They want you to put these blindfolds on."

Thus the *Pueblo* became the first United States warship captured without a fight since June 22 1807, when HMS *Leopard*

forced the USS *Chesapeake* to surrender off the Virginia Capes
and impressed four of its crew into the British Navy.

Ten

CHARLIE LAW HAD GONE BACK to the mess deck for another cup of
coffee when he heard Bucher call over the 1MC for Klepac and
Bussell to go to the fantail to receive a boarding party. He
didn't hear a "repel boarders" call and he knew that there was
not going to be any resistance. Shortly after, Law heard Lacy's
voice on the 1MC warning the men that they were required to
give only their names, ranks, and serial numbers. Law went to his
quarters in the after berthing compartment and got the top to
his thermal underwear. He also picked up a foul-weather jacket.
On the way, he noticed some members of the crew ripping
their insignia from their left sleeves. He stopped by Murphy's
stateroom to see how Chicca was doing. Chicca was sitting on
the deck next to a little pile of papers from his wallet. Law lent
him his lighter and Chicca burned the pile, which included a
picture of his wife. Law saw Lieutenant Murphy sitting on a
chair in the head between Bucher's and Murphy's staterooms.

Law ran into Donald Peppard, who was also drinking a
cup of coffee. Peppard said it might be the last one he would
get for a while. They were talking about the situation when they
heard Bucher over the 1MC order all hands except those necessary to operate the engine room to go forward to the well deck.
Law and Peppard passed the gun locker on their way forward.
It contained a couple of submachine guns, several M1 rifles, and
about fifty grenades. The locker was closed and locked. Most of
the officers had already thrown their sidearms, which they usually kept in their staterooms, into the sea.

So the crew began wandering, bewildered and a little frightened, from all parts of the ship toward the well deck forward.
Angelo Strano took one last look as he left the research space and
noted with some satisfaction that the equipment he had spent
hundreds of hours repairing seemed to be pretty well smashed.

Glass and paper littered the floor, and some of the equipment hung from its bays dangling wire and shreds of metal. Strano had taken care of the radar detection gear himself after directing Hammond and McClintock in the destruction of other priority equipment.

Strano thought the crypto and research spaces were now empty of people, but Don Bailey and Chief Bouden were still in the crypto center.

Bailey was keeping the line open to Kamiseya with operator's chatter when he suddenly became aware that he wasn't getting any more information from the research space. He got up and walked into the passageway, puzzled by the sudden silence, and choking in the dense smoke. He rounded a corner and almost walked into a North Korean guard, who, fortunately, was looking the other way and shouting something in Korean. Bailey turned, ran back to the crypto center, and told Bouden that the Koreans were already aboard. Bailey sat down and requested permission of Kamiseya to secure the circuit and destroy the gear. Kamiseya answered: "Permission granted. Good luck." Bailey immediately began destroying the equipment with Chief Bouden's aid. Bailey, hard of hearing, was smashing the working parts inside the crypto cabinets when he felt a tap on his shoulder. He turned and saw a crewman, followed by a stocky, expressionless North Korean armed with a submachine gun. The crewman told Bailey he had to get out of there and go to the well deck.

Tim Harris and Schumacher were still on the fantail with their group. They could hear some chattering as the Koreans took the cover off the machine gun, and Harris wondered if they could depress it far enough to shoot them where they sat. He also listened for shots from the other end of the ship and wondered if he could get over the side before he was cut down. After several minutes, Bucher came up again and said in a quiet, dejected voice: "You guys can remove your blindfolds and follow me."

Most of the crew, meanwhile, had reached the well deck. When Law arrived, about sixty crewmen were standing around, quiet and subdued, most of them with their hands in their pockets. A Korean stood at the O-1 level about eight feet above their

heads, his submachine gun pointed at them. He was trying to
count the crew, but Mike O'Bannon kept moving. The guard
yelled at him and pointed his gun. O'Bannon took his helmet off,
waved it in the direction of the guard, and bowed. But he remained in place. When the guard yelled at him a few moments
later as he lit a cigarette, O'Bannon bowed again. As he flicked
the cigarette over the starboard side he looked up, and a tingle of
excitement ran through him. A large ship was on the horizon and
coming fast. O'Bannon was certain it was a U.S. Navy destroyer.
He suppressed a shout.

Like most of the rest of the crew, O'Bannon thought help was
imminent and strained his ears for sounds of jet planes. Don
Bailey stood near the railing, ready to go over the side if the
Koreans started shooting. So was Charlie Law, who saw the same
ship O'Bannon had spotted. His more experienced eyes told him
it wasn't a U.S. Navy ship, but he kept hoping. He couldn't believe they wouldn't get help. If someone would take care of
those ships out there, he was certain the crew could overwhelm
in seconds the half-dozen or so guards on board.

Jimmy Shepard was certain the crew was going to be shot
and hoped U.S. jets would get there in time. It never crossed his
mind that they wouldn't. No one, he thought, captures a U.S.
warship without getting clobbered.

Sergeant Hammond was of the same mind. He had been one
of the last to leave the research space and had gone to Murphy's
stateroom to see Chicca. Jimmy Layton and Murphy's roommate, Lieutenant Harris, were also in the room. Hammond saw
Harris reach into his foot locker and pull out a Bible, knocking
Chicca's leg off a helmet Layton had placed under it to help stem
the bleeding. Harris said in a quiet voice: "Well, I guess I'll get a
court-martial out of this."

Hammond wasn't sure what the problem was. He had not
seen Harris in the research space after the opening minutes of
destruction, but he thought the equipment had been bent out of
shape enough so that the Koreans could not make use of it. He
had seen some weighted bags being filled with classified material and assumed that they had been thrown over the side,
although he knew they could be retrieved from the two-hun-

dred-foot depth if the Koreans wanted them badly enough. Hammond, like most of the crew, thought they would be rescued anyway.

There was at least one dissenter to the rescue-or-murder theory held by most of the crew as they stood on the well deck waiting for something to happen. Chuck Ayling had read a series of articles in the *Saturday Evening Post* in October and was impressed by the fact that the major powers no longer shot spies. They kept them and traded them off. He told himself that he had to keep faith that the United States would get them out and that they were worth more to the Koreans alive than dead. It was just a matter of the sellers coming to terms with the buyers, and that would be only a matter of a couple of weeks. Ayling thought it would be nice if U.S. jets showed up, but he couldn't see how they could do much with the Korean ships clustered so closely around the *Pueblo*.

Still, Ayling was offended. He was standing next to Lieutenant Harris on the well deck, and he whispered to him: "Sir, do we have to submit to this?"

Harris growled, "Shut up and do as you're told."

Eleven

AMERICAN JETS WERE ON THE WAY to rescue the USS *Pueblo*. And a huge carrier, the *Enterprise*, was beginning a slow turn northward as the *Pueblo* crew stood in the bitter wind six hundred miles away.

Lieutenant General Seth J. McKee, commander of the U.S. Fifth Air Force, received word by telephone of the *Pueblo*'s predicament about 1:55 P.M., or approximately two hours after Charlie Law first spotted the North Korean subchaser off the *Pueblo*'s port quarter. McKee's headquarters received the *Pueblo*'s position and the first call for help a couple of minutes later. McKee quickly ordered his commander on the island of Okinawa (about three hundred miles south of Kyushu in Japan, where the Fifth Air Force had its only combat-ready planes) to prepare all available planes for launch as soon as possible.

Had the Navy requested an alert status to protect the *Pueblo* on its mission, the planes could have been in the air in thirty-three minutes. As it was, the first two F105 fighter-bombers, armed with twenty-millimeter cannon, left Okinawa for Osan, South Korea, at 4:11 P.M. They would refuel at Osan and head for the *Pueblo* twenty-five to thirty minutes away with orders to attack on arrival. U.S. planes in South Korea suitable for the mission were ruled out because they were armed with nuclear bombs.

McKee also sought help from South Korea through the commander of U.S. forces there but was advised not to contact the South Koreans. He never learned why.

Meanwhile, the commander in chief, Pacific, ordered the Seventh Fleet to dispatch a destroyer to the area of Wonsan harbor to recover the *Pueblo*. The carrier *Enterprise* was ordered north and to prepare for launching aircraft "as would be directed by the commander in chief, Pacific." The only trouble was that the destroyer could not reach the area until the next afternoon.

Rear Admiral Frank L. Johnson, commander of U.S. Naval Forces, Japan, had returned from Tokyo to his headquarters at 3:10 P.M. in response to an urgent phone call. Johnson thought his staff had taken proper action while he was en route, but he was hampered somewhat in any action he could take from Japan because of the Status of Forces agreement with Japan, which made it impractical to stage military planes through that country in an emergency. He dismissed the idea of sending unarmed search and rescue planes to the scene since there was no indication that the *Pueblo* was sinking. Sunset at Wonsan was 5:41 P.M. and absolute darkness at 5:53 P.M. It would be too late to help once darkness had fallen.

The USS *Pueblo* was on the end of a long and shaky limb.

Twelve

STEVE WOELK WAS ON THE WARDROOM DECK, and Baldridge and Ralph Reed were still tending Hodges in the passageway, when a North Korean soldier appeared in the doorway and glanced at Woelk. In a moment the soldier was prodding Baldridge and Reed through the door and into the wardroom. Baldridge protested that he had to tend to Hodges, but the soldier merely grunted and made them sit at the wardroom table. After looking over the wardroom, the soldier rifled Woelk's pockets, and took his cigarettes, lighter, and watch. He took watches from Baldridge and Reed, but returned Reed's. It was a combination timepiece-stopwatch which Woelk figured the soldier didn't know how to run.

Hodges groaned once and tried to sit up, and Baldridge, ignoring the soldier, got up and settled him down. A few minutes later Baldridge went to check Hodges again. When he came back, he told Woelk and Reed that Hodges was dead. Woelk lay back on the deck and said a prayer for him. It was about 3 P.M.

Bucher came in shortly after, followed by an officer with a pistol, and Baldridge told him Hodges was dead. Bucher said, "I'm sorry," and turned around and said something to the officer. The officer spoke to the soldier in Korean, and then Bucher and the officer left. The soldier motioned to Baldridge and Reed, indicating they could lift Woelk to the wardroom table. They took the plastic table cover off the table and laid it next to Woelk, lifted him onto it, then put him on the table. Baldridge changed the bandages on Woelk's gaping wounds and gave him a shot of morphine. Then Baldridge and Reed were marched out of the room, leaving Woelk alone with the soldier. For the first time, the young man from the Kansas farmland who liked to play and sing country and western music was frightened.

The men on the well deck were frightened, too, and bewildered. They were still standing there shivering in the ten-degree temperature when Bucher, looking harassed, came to the

O-1 level and looked down at the crewmen. He asked Yeoman Armando M. Canales, thirty-four, of Fresno, California, how many men were aboard. Canales said, "About eighty, sir."

Bucher said, "Goddamn it, I know *about* how many. How many do we have?" Peppard spoke up: "Six officers, seventy-five enlisted, and two civilians. Eighty-three in all."

Bucher asked Gunner's Mate Wadley for the keys to the ready locker, which held the ammunition for the machine guns. Wadley pointed to a guard and said, "I've already given them to him."

After Bucher left, the officer still trailing him, a soldier came down to the well deck and ordered the crew to sit. He was holding a couple of bedsheets, and he began tearing them into strips and passing the strips among the crew. He made it plain he wanted them to blindfold one another. There was some whispering among the men as the blindfolds were passed out. They didn't like what was happening and they were frightened. It was getting colder, and as someone behind Law blindfolded him, Law took one last glimpse at the ship he had seen on the horizon. It was definitely not American, and Law lost all hope of rescue.

Bucher by then was in the pilot house with a Korean pilot, steering the ship toward Wonsan harbor. He requested that his crew be allowed to go below where it was warmer. When the request was granted he spoke over the 1MC and told the men on the well deck to remove their blindfolds and file down to the forward crew's compartment. Crandell, who had shrapnel wounds in his leg, and Chicca had been lying on the deck. When the order came for them to go below, Law helped Chicca down the ladder to the compartment and laid him on a bunk, then sat down next to Jimmy Layton and replaced his blindfold. After a few minutes, the men from the fantail shuffled in and sat down, their teeth chattering.

Most of the men were in the compartment now, their blindfolds replaced, sitting on bunks or on the deck. They were silent, and they could hear the Korean soldiers chattering and going through their lockers. Francis Ginther was peeking under his blindfold and could see Lieutenant Harris hunched over on top of a bunk. Lieutenant Murphy was lying on a bunk, one arm thrown across his forehead. He overheard Stuart Russell whisper that he hoped the Koreans would find the Ex-Lax in his locker.

Mike O'Bannon, also peeking under his blindfold, could see a soldier rummaging through foot lockers. O'Bannon saw him take some coins and drop them in his pocket. The soldier went to another locker and found a copy of *Playboy* magazine. He thumbed through it, his submachine gun leaning against his knee, then ripped out several pages and stuffed them into his pocket. He seemed to be curious about the pillows on the bunks and pushed and squeezed one until it started to come apart. Another soldier came through, systematically tearing down pinups and sticking them in his pockets.

After a while the call of nature began to trouble the crew. Several called out "Benjo," Japanese for "toilet," but the Koreans ignored them. Finally one of the crewmen just stood up and urinated in a helmet. A guard got the message and began allowing the crewmen to go to the head.

One man knocked over the helmet, and three or four of the crewmen, including Russell, instinctively jumped out of the way. The guard pointed his gun toward the sudden movement and Russell froze, thinking: "Oh no, what a reason to get shot." Incongruously, the thought flashed through his mind that he should have been kinder to his parents.

The men were allowed to remove their blindfolds while going to the head, and as Chuck Ayling went through a passageway he saw a huge pile of paper unburned. The thought of all that material falling into the hands of North Korea made him sick. Since Ayling had been in a damage control party forward while other CT's were destroying equipment, he didn't know how much they had broken up, and he worried about that, although he knew most of the equipment was available on the open market in the United States. There were just a couple of highly classified pieces in the research space, plus schematics of all the equipment. He found out later that the schematics had not been destroyed.

The crew, with the exception of Bucher in the pilot house, Blansett and Goldman in the engine room, and Woelk in the wardroom sat in the compartment for nearly two hours. Bewilderment slowly turned to rage and frustration. Some still held out hope that they would be rescued.*

About 6:30 P.M. the crew heard bumping and scraping. The *Pueblo* had arrived in Wonsan, a seaport with a large, deep natural harbor and a population of about 113,000 people on the east coast of North Korea.

They were entering a country into which no American had entered except as captive or conqueror in more than twenty years.

Thirteen

As THE MEN slowly and stiffly got to their feet, they heard a Korean address them.

"You have violated the laws of our country," he said in good English, "and you will be punished." Many wondered what that punishment would consist of.

They were led one by one to the top of the ladder of the compartment and frisked. The soldiers went through their pockets, saying over and over again something that sounded like "pistola" to the crewmen. Stuart Russell lost his eyeglasses to a soldier, who probably thought the case enclosed a weapon. Angelo Strano was unlucky, too. A soldier ripped the pockets off his jacket and Strano's watch and a $300 ring fell to the deck. He got the watch back but never saw the ring again. Jimmy Layton lost three packs of cigarettes.

Immediately after they were frisked, the hands of each crew member were tied tightly in front of them with what seemed like heavy fishing line. Then they were pulled one by one by their hands across two wooden planks laid between the *Pueblo* and the pier. If they stumbled and fell, they were dragged until they could regain their feet. Vic Escamilla fell as he crossed the planks, and he dangled between the ship and the pier for a mo-

---

* Lieutenant General McKee by then had decided that it was too late to help the *Pueblo* because of darkness, and ordered his F105's to remain at Osan. The carrier *Enterprise* continued its movement north in what turned out to be a useless and empty bluff.

ment before he was hauled roughly onto the pier.

For Steve Woelk in the wardroom, a special ordeal had just begun.

Several Korean soldiers, led by an officer with a pistol, came into the wardroom with a stretcher they had found somewhere on the ship. While the officer held his pistol on the helpless Woelk, the soldiers picked him up in the plastic table cover and lifted him onto the stretcher. They threw a blanket completely over him, including his head. When Woelk tried to pull the blanket away from his mouth one of the soldiers slapped him and re-placed it. The shot of morphine Baldridge had given him had worn off and the lower half of his body hurt terribly. By now, Woelk had deduced that a piece of shrapnel had struck him in the upper right thigh, passed through his body, and come out his right buttock, laying open wounds in both areas. He learned later that the piece had also knocked two inches off the base of his spine, and that was what was paining him the most.

The pain became worse from the movement and from the stretcher, which bowed in the middle and scraped the floor. The soldiers were not careful going around corners on their way to the well deck. Woelk could feel the bleeding start again as he bumped through the passageways and out into the cold air. But he was too frightened under his blanket to cry out. He could feel himself being carried over planks that bent and sprang back with each step. He groaned as they slid him onto the pier. He could feel gravel rubbing against his back. The groan brought a solid cuff to the face, and Woelk tried to keep himself under con-trol. He could hear people shouting and children giggling, and he surmised there must be civilians at dockside. He hoped there was a hospital nearby, but he had given up hope that it would be U.S. Navy.

Finally, he was laid down in the aisle of a bus. His blanket was stripped off and he was blindfolded and his hands tied in front of him, just like the rest.

Tim Harris could also hear people shouting and laughing as he was led off the ship. He was placed in the back end of what he thought was a van; and while he sat on the bench waiting for something to happen, he raised his hands and wiggled them in an effort to increase the circulation. A guard hit his hands hard with the barrel of a rifle and Harris put them down. A few minutes later he felt small hands touching his ankles and he heard giggling. Then someone yanked his hat down hard by the brim. It hit the bridge of his nose and hurt. He could hear feet running away and loud giggling and laughter.

Escamilla and Bailey were on the same bus with Lieutenant Steve Harris. While they were waiting for the bus to move, Escamilla heard a Korean ask Harris if he was the research officer on the *Pueblo*. He said he was, and the Korean asked him for the keys to the radio room. Haris said he didn't have them, but the Korean kept insisting that he did. After a few minutes, Harris was pulled off the bus and the bus started over a bumpy road, the crewmen sitting silently with their hands hooked around projections on the seats in front of them.

The bus stopped after about fifteen minutes and everyone was ordered off and into a building, which smelled like a barn. Escamilla guessed that it was a police station. After a few moments, he began to hear thuds and cries. He also heard Commander Bucher's voice, protesting. It was followed by more thuds and a lot of voices and commotion.

The Koreans were conducting their first interrogation. They were particularly interested in three Filipinos: Rizalino L. Aluague, twenty-seven, of Subic City, the Philippines; Policarpo Garcia, thirty-three, of Point Mugu, California; and Rogelio Abelon, twenty-three, of Ambabaay, the Philippines; and a sailor of Mexican descent, Ramon Rosales, nineteen, of El Paso, Texas.

Aluague and Abelon were steward's mates. Garcia was a storekeeper. Rosales was a seaman. The Koreans accused them of being South Korean spies and beat them about the body and face, threatening to shoot them if they didn't confess. None had anything to confess to, and they didn't even know what the *Pueblo*'s mission had been. A couple of the sailors still didn't know what country they were now in. Finally, an officer leaned down and raised the pants leg of one of the Americans. The leg was hairy. Koreans have little hair on their bodies. The men were taken, stunned and bleeding, back to the bus.

Don Bailey was wriggling his hands, trying to get some circulation into them, when someone touched them. He looked under his blindfold and could see it was a woman. She said something in Korean, and a guard untied him. She took hold of his arms and pushed them together in a rubbing motion, talking in Korean. Bailey got the idea and began to rub his hands together until the circulation returned. His hands were then retied, and the woman checked to make sure the rope wasn't too tight.

Then he heard a Korean speaking in English. "You are now in our country," he said. "If you don't follow our rules and obey our laws, you will be killed."

As Bailey was led back to the bus, he wondered how he would know what the rules and laws were.

The other buses were waiting, the motors running, when Bailey and Escamilla and the others were led out.

They were driven for about twenty minutes over what seemed like the same bumpy road they had traveled before. O'Bannon and Russell were on a bus with Woelk, who was in the aisle near the front. O'Bannon, sitting on the floor, could hear a woman up front giggling and laughing. He also heard a Korean ask a crewman behind him: "Are you mad, are you mad?" The crewman, Jimmy Shepard, said he didn't know what he was talking about. Then the Korean asked: "Who dead guy?" Shepard said he didn't know that either. The conversation shook up O'Bannon, who hadn't known anyone had been killed. He spent the rest of the trip trying to figure out who it was. He also remembered that it was his twenty-first birthday, Korean time.

The buses had air whistles instead of horns, and the drivers used them frequently. The crewmen could hear shouts and people banging on the sides of the buses. At one point they held their breath as the buses tried to negotiate a steep hill, failed, then backed down for another run. They didn't want to be stalled in the midst of wild civilians.

After a while the buses stopped and the men were pulled off. Tim Harris was yanked by his hands off the back of the van and someone caught him flush on the jaw in midair with a hard punch. Harris saw stars and fell to his knees as he hit the ground. He was dragged by his hands until he could regain his feet. His hat fell off. Someone caught up with him and jammed it back on his head.

Others were getting similar treatment. Don McClarren was struck in the right eye when his blindfold slipped, and he too saw stars as he was dragged along by his hands. The men were outraged and humiliated but helpless as the North Korean soldiers pushed and shoved them along.

Steve Woelk lay in the aisle, the pain in his hip excruciating, as crewmen filed past him and off the bus. He listened for shots but didn't hear any. In a moment he felt himself being lifted and carried off the bus, across a platform, and into what was obviously a train. His stretcher was laid across an aisle, with each end resting on a bench. The stretcher sagged almost to the floor, placing him in an uncomfortable position, but he was afraid to move because he didn't want to start the bleeding again. The plastic tablecloth had stuck to his bandages. When he tried to move, pain shot through the lower part of his body and made him dizzy. He wanted to urinate but didn't know what to do about it. He wanted to cry but didn't. So he lay there and thought about his mother and father, and the wheat and corn fields around his home in Alta Vista.

The crewmen had been led onto the train and seated on long benches, facing each other. They were still blindfolded. After the train began to move, Angelo Strano heard a voice call out: "Ayling here. Who else is here?" Strano heard a growl and a couple of thumps, then silence.

The Korean soldiers were moving through the train now, loosening the ropes around the wrists of the crewmen. Later they placed a piece of bread in the hands of each crewman. They also got water for them to drink.

Don Bailey tried to look under his blindfold to see who was sitting next to him, but when he tilted his head he was hit hard with the butt of a gun in the back of the head. He sat there half-stunned, and when someone shoved a piece of bread into his hands he was afraid to eat it for fear it was poisoned or doped. He was afraid to drink the water for the same reason, although he was terribly thirsty.

Steve Woelk was also terribly thirsty, but he didn't get water, apparently because of his wounds, and he cried out, begging. He heard someone shout: "For God's sake, give him some water," and someone came by and gave him a drink. He threw the bread on the floor because it was so dry and hard. He still had to urinate. He kept calling out, "Benjo, benjo," and a soldier came with a bucket and untied his hands. Woelk removed the blindfold himself, and the first man he saw was Francis Ginther. Woelk was glad to see that he was alive and seemed to be well. Ginther had been his principal benefactor. He had heard Woelk, half conscious, calling over and over for a doctor and then for water. Then he heard him call, "Benjo," and Ginther had shouted at a guard for help. When the bucket arrived, he removed his blindfold and helped Woelk turn on his side and urinate in the bucket. He didn't see any bandages, and he was sickened at the sight of Woelk's wounds.

Woelk didn't have any sensation in the lower part of his body and he kept asking Ginther if he was finished. Ginther took the opportunity, while his blindfold was off, to glance at his watch. It was 9:40 P.M.

One by one, the men were being led to one end of the car and set in front of a makeshift desk. Each was asked his name, rank, serial number, and his duties on the ship. Wallets were searched and handed back, and some crewmen had their blindfolds removed and their pictures taken. Then they were led back to their original seats. Tim Harris overheard Commander Bucher say to someone that the *Pueblo* was an oceanographic research ship. Bucher asked why his men were being beaten and humiliated. A Korean answered in English that he had no right to ask questions.

Jimmy Shepard wondered why the United States wasn't attacking right then. He no longer cared what happened to him.

Fourteen

IT WAS A LONG NIGHT for the men of the *Pueblo*. They tried to doze, but they were forced to remain in a sitting position and the benches were hard. The compartments were cold, and if a crewman made a move that displeased a guard, he was cuffed. Woelk mercifully lost consciousness.

About 6 A.M. the train ground to a stop and soldiers moved through the compartments untying hands and removing blindfolds. Tim Harris blinked and looked around the dark, dirty interior. He tried to look outside, but paper covered the windows. In a few moments he was pulled out of his seat and led to the end of the car, where he saw his roommate, Lieutenant Schumacher. They looked at each other without expression, and Harris shrugged. Soon after, Bucher and Lacy joined them. There was a lot of commotion. Several Korean officers in their long black greatcoats stood about in the aisles, their coats open and their hands on their hips. Harris could see pistols strapped to their waists.

An officer came in and said in barely understandable English: "You have now arrived at your destination." Harris guessed it was Pyongyang, the capital of North Korea. The previous U.S. military men to arrive in Pyongyang had been members of the U.S. Eighth Army on October 19, 1950. They had come as conquerors.

Bucher, Harris, Schumacher, and Lacy were told to line up in order of rank and walk in single file off the train. As they went down the steps, Tim Harris looked around for Murphy and Steve Harris, but apparently some of the Koreans didn't know yet that they were officers.

The train station was crowded with people, and there were floodlights all around the perimeter. As Bucher stepped off the train a man in his early twenties dressed in civilian clothes rushed up and kicked him in the left thigh. Bucher had seen him coming and tried to dodge the blow, but it caught him flush. The man was yanked away by guards, and off to the right Harris saw many civilians being held back by heavily armed soldiers. An officer told the crewmen to follow him and motioned for them to raise their arms. Tim Harris could see photographers' flashbulbs pop and he heard a great hubbub of excitement as the crew began filing onto the platform. He could see some civilians behind the lights, shaking their fists and shouting and making faces.

While the crewmen were forming ranks with the officers in front, Ginther, Lieutenant Murphy, Dale E. Rigby, twenty, of Ogden, Utah, and Norman W. Spear, twenty-five, of Portland, Maine, were told to remain behind and carry Woelk, who was conscious now and smoking a cigarette someone had given him. Murphy and Rigby took the front of the stretcher, and Ginther and Spear the back. They carried Woelk to a bus nearby and laid him in the aisle. Rigby dropped his lighter on the way, and Woelk leaned halfway out of his stretcher to pick it up and hand it back to him. He expected to be in hospital in a few minutes and looked forward to it.

After a few minutes more of picture taking the rest of the crew filed onto two large buses. It was still dark, but there were no coverings on the windows, and even in their desperation the men looked forward to a little sightseeing. Bucher and Schumacher were sitting together in the back of one bus looking out the window when it started. But a soldier reached over and smacked them both hard in the back of the head and they had to keep their heads bowed the rest of the trip. They still managed to look out of the corners of their eyes.

There were faint glimmers of light as the buses pulled out of the train station and turned onto a large, four-lane highway. It was bitterly cold in the buses, and the crewmen sat hunched together for warmth in the three-passenger seats.

There was no traffic as they drove into Pyongyang and down a broad boulevard lighted by mercury-vapor street lamps. The crew could see long rows of four-story buildings on each side of the boulevard. The bottom stories were stores with consumer goods, mostly clothing, in the windows. Sergeant Hammond, sitting next to a window, guessed that the upper stories were apartments. The buildings were western style and covered an entire block. Hammond was surprised at how modern the city looked. He was also surprised to see a group of about forty people jogging along in formation in the gray dawn, their breath steaming in the cold air. They took no notice of the buses or the jeep escort.

The buses passed through a couple of traffic circles and turned onto another broad boulevard with an island in the middle. Hammond noticed the absence of traffic lights.

After about forty minutes the buses angled to the left off the main boulevard and onto a rougher road and then through an archway onto a dirt drive. The men could see a long building of about four stories and a smaller building, both of concrete construction. The buses pulled up to the back door of the larger building. The crewmen had arrived at their new home.

Charlie Law thought it was a hell of a predicament to be in. Instead of the Koreans being in a whole bunch of trouble, the crew of the *Pueblo* was. He wished the United States would drop a bomb; he'd take his chances.

Ginther, Spear, Rigby, and Murphy picked up Woelk again and the men filed off the buses into the building. As Law went through the small door and into a hallway, he saw a Korean in his underwear come out of a room and watch. Law figured that they were in some sort of army barracks. The men later named the building "The Barn."

Law wasn't hungry, but he was thirsty and he had to go to the head again. This was a common problem with the crew at this point. For the next several days the problem would be constipation.

Without much ceremony the men were led up three wide flights of stairs and assigned to rooms—ten men in one, eight in each of two others, two to another, and the rest to rooms in groups of four.

The officers had separate rooms. Tim Harris's was about fourteen by twenty feet, with a wooden floor, one wooden table, a straight-backed wooden chair, and a bed just long enough for his five-foot-ten-inch frame. The mattress was no more than a sack with lumpy padding. One dim, bare light bulb hung from the ceiling. There was a big window at one end of the room, but it was covered by a piece of cloth. There was a radiator just below it. The door had cracks through which Harris could see guards look from time to time. The room was dusty as though it hadn't been used for some time.

Harris had just sat down in the chair when a Korean officer, a senior captain, walked in and said in almost perfect English: "You may go to sleep now." Harris lay on the bed and tried to doze off, but it was very cold in the room and the one thin blanket was of little use. He closed his eyes. He had been lying there shivering for about an hour when the door opened again and a fat, dumpy Korean woman in her twenties brought in a wooden tray which held three slices of hard, stale bread, a small piece of butter, and a bowl of small turnips. She also carried a teapot filled with water, and a cup and saucer. Harris was thirsty, and he poured some water while the woman set the food on the table and left. Her flat expression never changed, nor did she say a word. She didn't even look at him.

The water was filthy, but Harris drank it.

The woman came back almost immediately and laid a package of cigarettes and some wooden matches on the table. The cigarettes where Korean, loosely packed in a green package with a picture of a sea gull on the front. Harris lit one. It was strong and liberally sprinkled with small sticks and weed. Harris then ate all the food but found it tasteless and unfilling. He looked at the watch he had borrowed from Barrett so long ago in the *Pueblo*'s pilot house. It was 10 A.M. on January 24, 1968. Harris lay down and went to sleep.

Fifteen

EXCEPT FOR WOELK, CHICCA, AND CRANDELL, the enlisted men were in slightly better condition than the officers. At least they had one another and were not confronted with the terrible and sudden loneliness that assailed the four officers who had been separated from the rest of the crew. Murphy and Steve Harris still hadn't been uncovered as officers, or else the Koreans had forgotten. Murphy, in a room with Ginther, Rosales, and Spear, told them that the *Pueblo* had not come close to intruding on Korean waters.

Woelk had been carried by his crewmates from the bus to a room and laid on the floor. Korean guards came and placed him on a bed, stretcher and all. He told Chicca, Crandell (who had a long wound on his leg), and Rigby (the only unwounded crewman in the room) that Hodges was dead, and then waited for the Koreans to take him and Chicca and Crandell to a hospital. But the three wounded lay there the rest of the day and all the next day without attention.

Finally they got some water, but the amount was so meager they had to ration it. Woelk didn't get anything to eat and finally lapsed into semiconsciousness, overwhelmed by pain. Rigby tended his three shipmates. All he had to rely on was Boy Scout training in first aid, but it was useful. He got a bottle from the guards so Woelk could urinate. He tried to make all three as comfortable as possible, but it was a losing battle. Woelk was stuck to the stretcher where his blood had dried and he couldn't move. He lay there, unaware of what was going on, crying out for help in rare moments of consciousness. The room stank from the wounds.

Chicca, Crandell, and Rigby begged for help for him, and finally after three days some Korean soldiers came in late at night and lifted him by the plastic tablecloth off his stretcher and onto another one, then carried him three rooms down the hall. It had the same dim light bulb hanging from the ceiling, but there was only one piece of furniture in it, a table underneath the bulb, with some surgical instruments on it.

The soldiers laid Woelk in the stretcher, on the table. He was wearing a T-shirt, a dungaree jacket, and shoes. His pants had been cut off by Baldridge on the ship. There were two doctors, a nurse, and an interpreter in the room, all wearing gauze masks, and the interpreter leaned over and said it wouldn't hurt. Woelk didn't think the interpreter gave a damn whether it hurt or not.

He was blindfolded and his hands were tied behind his head, and he shortly discovered that this was the Koreans' substitute for anesthetic. When the operation began, the nurse held his feet down because he was kicking so much.

The doctors took two pieces of metal out of him and cleaned his wounds, which had become infected. Then they put on fresh bandages, took the blindfold off, and untied his hands. The operation had taken half an hour. Woelk, dizzy with pain and fear, was carried back to his room and put in his bed.

For Commander Bucher, the worst was just beginning. Almost immediately after he had been led to his room he was taken to a large room at the end of the hall for questioning. He was told over and over again that he and his men were spies, which he denied. He told his interrogators that he and his crew came under the provisions of the Geneva Convention and that they were military prisoners. His captors laughed at him and told him he and his crew would be treated as civilian espionage agents, tried under Korean law, and shot. Bucher was asked to sign a typed confession stating that he was a spy and a member of the Central Intelligence Agency (CIA) and was trying to start a war. He refused.

He noted that one interrogator had his personal file from the ship, and he saw no reason to deny the personal history contained in it.

He thought the Koreans were apparently confused by references to CIC (Combat Information Center) School in his personal history and were convinced that he was a member of the CIA. Bucher learned that the Koreans were obsessed with the CIA.

Tim Harris, meanwhile, had slept until about 3 P.M. on the afternoon of the 24th and was sitting in his chair wondering what was going to happen next. He felt certain that they would be out of this in two weeks at the most and was just considering how he could stand the utter boredom that long when a Korean officer came into his room and ordered him into the hall. The other five *Pueblo* officers, their heads bowed, were there waiting, and Harris thought that it hadn't taken long for the Koreans to find out about Murphy and Steve Harris. They were lined up in order of rank and then led to the same big room at the end of the hall where Bucher had been questioned.

In the middle of the room was a desk with a Korean officer, a general, behind it. The officer was in his middle forties, with a bland, chubby face. He was wearing a big gray quilted overcoat, and there was a smirk on his face as the American officers filed in and sat down in chairs in front of his desk. To the left of the chairs was a table, behind which were seated three Korean officers, including the one who had told Harris to sleep. He was an interpreter, a man with a soft, even voice who always seemed to be smiling.

The Korean officers at the table were wearing Nehru-type olive-green jackets that came down to the top of the thigh and buttoned tightly around the neck. Their pants were cuffless, and they wore ankle-high black boots. Wide brown belts went around their waists and across their chests. On each collar was a two-inch-wide yellow stripe with a red stripe in the middle. Metal stars gave their ranks.

The general, his manner calm and deliberate, got down to business without ceremony, asking through his interpreter what the *Pueblo* was doing in Korean territorial waters. Bucher stood up and said the ship was conducting oceanographic research and had not violated territorial waters. The American officers were asked what their jobs were on the ship. They stood up one at a time and answered. Tim Harris half stood and said, "Supply officer." Each was asked whether the *Pueblo* had violated Korean waters. Each stood again and said, "No." Then they were asked why American troops were in South Korea.

Bucher stood and said, "To my understanding, the South Korean government asked us to be there."

This infuriated an officer sitting at the table on the left. He raised up and banged the table, shouting loudly in Korean and stomping his foot. The American officers immediately switched their attention to him. Something in his manner told them he was no ordinary person and they watched him closely as he delivered his tirade in a hard, strong voice. The Korean officer had a thick shock of jet-black hair combed straight back without a part. He was about forty and very thin, with high cheekbones and large, protruding front teeth that gave him a horsy look. He was exceptionally well-groomed, and his eyes were quick behind green-tinted glasses. Except for the teeth, Harris thought he would be regarded as handsome, even by American standards. He was a senior colonel and he would soon become known to the crew of the *Pueblo* as Super C. In a short while, the general, who eyed them so deliberately while he chain-smoked and toyed with his cigarette lighter, would leave and the crew of the *Pueblo* would be in the hands of the senior colonel.

Until the outburst by Super C, the discussion had been reasonably calm. Harris was dazed and a little frightened by the display and realized that it was no act. American troops in South Korea were also an obsession with their captors.

When Super C had finished his tirade, the general calmly looked them in the eye one by one, then said in a hard, even voice: "You are spies and you will be shot. How do you want to be shot? One at a time or all together?"

Bucher stood without being asked and said, "You should release my crew and ship and just shoot me." After that was interpreted, the general laughed and said, "You will be shot at dawn." Then they were dismissed. The whole thing had taken half an hour. As they went back to their rooms, Tim Harris thought that the man was bluffing. If they had been going to shoot the Americans, they would have done it a long time ago. But Harris was frightened nevertheless.

He went back to his room after the meeting with Super C and lay down, but he couldn't sleep. About 5:30 P.M. the same Korean woman brought in a wooden tray and set it on the table. The food was soup in a tin bowl that reminded Harris of a dog dish, and the same hard bread. The soup was hot and contained turnips, radishes, and one small piece of fish. The fish was good, but the soup was watery and tasteless, without salt or pepper. Harris ate every scrap, but he was still more nervous than hungry, so he chain-smoked until an officer came in and told him to go to bed. Harris knocked on the door to get the guard's attention and motioned to the light switch. The guard shook his head, and the light remained on. It remained on for the next forty days.

Harris was restless and still couldn't sleep. About midnight he heard movement in Bucher's room next door. There were shouts in Korean, the noise of scuffling, the thump of someone being thrown against a wall. Harris strained for Bucher's voice but didn't hear it, just more commotion and doors slamming.

There were footsteps in the hall constantly. Each time they went past, Harris tensed, expecting his door to open. The sounds, the footsteps, and the commotion went on all night. Harris, exhausted, finally went to sleep about 5 A.M.

The Koreans were desperate, and they were showing their desperation to Bucher in raw form. They had to justify their seizure of the *Pueblo* to the world, and to do that they thought they had to get a confession from Bucher that the *Pueblo* had intruded on Korean waters and that Bucher was a spy.

About 8 P.M. he had been taken to the large room at the end of the hall where Super C and another officer waited with drawn pistols. Several interpreters and three or four guards with rifles and fixed bayonets were also present.

Bucher was again told to sign the typed confession. When he refused he was told to sign or he would be shot. He was forced to kneel on the floor, and an officer placed a pistol at the back of his head. He was told he had two minutes to sign. After the two minutes were up, he heard Super C say, "Kill the son of a bitch!" The gun clicked but nothing happened. Bucher was told the gun had misfired. He was told he had another two minutes, and he felt now that the Koreans were playing games with him. When he refused again to sign, he was told that he was not worth a bullet and that he would be beaten to death.

The officers stepped back and the guards moved in and beat him about the body for several minutes with their rifles and fists until he lost consciousness. He was carried back to his room.

Bucher's famous stamina, known in a score of liberty ports around the world, was about to give out. He had not eaten or slept since the capture and he had been roughed up and questioned constantly almost since the time he stepped off the *Pueblo*. His wounds, while superficial, were painful and untreated. When he came to in his room he was pulled from his bed and slammed around and beaten some more, then taken to the interrogation room again and told by Super C that he would now see what happened to spies.

Groggy and sore, Bucher was taken downstairs and outside to a staff car and driven to a building about ten minutes away, according to the story he told Tim Harris later. He was led into the basement and shown a man, allegedly South Korean, strapped to the wall; his arm was broken and one eye hung from its socket. Super C, his pistol in his hand, said, "Now you know what happens to spies."

Then Bucher was taken back to the interrogation room. After another hour of questioning he was told that his crew would be shot one by one in his presence, starting with the youngest member.

He was told that Fireman Howard E. Bland had already been
sent for. Bland, twenty, was not the youngest nor had he been
taken from his room, but Bucher was by now convinced that the
North Koreans were up against it and would stop at nothing to
prove their case before the world. He signed the confession.

It was a remarkable document.

It was carried in full in the English edition of the Pyongyang
Times of February 1, 1968, under this heading: "Confession of
Criminal Aggressive Acts by Captain of Armed Spy Ship of U.S.
Imperialist Aggressor Forces Captured While Committing Es-
pionage Activities After Intruding into Coastal Waters of
D.P.R.K."

It read, in part:

I am commander Lloyd Mark Bucher, captain of the USS *Pueblo*
belonging to the Pacific Fleet, U.S. Navy, who was captured while
carrying out espionage activities after intruding deep into the territorial waters of the Democratic People's Republic of Korea. . . .

My ship had been sent to Sasebo, Japan, to execute assignments
given by the U.S. Central Intelligence Agency. . . .

The U.S. Central Intelligence Agency promised me that if this task
would be done successfully, a lot of dollars would be offered to the
whole crew members of my ship and particularly I myself would be
honored.

Soon after that I reinforced the arms and equipment of the ship
and made detailed preparations for espionage activities.

Then we disguised my ship as one engaged in researches on oceanic
electronics and left the port of Sasebo, Japan, and conducted espionage
acts along the coast of the Democratic People's Republic of Korea via
the general area off the Soviet Maritime Province. We pretended
ourselves to conduct the observation of oceanic conditions on high
seas, electronics, research on electric waves, magnetic conditions and
exploitation of oceanic materials. . . .

Furthermore we spied on various military installations and the
distribution of industries and the deployment of armed forces along
the east coast areas and sailed up to the point 7.6 miles of Ryodo
Island (39 degrees 17.4' N., 127 degrees 46.9' E.), when the navy patrol
crafts of the Korean People's Army appeared.

We were on the alert instantly and tried to escape firing at the
navy patrol crafts of the People's Army.

But the situation became more dangerous for us and thus one of
my men was killed, another heavily wounded and two others lightly

wounded.

We had no way out, and were captured by the navy patrol crafts of the People's Army.

Having been captured now, I say frankly that our act was a criminal act which flagrantly violated the Armistice Agreement, and it was a sheer act of agression. . . .

The crime committed by me and my men is entirely indelible. . . .

Therefore, we only hope, and it is the greatest desire of myself and all my crew, that we will be forgiven leniently by the Government of the Democratic People's Republic of Korea.

Beneath the confession was a picture of Bucher hunched over a table signing a piece of paper, his hair hanging down in his face. When they had time later, the Koreans got a much longer and more detailed confession from Bucher.

Sixteen

FOR THE FIRST COUPLE OF DAYS the *Pueblo* men had it fairly easy while the Koreans worked on the officers. Charlie Law had been led to Room No. 23 with Bland, Layton, and William W. Scarborough, twenty-five, of Anderson, South Carolina, and told to go to sleep. About 8 A.M. a woman came in and set four plates of bread and turnip stew on the table. Lunch came about 1:30 and dinner about 7. Otherwise, the men just lay on their beds or walked about the room smoking, talking, and wondering how long it would take the United States to get them out of there.

On the second evening an officer wearing a gauze mask over his face came in and led them to a room down the hall which contained stacks of clothing. The men were told to strip to the skin and remove everything from their pockets. They were allowed to keep their watches, rings, lighters, pens, and pencils but had to hand over their wallets and dog tags. These were bundled together with their old clothes and tagged with their names. The men never saw them again.

Two Korean enlisted men and an officer, all wearing gauze masks, issued them their detention uniforms: undershorts, long underwear with drawstrings at the ankles and waist, a coarse cotton slipover shirt, a dark blue suit, and heavy quilted pants and jacket. They also got heavy quilted tennis shoes, with rubber soles, that laced above the ankles, and fur hats with earflaps.

The atmosphere was such that a simple thing like the gauze masks the Koreans wore heightened the tension, but the men had to laugh at one another when they got back to the room. Someone said they looked like commies. All they needed was slant eyes and horns. They quickly named their new outfit C.B.O., for Charlie Brown Outfit, a term straight out of the *Peanuts* comic strip.

The next evening, the crew's third in North Korea, the men in Room No. 23 received their first harsh words. They were sitting at their table when an officer and two guards came in. The officer barked at them to stand at attention and told them they were disrespectful. He said this would not be tolerated, then handed out mimeographed personal-history forms, two sheets to each man, and told the men to fill them out.

Law, Layton, Bland, and Scarborough discussed whether to fill them out even though to do so would violate the Code of Conduct, which had been instituted in 1955 for U.S. prisoners of war. It suggests to prisoners that they reveal only name, rank, and serial number.

The forms the Koreans distributed went much further but asked no questions of a military nature, so the men decided to fill them out. They figured the Koreans had their service records from the ship anyway. They answered all the questions—falsely as much as possible.

Two days later an officer brought the forms back and told them to fill them out correctly. He was holding their service records from the ship in his hand, so the men decided to comply. Then they stood up against the wall to have their pictures taken. Each got an extra blanket.

Things were even easier than that in Room No. 14 for a while, although the room had made a bad name for itself almost immediately. Mike O'Bannon, Charles Sterling, Larry E. Strickland, twenty, of Grand Rapids, Michigan, and Michael W. Alexander, twenty-one, of Richland, Washington, didn't get the message about the proper way to go to the head. They were supposed to knock on the door, wait for the guard to open it, and ask permission to go.

But Room No. 14 would stick its collective head out the door, yell, "Benjo," and then troop off to the bathroom at the end of the hall. The guards seemed to be afraid of their cocky attitude, and they got away with it for five days.

Going to the head was an unrewarding experience, however. It had four badly cracked urinals, and until the crew learned how to handle the situation they found themselves urinating on their own feet.

The behavior of Room No. 14 made the Koreans do some strange things. On the second day a guard caught O'Bannon sitting on the window ledge with his feet on the table. The guard seemed insulted and left, slamming the door. The next day their good table was removed and replaced with a rickety one with several boards missing. O'Bannon was caught sitting on the table, and it was replaced with a white table, in good condition, about five feet long. The men used coins to play shuffleboard on it.

When they got their new clothing the coins were taken away, so they made a deck of cards out of toilet paper, which was no more than rough brown wrapping paper. The guard caught them playing cards with their makeshift deck and apparently didn't understand what they were doing. But he seemed to think that it was something sinister. After giving them all a hard look, he took the cards away. A Korean duty officer came in shortly afterward and told them they mustn't do that. They asked the duty officer for more toilet paper. When he went and got it, they promptly nicknamed him Fetch.

After about four days a Korean officer came in with the personal-history forms. The crewmen told him they had already done that, and he went away.

But, for other rooms, reckoning came quickly.

Vic Escamilla was in Room No. 18 with Signalman Leach, Fireman Richard I. Bame, twenty, of Maybee, Michigan, and Clifford Nolte. Escamilla had some idea of what the Koreans were really like because he had been in the police station and had heard some of the crewmen being beaten. He had walked off the bus to The Barn with his hands in his pockets and had received a sharp karate chop in the throat from a guard. It had left him choking and gagging.

Escamilla, like many aboard the *Pueblo,* didn't know the ship's mission and had learned from scuttlebutt only a couple of days before the capture that they were off North Korea. He wasn't prepared for what was to come.

On the third day of captivity the personal-history forms were brought to Room No. 18 and left for the crewmen to fill out. Escamilla warned the others that they were not supposed to reveal more than name, rank, and serial number, and that is all they put on the forms.

The Koreans were angry and told Escamilla and Nolte, who was also against filling out the forms, not to talk to the others. Escamilla and Nolte were taken into the hall and told to get on their knees and raise their arms over their heads. After about ten minutes they were asked if they would sign. They refused and asked to see Commander Bucher.

They were kicked in the ribs.

After about half an hour they were taken to separate rooms. Escamilla was told to take his pants off. He thought he was going to be castrated and closed his eyes and prayed.

But instead Escamilla was told to kneel on the floor, raise his arms, and walk on his knees in circles. When he dropped his arms, he was kicked in the ribs and under the arms. The officer kept calling him a son of a bitch and told him the Geneva Convention didn't apply to him because he was a prisoner of espionage. The officer said no one could help him now, not even the great United States, and his fate was to be decided by Korean law.

Then he asked Escamilla to fill out the forms. He refused and asked again to see his captain. He was kicked again and a chair was placed in the center of the floor. He was told to circle it on his knees, his arms still raised. After an hour and a half he was given a drink of water and an officer came in with some papers under his arm. Escamilla, his knees now raw and bleeding from the rough floor, saw that the papers were Gene Lacy's personnel file. He realized for the first time that there had been a terrible oversight. The crew's service records had not been destroyed, a mistake that the Koreans were using to great effect. He agreed to fill out his questionnaire, but he was shaking so badly that he couldn't write.

After about an hour he was able to fill out the form and was taken back to his room. About an hour later Nolte was brought in, his knees in even worse shape than Escamilla's. He had filled out his forms after the Koreans had shown him Escamilla's.

It wasn't the kind of "torture" the crew might have expected from the Koreans, but it was effective. The Koreans were ignorant of American ways, but they were masters of the art of getting what they wanted.

It took the Koreans longer, but they finally got what they wanted from Marine Sergeant Bob Hammond, a blond youngster who looks a little like Alan Ladd. Hammond had come aboard the *Pueblo* with Chicca to monitor Korean radio signals and warn of possible danger. After their capture, their knowledge of the language made them marked men.

Hammond had trouble almost from the beginning of captivity. He had been struck in the mouth on the bus for moving, and a Korean woman had come by and rapped him hard two or three times on the top of the head for no apparent reason. Getting on the train, Hammond had asked if they were in Wonsan. An officer laughed and squeezed his face until it hurt.

Once in The Barn, he refused to tell the Koreans his age, and they put a gun against his stomach and told him he had one more chance. When he remained silent, the trigger was pulled, but the gun was empty.

He had figured they wouldn't shoot him because a guard was standing right behind him. The guard told him to go to the head, but he was afraid. He thought they would beat him once they got him in the hallway.

Strangely enough, Hammond filled out his personal-history form without argument, although, like many of the others, he falsified many of the answers. But the Koreans wanted to know if Hammond spoke their language and he denied that he did.

They accepted his denial the first three times, but the fourth time they made him kneel in a corner holding a chair over his head while four guards kicked him under the arms and in the ribs.

Hammond figured that the Koreans knew he spoke their

language or they would have never asked the question, but he was determined not to give in. The punishment increased after each denial, and finally all the furniture was removed from the room and he was dragged to the middle, where four or five guards took turns beating and kicking him. A piece of wood was placed behind his knees, and one of the guards stood on the backs of his ankles while the others took turns hitting him in the face with their fists. When he fell over they picked him up again. Once someone stepped on his throat and he thought he was going to die. His back hurt so badly he couldn't get up by himself. When he began to yell, a rag was stuffed into his mouth.

He was held in a standing position while the backs of his legs were beaten with a board. Then he was kicked in the groin. Finally, after six hours, he mumbled through swollen lips, "Okay, okay."

This didn't suit the Koreans now. They plainly wanted to make an example of him. He was given some water, which revived him enough so that he tried to stare one of the officers down, although his eyes were almost closed from the beating. The officer became furious and struck him with several hard karate chops across the face and neck. Then he was alternately beaten and questioned for thirteen more hours, with only an occasional drink of water for respite.

When he was taken back to his room, his roommates were shocked at his condition. Nothing had prepared them for this sort of treatment. They thought they were prisoners of war and that, except for some minor infringements, they would be treated as such.

Hammond couldn't stand without help for almost a week, but he received no mercy from the Korean guards, who demanded that he follow the same routine as his roommates. Hammond was deeply disappointed in himself. He had thought he could outlast the Koreans.

Seventeen

ONCE COMMANDER BUCHER HAD SUCCUMBED to their threats and beatings, the Koreans concentrated on the other officers. They were also beaten, threatened, and questioned. The treatment accorded Ensign Tim Harris was typical, although he wasn't beaten as severely as some of the others.

On the second day of detention he was taken to the big interrogation room two doors to the left of his room. An older officer whom Harris had not seen before and would not see again was sitting with a bored expression behind Super C's desk.

Harris was still wearing the clothing he had left the ship with. To hide his fear, he flipped his hat from hand to hand as he sat down. Harris was certain that Commander Bucher and the others had been beaten, but he had seen no one in the crew since entering his room two days previously. The fear of physical harm was bad enough, but the uncertainty and the loneliness were doing the real damage. As Harris faced this bored-looking old man, he tried to fight him with flippancy.

The officer asked him if he would answer some questions.

"All depends on what they are," Harris said, flipping his hat in his hands, his elbows resting on his knees. He thought his personnel record had been destroyed and figured he would lie his way through the interview, although he noticed an interpreter to his left writing down everything he said. Harris told them the correct names of his mother and father but lied about their ages. He admitted he was married but lied about his wife's age and told them she was living in Florida when she was actually in Japan. He said his father was a carpenter. His father was a Navy veteran of twenty-six years, and his mother had been a Wave. They asked him if he had had a .45-caliber pistol on board the ship, and he said no.

An interpreter raised up and shouted, "You lie! If you lie we knock you out!" Harris thought he did it for form's sake, to keep things alive.

The older officer seemed to come awake at this and admonished Harris to sit straight up and keep a military bearing. Harris laid his hat on the floor and thought to himself, "These guys are really screwed up."

The Koreans asked him where the Naval Academy was. Harris said to himself, "If you're really that dumb, let's see how dumb you are." He told them it was in the Great Lakes. They asked him where the Air Force Academy was. Harris said it was in Texas. The officer asked, "Is it on Johnson's ranch?"

Harris leaned back and said, "Heell yes," in a simulated Texas drawl. They wanted to know about the National Guard. Harris pulled his chair up, leaned back again, and began to talk expansively. The Koreans leaned forward in their chairs eagerly.

"There are thirty million National Guardsmen," Harris said. "Every city no matter how small has a National Guard unit." He said the National Guard was as tough as nails.

"Why does the National Guard beat up people in the American people's struggle for liberation?" he was asked. Harris said the people were beaten only when they deserved it. "You lie," an officer said, hitting the table. "Johnson calls for the National Guard to beat up people," the officer said.

The Koreans wanted to know how many Army bases there were in the United States. Harris said he was in the Navy and didn't know. They said, "You know, you in military." Harris finally said there were four hundred bases, and six thousand ships in the Navy.

The questioning lasted over an hour. The Koreans wrote down faithfully every one of his outrageous lies. It all seemed nonsensical to Harris, a little bit like low comedy, and he was puzzled.

He was questioned again the next night by the same men. This time they wanted to know about his job as supply officer on the *Pueblo*, and they asked him to list all the supplies he had ever ordered for the ship.

When he said that was impossible, he was made to get on his knees and sit back on his ankles. He thought that, too, was nonsense and began to reel off anything that came to his mind, the first one being fifteen hundred sheets of toilet paper. He remained on his knees for forty-five minutes, listing supplies. They always wanted to know the amount and wrote down faithfully every nonsensical figure Harris gave them.

The Koreans wanted to know about the poor people in the United States and why something wasn't being done for them. Harris said there were programs to take care of them. Sometimes the Koreans just preached to him. It was plain that their most cherished desire was reunification with South Korea, and they said over and over that the U.S. imperialist aggressor forces in South Korea were the greatest obstacle to reunification. The phrases became so familiar that Harris could see them coming and would recite them under his breath along with the officer.

This went on for a week, and then the Koreans suddenly stopped playing with him. Harris was brought before a colonel one night and was read the Rules of Life under which he would live while a captive.

The colonel told Harris he must stand at attention when someone entered the room; he must clean his room every morning; he must knock on the door for permission to go to the bathroom; he must not attempt to communicate with other rooms; he must obey orders unconditionally; he must lie on his bed at the required time; and he must sit in his chair unless specifically required to do something else.

The colonel told him that everything not mentioned in the Rules of Life was illegal and forbidden.

Life began to fall into a pattern for Harris during that first week. He had to be in bed at 10 P.M. and up at 6 A.M. The food was virtually the same for all three meals: turnip soup and a small piece of fish. The quality of the fish deteriorated steadily until it was all Harris could do to eat it. Meals were served in his room, which was bitterly cold, and the light suspended from the ceiling burned twenty-four hours a day. He was hungry and cold all the time, and terribly lonely. He could hear movement in the hall, but he didn't know whether his crewmates were dead or alive, maimed or insane. No one ever mentioned them, and he didn't see them.

The Korean structure of organization began to take shape to him, and so did the Koreans. They all looked alike at first, but now they began to separate into personalities. There were nearly a dozen duty officers, all in their late twenties or early thirties. The guards were young, in their late teens, and mean. They kicked and cuffed Harris whenever he went to the bathroom at the end of the hall.

The duty officers were frequent visitors to his room. They seemed to like Harris because he was a junior officer like themselves, and they considered him almost like one of them, perhaps because of his youth.

Fetch, in particular, was a frequent visitor. Harris hadn't learned of the name Room 14 had given him, but he would have agreed with it. Fetch was about 5 feet, 5 inches, and weighed about 120 pounds. He had a smashed-in face, slanted eyes, a flat, yellow complexion, and bushy black hair. He spoke bad English through a small mouth and in a low, soft voice. His laugh was a sort of double grunt.

Fetch told Harris in his naïve way that although he had been in the Army most of his life and hadn't had time to get married, he had a girl friend and would get married as soon as the country was unified. Fetch appeared to be sympathetic and kept asking Harris if he missed his wife.

"Yes, I understand your feelings," Fetch would say. "You are lonely. In order to return home to your wife, you must tell complete truth about all things. You must confess everything and do not lie. You lie and we will find out. You must confess for your criminal acts, and your government must confess and apologize."

That was the official line, and Harris was aware that the Koreans were working on him in a subtle way, holding out hope that he would be released if he did as they said. The duty officers tried to get Harris to feel sorry for himself, which made Harris angry because their motives were so transparent.

He could tell Fetch this and get away with it. Fetch would change the subject quickly, and one day he asked Harris if he had children. Harris said he had been married only four months. Fetch looked surprised and asked if he slept with his wife. "Yes," Harris answered, "but no children."

Thus he learned about Fetch's intense curiosity about sex. Fetch said that one day, when the whole world was socialistic, he would go to Hawaii. He was fascinated when Harris told him he had been there. Fetch wanted to know all about Hawaiian women. Harris figured that someone had told Fetch once that Hawaii was running over with beautiful, available women and Fetch would have happily chucked the whole Communist bit for a chance to go there.

After several days of soft treatment, Harris came face to face with reality again.

Harris was given an outline of a confession early one day and told to fill it out. He wrote four pages, which said essentially that he was a supply officer and didn't know what was going on otherwise. A duty officer brought it back during the afternoon and told him it wasn't good enough and said he must tell the complete truth. Harris wrote the same thing, only in eight pages, and handed it in. Late that night Harris was taken to the interrogation room and put in a chair in front of Super C, who looked grim. He was playing with his cigarette lighter with well-manicured hands while his translater interpreted for him.

"You have not told the complete truth," the colonel said. Harris said he was only the supply officer and didn't know anything. The colonel said, "We think you are lying. Do you want to see proof?" Then he waved a sheaf of classified documents in Harris's face. Harris was surprised. He thought the documents would have been included in the first group to be destroyed. Harris said he had never seen them before.

The colonel said that Harris must write a confession admitting espionage and intrusion. Harris said: "We didn't do that." An officer with a large scar on the back of his head came in, listened for a moment, and called Harris "son of a bitch" in perfect English. Most of the Koreans knew all the American curse words. Super C left the room then, and Harris became frightened.

The officer with the scar gave Harris a pencil and paper and dictated questions that he wanted answered. He wanted to know who gave the *Pueblo* its orders; what the orders were; what information had been collected; what Harris's espionage activities were; and what the espionage activities of other crewmen were. The latter question was Harris's first taste of a typical Korean ploy. They continually put the crewmen under pressure to rat on each other.

He told Harris to write down the names of those who held
the ultimate responsibility for the aggressive action against the
Democratic People's Republic of Korea, and demanded that
Harris beg forgiveness from the Korean people for his criminal
acts.

Harris wrote the questions down but said he couldn't answer
them because he didn't know. The officer paced the room in a
rage and cursed Harris again. Super C returned to the room, sat at
his desk, and pointed his finger at Harris.

"Go back and write confession. No more double talk," he
said. For the first time, the colonel pounded the table and
showed anger. Then he dismissed Harris with a wave of his hand.

Harris went back to his room. He was supposed to write the
confession right then, but it was late. So he went to bed. An hour
later the interpreter came in and took him back to the interrogation room.

A senior captain whom Harris had never seen before was
sitting behind the desk, and there was a new interpreter. The
captain said he was going to test Harris's honest mind, and
asked who Syngman Rhee was. Harris said he didn't know. The
captain asked if he knew who Westmoreland was. Harris said he
was the general in charge of U.S. forces in Vietnam. Harris was
asked what espionage acts he had taken part in, and who among
the *Pueblo* crew was a CIA agent. Harris said he took part in no
espionage acts, and he didn't know about any CIA agents. The
captain stood up and shouted: "I will give you one more chance.
Are you going to make a true confession?"

Harris said he already had.

He was told to go to a corner of the room and get on his
knees, and hold a chair over his head. A guard stood behind him.
When Harris's arms got tired and he let the chair slip, the guard
kicked him under the arms, in the ribs, and in the back. The captain came over and said: "Didn't you log thirty-five to forty
radar contacts while you were officer of the deck?" Harris said
he had not, although he had, and he wondered how the Koreans
had got that information. He thought all the logs had been destroyed. The captain wanted to know how he had gotten from

Pensacola to the *Pueblo*, which startled Harris. He thought the personnel records had been destroyed also. The captain told him the operational code name for the *Pueblo*'s mission was "Pink Root," which Harris denied. He said they didn't have an operational code name.

"I know all about your mission," the captain said, and walked away.

After two hours of being kicked and punched, Harris said he would write a new confession. He was taken back to his room and given three hours to complete it. The captain told him that if he didn't do it right this time he would never eat again. Harris was tired, hungry, and sore, and so he wrote what he thought the Koreans wanted. He figured they knew everything anyway, and then admitted to himself that he was rationalizing and that he shouldn't confess to anything. But his spirit was deadened. The interpreter came in, and Harris read the confession to him.

The captain came in a few minutes later and asked the interpreter if he thought the confession was satisfactory. The interpreter nodded yes. Harris thought they, too, were weary and just wanted to get it over with. Harris never signed the confession or saw it again.

Eighteen

LIEUTENANT MURPHY AND QUARTERMASTER LAW were of great interest to the Koreans because they had navigated the ship. It was one thing to charge the *Pueblo* with intruding, and it was another thing to prove it, but the Koreans had their ways.

The Koreans began to interrogate Murphy shortly after the crew arrived at The Barn. Two officers worked with Murphy in preparing documents to support allegations of intrusions, but they found Murphy an unwilling accomplice. He denied all such allegations, and his denials were accepted without physical violence.

On the fifth day of captivity the Koreans tried to get Murphy to concur that the *Pueblo* had come within four or five miles of a small island. He denied it, and a stick was placed behind his knees as he knelt on the floor and extended his arms over his head. He wasn't beaten, and when he again refused to cooperate he was returned to his room.

The next day he was forced to assume the same kneeling position, this time holding a chair over his head. Then he was kicked and beaten, one kick bloodying his mouth and another tearing his ear. He finally agreed to confess and was taken to his room. But he changed his mind and demanded to see Commander Bucher. Super C then offered to play a recording of Bucher's confession, but Murphy said he wanted to see him instead. Then Super C told Murphy that the North Koreans had been expecting to capture the *Banner* rather than the *Pueblo*, and he showed Murphy a copy of a message captured from the *Pueblo* that showed the schedule for the *Banner* and the *Pueblo*. Murphy later heard what seemed to be a recording of Bucher's confession being played somewhere in the building.

Later, Murphy was told by an officer that he had the authority to shoot him and asked him if he was prepared to die. Murphy said he was, and the officer asked him if he would like to write a will. Murphy declined. He was then stripped to his shorts and his hands were bound with wire. He was kicked and beaten. After passing out several times he agreed to write a confession and help the Koreans with the charts.

Charlie Law also was being questioned on navigation by a junior colonel whom Law considered knowledgeable on the subject.

The colonel was curious about Loran (long range navigation) and asked Law how many Loran stations the United States had in the Pacific. Law said there were fifty. The colonel broke out a chart with the Loran stations marked on them and made Law count them; there were thirty-two. The colonel asked Law why he said fifty, and Law said: "I don't know. The Coast Guard is in charge of that anyway."

Actually, there are a Loran A and a Loran C. The colonel couldn't understand why there was no Loran B and refused to accept Law's explanation that there just wasn't one. That problem was never resolved, and after the Koreans had called him a liar several times, Law said: "Well, you'll just have to punish me," An officer hit Law on the right side of the head three or four times with his fist. Law thought that was silly since he was telling the truth.

Eventually, the Koreans got what they wanted. The position of a ship is kept on several logs. In the case of the *Pueblo*, some of the logs had been destroyed but a couple had not. The Koreans had captured an alternate-day log, which gave the *Pueblo*'s position on every other day, and they tried to work from that.

They plotted six intrusions. One placed the *Pueblo* fifty miles inland. Another had the *Pueblo* going 2,500 knots in order to maintain the intrusion. When Bucher heard about it, he said the Koreans should at least have the courtesy to keep them at sea.

The log was kept in pencil, and the Koreans, in altering the figures, had fouled them up beyond recall. Later, they came up with eleven more intrusions, plotted off the Loran log.

It was all ridiculous, Law thought. Even if the Koreans were correct on the intrusions, that hardly justified one man's death and the risk of another war.

For other members of the crew, isolation was less of a problem than the sheer uncertainty of the situation. Almost all thought they would be released in a couple of weeks.

Chuck Ayling was in Room No. 11 with Norbert Klepac, Larry Mack, and Harry Lewis, thirty-one, of Springfield Gardens, Long Island, New York, the ship's cook and one of the two Negroes on the *Pueblo*. The four were fortunate in that they were on the sunny side of The Barn and hardly needed the old cast-iron radiator that stood under the window. But it was useful for another purpose. On the first day Ayling heard tapping and scraping coming from the direction of the radiator. He went over to it and listened. The tapping and scraping sounded like Morse code to Ayling, who had learned the code as a Boy Scout. He thought at first it was a Korean trick, but when he heard it again the next day he took out his pocket comb and tapped out his name. He listened closely to the answer, calling out the letters to his roommates as he deciphered them. They thus discovered that their neighbors were Stuart Russell and Radioman Lee Hayes.

Ayling sent the names of his roommates and asked for any news Russell and Hayes might have. A message came back slowly and Ayling called out the letters. It read: "Hodges is dead." Until then, Ayling and his roommates hadn't known that anyone had been killed.

Room No. 11 soon got the treatment on the personal-history forms. Ayling and his roommates just filled out the top part, which listed name, rank, and serial number. The Koreans took Larry Mack out of the room and threatened him, then showed him Bucher's personal-history form, filled out in entirety. Room No. 11 then filled out the forms. The divide-and-conquer trick continued to make things easy for the Koreans.

Ayling was particularly worried at the attention he expected to get from the Koreans because he was a communications technician and had much valuable information in his head. Don McClarren in Room No. 12 was also worried because of the valuable information he carried in his head about U.S. codes, and Don Bailey in Room No. 20 was concerned because of his knowledge of the Navy's communications system. Bailey was also concerned about an address book in his pocket the Koreans had overlooked. Five pages in it were filled with the names and addresses of family and friends. He wanted to get rid of them but didn't know how. He finally tore them out of the book and ate them a page at a time.

He tore the rest of the pages in two, and he and Langenberg made a full deck of cards out of them. They played gin rummy and hearts until a guard caught them and took the cards away.

Bailey was one of two men of the *Pueblo* who had had SERE (Survival, Evasion, Resistance, and Escape) training, but he found out quickly that, while the training was helpful in resisting the Koreans, it didn't prepare him to outlast them. The SERE training that Bailey had taken was contained in a one-week course. Bailey thought he could stand almost anything for a week, but the indefinite captivity now facing the crew frightened him. He didn't know how long he could hold out.

Bailey's SERE training was put to the test almost immediately by the personal-history forms. The Koreans left the forms in the room, and Bailey told his roommates to fill in only what was permitted, which they did. The Koreans came back, looked at the forms, and were furious. They made the men get on their knees and hold their hands over their heads. Then they slapped and kicked them for three hours. The solid front began to crumble. The men gave in one after the other. Bailey finally falsified his forms. He knew that his service records were still in Japan and figured he could get away with almost anything. A few minutes after turning the forms in, Bailey was called from the room. A Korean officer had Bailey's medical record in his hand. He showed it to Bailey, then turned it over. On the back, written in ink, was a copy of his service record. Bailey then filled out his form correctly, cursing the efficiency of CT yeoman Peppard.

Bailey, McClarren, and Ayling were all questioned eventually on their duties, along with most of the others. The Koreans got some strange answers. Ayling told them he was a cleaning and maintenance man aboard the *Pueblo*. Hammond said he kept the machine guns clean. McClarren and Bailey said they were cleaning and maintenance. The Koreans probably wondered why a small ship like the *Pueblo* needed so much cleaning and maintenance.

One day, an officer the men called Maximilian came for Ayling and took him to the interrogation room. When Maximilian started to question him, Ayling said he wanted to see his commanding officer. Maximilian ignored the remark and said: "Will you answer questions, yes or no?" Ayling said: "Well, since you put it that way, no."

Ayling was put in a corner and forced to kneel, then beaten and kicked for more than an hour. He thought at the outset that he could last through it, that it wasn't too bad. But they took him to another room and made him strip, then walk on his knees around the room while four guards circled and kicked at him. Ayling thought he could fake it and fell down, trying to show more damage than he had actually received, but that just meant the guards could stomp him more easily. He staggered back to his knees. Besides being frightened, Ayling was angry. He could hear some Korean women standing by the door talking and giggling. The carnival atmosphere infuriated him.

He finally decided to tell them a false story. When Maximilian came back, Ayling told him that he cleaned the teletype machines and that it was a full-time job. Maximilian told Ayling he actually maintained the crypto equipment, a statement that

nearly floored Ayling. He decided that since the Koreans knew
it all anyway he would give in. He told Maximilian he would cooperate and was allowed to go back to his room.

The Koreans brought in some technicians, including one naval
officer, to question the CT's, but the *Pueblo* crewmen found they
lacked knowledge and were easily fooled. The CT's relied on
confusing them, talking at length on unimportant points and going around in circles.

Bailey was convinced that the Koreans never understood
what they had in their possession. Many of the CT's had worked
at some of the Navy's most advanced installations, and their
minds contained information beyond price, a hundred percent
more valuable than their knowledge of the electronic equipment
in the *Pueblo*, most of which could be bought on the open
market anyway. But the Koreans were much more interested in
the location and organization of military bases in the Pacific than
they were in American electronics. And they seemed to lack the
technical knowledge to enable them to drain the information
from the Americans. It would be a bad situation, Bailey thought,
if the Koreans ever found out what they had in their hands.

The Koreans were much more interested in the propaganda
value of the capture than they were in technical information. It
became clear that they didn't want to bruise the crewmen so
that the bruises showed, nor did they want to maim anyone per-
manently if they could avoid it. They wanted to send pictures out
to the world showing how well Koreans treated people even
though those people represented the U.S. imperialist forces and
had intruded on their territory. Bailey agreed with some of the
other crewmen who felt that the Koreans had a deep inferiority
complex and a need for world recognition, sympathy, and understanding. It was probably the only thing that saved them from
being shot.

Nineteen

STEVE WOELK DIDN'T REMEMBER being carried back to his room after the operation, but he did remember waking up and finding his bandages blood-soaked again. He asked for water, but none was left, and Rigby had to plead with the guard to get some. Woelk couldn't move in his bed and soon regretted regaining consciousness because he couldn't get back to sleep.

So he lay there, and after a while a nurse came in and took his temperature. It must have been high because she grimaced when she read it. But she left without a word and didn't come back that day. Although Chicca and Crandell had also been treated, the room smelled so bad that Woelk sometimes found it hard to draw a deep breath. For the first two weeks, the nurse came in about every three days and changed his bandages and gave him a shot, but the sheets were never changed and they soon became saturated with blood and fluid from his wounds, which drained constantly.

Woelk couldn't sleep except occasionally during the daytime. He lay in his bed hour after hour shivering from the cold and thinking about his home, and food. Rigby sponged him off whenever he could get extra water, fed him soup, and helped him go to the toilet, but Woelk's condition worsened and the pain was unceasing.

After a little more than two weeks, four Korean soldiers came in the room about midnight and lifted him onto a stretcher. He was carried downstairs and outside to a jeep, covered with a blanket, including his head, and driven over a bumpy road. The driver was plainly unconcerned with his cargo, and Woelk groaned constantly during the cold two-mile ride. The jeep stopped and everyone got out and left Woelk alone in the jeep. After a few minutes, Woelk pulled the blanket from his face. He could see stars out the window and was happy that something he once knew still existed. When he heard footsteps he pulled the blanket back over his face.

Four soldiers lifted his stretcher out of the jeep and carried him into a building, up a flight of stairs, and down a long passageway. He was taken into a small room much like the one he had just left and unceremoniously rolled off the stretcher and onto a bed, where he lay facing the wall. In a few minutes a doctor came in and stood by his bed wordlessly, then gave him a cigarette.

Woelk thought he was going to have another operation and didn't like the idea after his previous treatment, but as quietly as he had come the doctor left, leaving the light burning.

Nothing had really changed for Woelk, except that now he was indeed in a hospital. He heard babies crying and nurses swishing through the hall, and about every three days his bandages were changed and he got a shot. But he had no one to talk to except the doctor, who came in occasionally and tried to talk to Woelk with a combination of sign language and poor English. The doctor was the first friendly Korean Woelk had met, and as his condition improved slowly he was able to sit up and read the English-language propaganda material that was brought in. The doctor was fairly tall for a Korean, with a medium build and a long face, and was probably in his early forties. He wore a white robe over his Korean army uniform and had two stars on his collars. Woelk wasn't sure what that meant.

The doctor visited every three or four days, and after checking Woelk's wounds he remained for a few minutes trying to read the propaganda material. When he stumbled over a word, Woelk would help him out. And on each visit, just before leaving, the doctor would point in the air, make a flying motion with his hands, and say in a soft voice: "Go home. Real soon."

The wounds continued to drain, but at least the food improved. Woelk got milk and an apple with every meal, cold soup, and rotten meat that looked like ham. He got rice for a while, but when he got sick from it one time he didn't get it again.

He had dysentery the entire time. The room quickly began to smell like the one he had just left. The loneliness became more painful than his wounds, and Woelk longed for his friends, and his home, and his parents.

The windows were covered and the door to Woelk's room

was padlocked. The head nurse, although her face was usually stern, seemed to be concerned about Woelk's condition, and visited him frequently. The other nurses, most of them in their mid-twenties, were also pleasant, except for one who gave Woelk a dirty look each time she saw him.

One nurse, a short fat girl about twenty, apparently fell for Woelk and came into the room frequently to stare at him, giggling. The other nurses seemed to be kidding her all the time, and Woelk could see her blush even through the olive skin. He called her Miss Dilbert because she kept forgetting to take his bedpan. The only English word she knew was "goodnight" and she said it over and over again.

After about a month he was given glucose intravenously. Until then he felt he had made no progress, but he began to feel much better after that and was able to get to his feet for two or three minutes once a day. The Koreans brought him five packs of cigarettes every two weeks. He was never allowed to leave the room, so he lay on his bed most of the time reading the propaganda and smoking. He kept track of the days by breaking matchsticks and sticking them in the window ledge. After three weeks he was brought a deck of cards. He played endless games of solitaire.

One day a Korean officer came into his room and sat down. He asked Woelk what he thought about Communism. Woelk said he didn't know much about it but he could see he'd rather live by his own system. The officer, about forty, with big, dark-rimmed glasses, wasn't inclined to argue and left after a few minutes. Woelk figured he was just curious.

The wounds were still open and continued to drain, but after the intravenous feeding Woelk got steadily better until he was able to walk around his room once a day. Once he got a look at himself in the transom, which was open and slanted downward. Woelk was shocked at his appearance and didn't look again.

After forty-four long, pain-filled days Fetch came late one night and told him he was going to join the others. Woelk was relieved that there were others to join, and even though he was far from healed and still in pain, he was anxious to get back with other Americans. Fetch brought him a Charlie Brown Outfit and left the room while he changed. Woelk didn't blame him. He hadn't had a bath since before the capture.

He was escorted down the long passageway past closed doors to a stairway. He held on to the railing and went down the stairway unaided, but slowly and stiffly, then through the marble-floored lobby to the entrance.

Woelk's doctor and another doctor were there to see him off, along with the head nurse. Fetch suggested that Woelk shake hands with the doctors and the nurse and thank them. Woelk wasn't sure exactly why he was thanking them, since his own strong constitution had pulled him through rather than the treatment he had received in the hospital. But he had no ill feeling toward these people, who had at least treated him like a human being, and he did as Fetch suggested. Later, the Koreans sent a picture of Woelk in his room with the doctor to Woelk's parents. The accompanying letter said the doctor and the Korean people had saved their son's life.

Twenty

KOREA is a peninsula lying between the Sea of Japan on the east and the Yellow Sea on the west and is about the size of the state of Utah. For five hundred years the Chinese and Japanese fought over it until the Japanese annexed the country in 1910. Korea is about 80 percent mountainous and has much mineral wealth, but constant war and political turmoil have prevented the people from developing their resources industrially. Consequently, four-fifths of the Koreans are farmers, with rice and barley as their main crops.

The people resemble the Japanese and Chinese, usually having straight black hair, dark eyes, and olive-brown skin, but they are somewhat taller than the Japanese. Until the Communists took over, most North Koreans practiced the Buddhist faith. There is a heavy streak of Mongol blood, especially in the north, the result of an invasion of the Mongol armies of Genghis Khan and Kublai Khan in the thirteenth century.

The Japanese ruled Korea until the end of World War II, when Russian troops occupied the country as far south as the thirty-eighth parallel. The United States occupied the southern half of the country in September, 1945, but the two powers could not agree on a government for all of Korea, and referred the problem to the United Nations. In 1948 a United Nations commission supervised elections in southern Korea, but the Russians refused to allow the commission to work in the northern part, and instead set up a Russian-style dictatorship there under Kim Il Sung.

On June 25, 1950, North Korean armies poured across the thirty-eighth parallel on a self-proclaimed mission to liberate the South from the aggressor United States government. It took three years and the efforts of sixteen member countries of the United Nations to bring the war to an end, with the borders essentially the same as before the invasion. But more than 54,000 Allied and 415,000 South Korean troops died. The North Korean army was virtually destroyed and the country was saved by the Chinese, who sent an army of "volunteers" across the Yalu River, the border between Manchuria and Korea, in November, 1950.

Truce talks began in July, 1951, at Kaesong and were later shifted to Panmunjom, continuing until July, 1953, when a truce agreement was signed. The truce created a 2½-mile-wide zone between North and South Korea from which all troops were to be withdrawn, and provided for continuing talks between the United Nations and the North Korean government for a permanent settlement of the problem.

When the *Pueblo* was captured, those talks still were going on and North Korea was continuing to build its military power. And North Korea had lost some friends. By 1968 North Korea hated the Soviet Union and Red China almost as much as it hated the United States, and was considered a renegade nation, operating outside all established boundaries of civilized behavior. This left the United States with few levers with which to pry at the grip North Korea had on the eighty-two men it held captive.

If the men of the *Pueblo* knew this, they knew it only vaguely and could only wonder how it was possible that any country could hold them hostage and get away with it.

But twelve million North Koreans were doing it, and apparently getting away with it. The North Koreans were sensitive to world opinion, but only in the propaganda sense, and then only the people in the government. The populace heard only what the government told them, and reacted in the way that the government told them to react. North Korea was a tightly controlled police state, headed by a fifty-seven-year-old man who presented himself as a living god—Kim Il Sung.

Because of their almost total isolation, the North Koreans lacked technical knowledge and an understanding of the customs and idiosyncrasies of other people. The leaders were much more interested in running a tightly controlled state than in anything else anyway, and the *Pueblo* incident gave them one more opportunity to give their people something to think about besides their own misery. And it served their ego greatly to humble a great nation.

If the Koreans were ignorant of technical matters and foreign customs, they were experts at getting what they wanted from their captives. They operated with great cunning, playing one against the other, seeking out weaknesses in individuals and exploiting them, holding out hope and then withdrawing it, applying pressure and then easing it, using force only when necessary, and then applying it with great skill. They were patient. The Americans found that they could fool the Koreans on some matters, but they could never lie on anything of importance and get away with it. And, of course, the Americans had handed them some mighty weapons: their personnel records, some classified materials, and themselves.

The total effect was crushing. Taken out of their pleasant habitat and placed in harsh surroundings with the threat of death hanging over them, the unprepared Americans succumbed. They were crushed, angry, frightened, and bewildered, and their spirits were at a low ebb. They shivered in their miserable rooms, shuddered when a Korean gave them a hard look, complained of their fate. For a while they were bitter at the United States. They couldn't understand.

Twenty-one

FOR TIM HARRIS, REMORSE SET IN after his confession. Once carefree, he was now at the end of a long rope, isolated, fearful, uncertain as to the future, aching for home. In his mind he had committed the final sin by betraying his country, his family, and his friends.

He thought that his father, a career Navy man, would never have given in, and that he had done something terribly wrong, although he couldn't tell just then what was right and what was wrong. He was confused and weary after his long interrogation and eventual confession, and remorseful enough to consider trying to climb up to his window and jump out of it, or jump one of the guards and make a run for it. He saved himself by falling into bed and going to sleep.

Fortunately, after days of beating and questioning, life began to stabilize slightly for the men. They got new clothing, toothbrushes, yellow hard soap, and toothpaste in a white tube with blue lettering that said "Paik Zo" in Roman letters and tasted like soap. They also got buckets and one rag per room and were told they had to clean their floors each morning. Each room was allowed five minutes for washing in the morning. On the fifth day of captivity, Charlie Law caught a glimpse of Commander Bucher going into the head across the hall and was happy to see that he was still alive. Law didn't get a good look at his face, but he noticed that Bucher limped heavily.

The Koreans also brought them propaganda material—books, magazines, and pamphlets written in English and filled with accounts of atrocities committed by U.S. troops in South Korea and elsewhere. Stuart Russell read aloud from the Pyongyang *Times* to his roommates:

On September 15, 1967, three U.S. imperialist aggressor armymen— Robert and James of the Hq. Company, the U.S. 8th Army, and Joseph of the 38th Reinforcement Company, the U.S. 8th Army—in front of the gate of the U.S. 8th Army building, pounced upon taxi

driver Bae Jung Hwan (29) who had carried them, wrung his neck
and beat him right and left before fleeing away. The victim fell into a
critical condition. (South Korean Radio, Sept. 16, 1967.)

Russell said the assault sounded just like home.

The picture magazines were filled with accounts of North
Korea's great industrial progress, and long stories about labor
heroes and heroines. Every triumph was credited to the thoughts
and deeds of the leader of Korea, Kim Il Sung. Russell wondered
how the people could stomach it, then decided that they had no
choice.

The men received five cigarettes per person a day. In Law's
room the cigarettes were placed on a table. When someone
wanted a cigarette he asked permission of the others, and they all
smoked it, passing it from hand to hand. When Law came back
exhausted from one of his lengthy interrogations, his roommates
allowed him a cigarette all to himself. He was touched.

Meanwhile, the men in Room No. 14 were in trouble again.
The Koreans had finally caught up with them on the matter of the
personal-history forms. Each time the Koreans brought them
around, the Americans kept insisting they had filled out the
forms, but, of course, the Koreans couldn't find the filled-in
forms. One day a duty officer the Americans called King Kong
came into the room and told O'Bannon they would have to fill
them out.

O'Bannon told the same story again; he said they had already
done it. King Kong said: "Okay, but you lie on first one. Have
to do it again." They were given one hour. After a brief discussion, O'Bannon, Sterling, Strickland, and Alexander decided
to give their names, ranks, and serial numbers. King Kong came
back when the hour was up and collected the forms. When he
saw what they had done he became very angry, but the Americans told him they weren't going to fill in the forms.

King Kong seemed to be nonplused, ordered them to stand at
attention and put their hands in the air, and left the room, apparently to seek instruction. When he came back he ordered them
into the hall and made them get on their knees. Then he kicked
each one in the chest. After twenty minutes King Kong said:
"Okay, you want to play games. I think I going to have ciga-

rette." O'Bannon snickered at King Kong's attempt to play a big shot, and King Kong kicked him in the chest again, while a guard jabbed at Sterling with a bayonet and kicked Alexander under the arms. Strickland had been taken to another room. After two hours the men gave in and filled in the forms.

The next day O'Bannon was in trouble again. After eating, he dumped an ashtray into his food bowl; this appeared to offend the fat, heavy-legged Korean woman who served the room. She reported it to the habitability officer, charged with keeping the place clean among other things, and he came in and demanded to know who had done it.

O'Bannon admitted his guilt. The officer called Fetch, who took O'Bannon to the head and told him to clean the floor. O'Bannon got to his knees and started scrubbing. When Fetch left, the guard came up behind O'Bannon and kicked him hard in the rear. O'Bannon, surprised, jumped up, his face red, shook a finger at the guard and said: "Okay, okay, I'm doing it." The guard jumped back and seemed frightened, so O'Bannon pressed his luck and cursed him. The guard left the room.

A few minutes later the habitability officer came back and asked O'Bannon if he had shaken his fist at the guard. O'Bannon again admitted his guilt, so the officer left and got King Kong, who ordered O'Bannon to clean the long hallway with a rag. It was a very long hallway, and while O'Bannon cleaned it the guard stood behind him and kicked him in the rear whenever he paused. After an hour O'Bannon's legs cramped and he had to crawl to finish the remaining four or five feet. When King Kong saw O'Bannon crawling, he ran the length of the hall, got O'Bannon to his feet, and helped him to his room. King Kong was fearful that O'Bannon was injured and he didn't want to be blamed for it. So much, O'Bannon thought, for Korean mercy.

The Americans found out quickly that the Koreans, especially the duty officers, were constantly playing a role. They strutted, walked around with their hands on their hips in a haughty manner, whenever the occasion called for an act. It was as though the Americans had given them their one chance to lord it over someone and play a part, and almost without exception they took advantage of the opportunity. The Koreans loved to get a piece of information. They would hang on to it, parcel it out in fragments, then strut around when their fellow officers were able to confirm the information, no matter how meager it was. The Americans thought it was one-upsmanship in its most ridiculous form.

Morale stayed low, despite certain amenities which the Koreans began to grant after the first week. The men were still in isolation, with hardly a glimpse of the others, and they were still suffering from utter boredom, poor food, violence, and threats of violence. But now they felt that at least they were going to be allowed to live.

For Tim Harris, a red-letter day of a sort came on February 2, 1968, about 2 A.M. A duty officer whom Harris had named Chipmunk came and got him from his room. Harris had been asleep but it wasn't necessary for him to get dressed. He slept in his clothes, quilted jacket and all, because it was so cold in his room that the water in his pitcher froze. As he was led outside he didn't know what to expect.

A small school bus was waiting, its windows covered and its motor running. Harris climbed inside and saw Schumacher and Lacy. They glanced at one another only once, and then avoided each other's eyes. Harris thought they looked okay, although a little haggard. It was the first time he had seen anyone but a Korean since the day after the capture.

They were driven down a bumpy road and taken, shivering in the bitter cold, to what looked like a fieldhouse. Chipmunk warned them not to talk, then led them inside where there was a shower stall with four shower heads and a little pool. They were told to dip the hot water from the pool, soap themselves, then get under the shower, which was cold. Harris thought: "Oh boy, they let us take a shower. Maybe that means we're going home." All it meant, though, was that they were going to get a haircut and a shave on the following day.

Guinea, a junior officer, was Harris's escort for the shave and haircut in another room in The Barn. The Koreans never seemed to address one another by name, or, if they did, Harris could never catch it. Thus, Harris and the rest of the crew assigned their own names to the more prominent members of the detail assigned to guard them, according to their physical features or personality.

Guinea was bigger than most Koreans and more muscular, with a stocky build, a thick chest, prominent cheekbones, and a big, sloping head. He could speak some English. When Harris took off his shirt to get in the barber's chair, Guinea noticed the St. Christopher's medal around his neck. Guinea was curious and took it. He turned it over and over and asked Harris where he had got it. Harris said his wife was Catholic and had given it to him. Guinea tried to read out loud the inscription on the back. "St. Christopher protect U.S.," he said haltingly. "No, no," Harris said. "St. Christopher protect us." Guinea said: "No. U.S. God is only in U.S. No place else." Guinea returned the medal to Harris reluctantly.

In this period, a typical day started at 6 A.M. when the guards slammed open the door to every room and shouted something in Korean. Harris could hear the guards pacing in the hall waiting eagerly for the stroke of six so they could charge into the rooms and shout at the sleeping men. He started getting up ten minutes early to rob them of that little pleasure at least. The enlisted men could go by room and were allowed five minutes in the head. The officers, of course, went singly. Breakfast of soup, a piece of rotten fish, and water followed about 7 A.M., and until lunch the men just sat in their rooms.

They were supposed to read the propaganda material, but usually they just opened it to a page and half dozed. Lunch was like breakfast, and in this early period the rest of the day was passed in the same way, except for those being interrogated. But on February 7 they learned of a great day to come.

The duty officers went around to the rooms and announced to the crew that the next day was a holiday. "You will have beer and cookies," King Kong told the men in Charlie Law's room. "You will have a good time," he said as though it was an order.

It was the twentieth anniversary of the formation of the Korean People's Army. The men got sweet bread and a hard-boiled egg for breakfast; rice, a piece of good fish, rice cakes, bread and butter, and a large bottle of Korean beer per man for lunch; and turnip soup, chewy dried squid, fruit, and bread and butter for supper. They also got a big plate of hard candy and cookies. In Law's room the men immediately stuffed the candy and cookies into their pockets for later. The Korean women who served them thought they hadn't gotten any and brought them another full plate, a windfall they talked about for a week.

They were allowed to sleep after lunch, and the enlisted men were told it was a "free day." Each room was brought a deck of cards and the men were allowed to play most of the day. Law's room played hearts and poker, using matchsticks for chips.

And the enlisted men met Super C for the first time.

The colonel, touring the building with his staff on this great occasion, was very solicitous. He came into Law's room and asked each man his name and whether he was having a good time. He acted as though he were their best friend. Law thought he was formidable looking and guessed immediately that this was the head man. The men also got clean underwear and socks. The next day the food returned to its previous level.

Also about this time, Law got his first hard look at Fetch, who came into the room briefly one day and then left. In a few minutes he was back, flustered and worried looking. He glared around the room and then pointed to his wrist. "Lost wrist watchee," he said. Law thought to himself: "Who is this dummy, asking for his wrist watchee?"

On their second Saturday of captivity, Fetch came into the room and asked why the men were passing around one cigarette at a time. Law told him they only got five apiece a day. Fetch said they were supposed to get ten and left. He came back with a full pack and they started getting ten a day after that. Law changed his opinion of Fetch.

Twenty-two

CAPTAIN NICE WAS A FAIRLY TALL Korean officer with sleek black hair parted in the middle, a set of white teeth in good condition, high cheekbones, and a slender build. He earned his appellation because he smiled a lot and was usually pleasant, although the crew discovered later that he could be brutal.

On the evening of February 12 he came into Harris's room and told him that his confession had been accepted, and then said he wanted Harris to participate in a press conference on the following day. He gave Harris a list of four questions he said he would be asked and told him to prepare answers for them. The questions concerned Harris's so-called espionage activities on the *Pueblo*, the work that was done by Japanese workers on the *Pueblo* in Yokosuka, and information on the ports of Yokosuka and Sasebo. Captain Nice came back the following morning and asked Harris for his answers but seemed unhappy with them because he thought them incomplete. He then prompted Harris on the proper answers and left.

About 2 P.M. on February 13 Harris was taken to the interrogation room, and Harris saw his fellow officers together for the first time since the conference with Super C shortly after the capture. Dunnie Tuck, one of the oceanographers, was the only other American there. It was plain to Harris that his crewmates had been under great strain. They looked jumpy, their eyes were bloodshot, and Bucher in particular had a haggard look. But Harris was overjoyed to see them alive and reasonably well.

The room was filled with lights and cameras and many reporters, among whom Harris thought he recognized some officers in civilian clothes. He wondered why there were so many anyway, since there was just one story to be written, and that would be the way the Korean government wanted it written. Bucher was sitting in the middle of one side of a long table, and the other officers and Tuck sat on each side of him. There were several microphones on the table and some bottled soft drinks, cookies, candy, and cigarettes, a better brand than usual. The reporters were smiling and laughing and waving at each other. It was quite a festive occasion.

Robot, a senior major with a rough, pockmarked face who earned his name by the way he carried out orders with great determination, servility, and efficiency, was the moderator. He was very cheery, as though nothing had ever happened, and as the room quieted, he spoke in a high, soft voice in Korean. His remarks were translated for the Americans:

"Greetings, gentlemen. Today we are having a press conference with the officers of the *Pueblo*, and the various news representatives from the Pyongyang *Times* and other news media. Now we open the press conference."

Under other circumstances, the Americans would have broken up at the phrasing as it was translated, and at the naïveté of it all, but now they were nervous and shaky under the hot lights, didn't know what to expect, and were concerned about their performance.

The Americans were introduced and told to stand up when their names were called, and then the reporters began reading questions off slips of paper. Harris was asked one question: "What did the Japanese workers do to the ship in Yokosuka?" Harris answered that they had built a wind screen for the flying bridge, put in an air compressor, and corrected steering problems.

Lieutenant Murphy was asked at what points the *Pueblo* intruded on Korean waters. Murphy listed seven points. Bucher got most of the questions and he sat while answering them. Beneath the lights, the circles under his eyes were so pronounced that it looked as if his eyes had been blackened.

Bucher gave a brief history of the *Pueblo* from its conversion at Bremerton to the present, and recited the orders he had received in relation to the *Pueblo's* mission.

While Bucher was talking, Harris and Tuck were able to talk with each other out of the sides of their mouths, speculating on how long it would take for them to get out. There was one small bonus. They got a fifteen-minute break, and Harris was able to whisper to Bucher in the head. They exchanged greetings and Bucher said they might be released in a couple of months.

The press conference lasted five hours. It was a horrible, grinding, nerve-racking experience, and when Robot finally stood up and said to the jovial, laughing Korean reporters, "Thank you, gentlemen of the press," the Americans were limp with fatigue.

The press conference was not funny in any way. It made chilling reading for the crew of the *Pueblo* in the February 22, 1968, issue of the Pyongyang *Times*. The story was headlined "Officers of U.S. Imperialist Armed Spy Ship Reaffirm Brigandish Acts of Aggression of U.S. Imperialists Bent on Preparation for Another War on Korea."

In smaller type, the headline continued: "Press Interview with Officers of the Armed Spy Ship 'Pueblo' of U.S. Imperialist Forces.

As reported in the *Times*, the press conference went like this:

Correspondent: "Well, it's some time since you came here. I would like to hear your impressions of your life here."

Captain: "Yes sir. My impression, as commanding officer, has been that the Democratic People's Republic of Korea is very progressive and has a very gentlemanly and understanding people."

Correspondent: "Research officer, you said that you had a special detachment under your command and I want to know how the detachment performed its mission."

Research Officer (Lieutenant Stephen Harris): "Yes, I am research officer. I am in charge of special detachment of 30 people including myself whose primary purpose is to assist the commanding officer in his intelligence collection efforts by providing him with any information which has been intercepted through listening to radio signals or intercepting radar waves.

"The second function is to intercept, collect and record all radio or radar signals of interest to us, submit the recordings and copied transmissions for analysis to the National Security Agency near Washington, D.C. It is also to collect radar signals, make recordings of these, and submit them to the Pacific Command Electronics Intelligence Centre for analysis."

No crewman who read the account could now complain that he wasn't aware of the *Pueblo*'s precise mission. But if he had any doubts about the kind of pressure the officers were under, those doubts should have been dispelled by the following question and answer:

Correspondent: "Though you mentioned briefly about your life here, I would like to hear them in more detail."

Captain: "Yes, sir. I will answer that question. Our life here has been one of humane treatment. We have been provided with a clean surrounding, given more than adequate meals every day, and all those who have had dealing with me have been cordial."

If nothing else did, the press conference proved to the crewmen that they were living in a never-never land beyond reality, where anything could happen. Those who had read George Orwell's *1984* shuddered in horror at their situation.

There was more interesting reading matter for the crew in the Pyongyang *Times*. Besides the dreary succession of confessions from all the officers, all of them ending with a plea for mercy and leniency, there were the constant sword rattlers, like the long story boxed up on the front page of one edition and headed: "If U.S. Imperialist Aggressors Dare Make an Attack, Heroic Korean People's Army, Korean People Will Deal Exterminatory Blow at Them."

And there were official statements condemning the *Pueblo*'s "intrusion" from the government of the Chinese People's Republic, the German Democratic Republic, the National Peace Council of the United Arab Republic, the Political Bureau of the French Communist Party, and the Presidium of the Central Committee of the Japanese Communist Party. Everyone in the Communist world seemed eager to get in on the act.

There was one brief item of real news in the Pyongyang *Times*, however. It read:

"Major General Pak Jung Pak, senior member of our side to the Korean Military Armistice Commission, met John V. Smith, senior member of the U.S. side, on February 2 and 4 at the request made by the latter on a number of occasions.

"It is said that at the meetings, discussions were held on the question concerning the incident of the 'Pueblo' the armed spy ship of U.S. imperialism.

"There are indications that negotiations will continue in Panmunjom later."

Twenty-three

THE UNITED STATES WAS STUNNED and outraged by the *Pueblo* incident from the moment the Pentagon announced its capture on the morning of January 23. The first official reaction came from Secretary of State Dean Rusk, who said immediate steps were being taken "through the channels that are available to us." The White House described the situation as "very serious," but there was no statement immediately from President Johnson.

There was a wide range of reaction from members of Congress. Senate Majority Leader Mike Mansfield of Montana said: "Our information is quite sketchy and we should not let our emotions get the better of our reason. We should keep our shirts on and think this thing through."

Others were more blunt. Representative L. Mendel Rivers (Democrat, South Carolina), chairman of the House Armed Services Committee, said that the United States should do anything, "including declaring war if necessary," to get the *Pueblo* back. "I wouldn't fool with them," Rivers said. "If they didn't give the ship back, I'd turn loose whatever we have out there on them."

Governor Ronald Reagan of California urged President Johnson to send warships into Wonsan harbor and "get the ship back if it isn't released in twenty-four hours." He called the capture "the most disgraceful thing to happen in my memory in America."

Two prominent Republicans, Senator George Aiken of Vermont and Representative Melvin Laird of Wisconsin, said they believed the seizure of the *Pueblo* was a diversionary tactic connected with the Vietnam War. Aiken said the incident could be "a trap or a warning to South Korea not to contribute any more to the Vietnam War efforts."

But, with few exceptions, even the hawks in Congress were moderate in their reaction. Senator John Stennis (Democrat, Mississippi), chairman of the Senate Preparedness Subcommittee, said: "We must avoid precipitous and rash overreaction. We must not rush pell-mell into the diaster of World War III." But he added: "We must not pull back from a confrontation out of humility or overcaution."

The statement by Stennis was echoed by others, who were torn between outrage and the fear of a nuclear war, and thus played both ends against the middle. No one really knew what to do.

There were more substantial developments than mere rhetoric, however. On January 25 President Johnson called up 14,767 Air Force and Navy air reservists, and the carrier *Yorktown* and a screen of destroyers were moving toward the Sea of Japan to join the carrier *Enterprise* and the guided-missle frigate *Truxtun*. The South Korean Army was on a full alert along the 151-mile demilitarized zone. For the South Koreans, it was just one more in a long series of provocations. Two days before the *Pueblo* was captured, a thirty-one man team of North Korean infiltrators invaded South Korea in an attempt to assassinate the South Korean president. The United States, worried that the North Koreans were leading up to another invasion of the South, quickly beefed up its naval forces in the area.

The United States moved quickly on the diplomatic front. It protested the seizure of the *Pueblo* to the North Koreans at the 261st meeting of the Military Armistice Commission at Panmunjom on January 24. This brought nothing but insults from the North Korean negotiator, but, quietly, the United States approached certain North Korean duty officers at the MAC site and requested private negotiations on the *Pueblo*. Secrecy was essential if the meetings were to be effective; also the Koreans would be unable to make political capital out of the discussions.

After a National Security Council meeting, at which military force was ruled out for the time being, the State Department set up a special task force to handle the Korean crisis. It was headed by Samuel D. Berger, deputy assistant secretary of state for East Asian and Pacific affairs. It was soon decided to start "pushing all the diplomatic levers available" and to marshal world opinion against what was termed "this piracy."

There were two problems with this approach. The North Koreans had few friends who could serve as intermediaries, and the North Koreans considered world opinion only as it suited their purposes. The United States immediately appealed to the Soviet Union for help, but that country rebuffed U.S. advances and denounced the intrusion of the *Pueblo*. The State Department kept the Russians fully informed on all matters anyway in the hope that they would intervene at a key point. Later, the Russians, plainly concerned at the situation, gave some assistance with the understanding that the United States would never reveal the circumstances of that assistance.

The United States appealed to friendly countries as well as Communist and left-wing governments. Some countries later revealed in great detail what they tried to do on behalf of the *Pueblo*. Others said they would do what they could but never reported to the State Department any details of their efforts. The State Department concluded that they had done nothing. In any case, efforts by all other countries were quickly rebuffed by the North Korean ambassadors, who had no leeway to operate anyway.

On January 26 the United States carried its quest for a peaceful solution of the problem to the United Nations. UN Ambassador Arthur J. Goldberg requested an urgent meeting of the UN Security Council, charging that a "grave threat to peace" had arisen from the incident. He called the capture "an act of wanton lawlessness" and emphasized that the ship was operating in international waters.

At the same time, the State Department was reported working on a new overture to the Soviet Union despite the fact that Tass, the official Soviet news agency, called the North Korean action "rightful," and denounced the call-up of air reservists as a "threatening act."

All diplomatic moves were hampered by sketchy information. The Navy had first reported that the *Pueblo* was twenty-five miles off the coast of North Korea, and later amended that to between fifteen and sixteen miles. The government knew that there had been no armed resistance by the *Pueblo*, despite a claim by the North Koreans that the ship had fired on their patrol boats, and it knew that four men had been injured, one critically. The United States didn't learn that one man was dead until January 30, and didn't learn his name until a week after that. Everyone questioned why there had been no air support once the *Pueblo* had reported it was in trouble, and why a valuable ship with sparse armament had been allowed to go so close to North Korea without any protection. Richard M. Nixon called the *Pueblo* incident a "tactical blunder" and said it was an elementary precaution to provide air and sea cover in such circumstances.

Two days after the capture, Dean Rusk said that the United States was determined to recover the *Pueblo* and that the seizure could be interpreted as an "act of war." But he was careful to avoid saying that the United States interpreted it as such. Then he said: "My advice to North Korea is to cool it."

The country was shaken when Radio Pyongyang broadcast what it called a tape recording of Commander Bucher confessing to "deep intrusions" into North Korean waters. Mrs. Rose Bucher, wife of the commanding officer, said flatly in San Diego: "I don't believe it."

Phil G. Goulding, assistant secretary of defense, denounced as "a travesty on the facts" the North Korean claim that Bucher's confession represented the true circumstances and said that the *Pueblo*'s last position report and North Korea's own radar "tracked by U.S. monitors show conclusively that the *Pueblo* was in international waters." Goulding said of the confession: "The style and wording of the document provide unmistakable evidence in themselves that this was not prepared by an American."

At the United Nations, Ambassador Goldberg started the State Department's campaign to rally world opinion and confronted Soviet Ambassador Platon D. Morozov with two maps proving that the *Pueblo* was in international waters. Morozov said: "I wasn't very much interested, although the second map was particularly handsome to look at—all in color." Then he countered Goldberg's statements with a stock speech, attacking South Korea as a "U.S. puppet." North Korea, not a member of the United Nations, said that body had "no right" to meddle in this affair and attacked the UN through Radio Pyongyang as "a tool of the U.S."

Finally, on January 27, President Johnson ended his silence on the *Pueblo* with a somber three-minute appearance on television. He called the seizure a "wanton and aggressive act" and said: "Clearly, this cannot be accepted." He said the country would rely on diplomatic efforts to solve the crisis, but added,

"We have taken and we are taking certain precautionary measures to make sure that our military forces are prepared for any contingency that might arise in this area. These actions do not involve in any way a reduction of our forces in Vietnam." Johnson said: "The United States will not back down." He made it plain that he hoped the North Koreans would "recognize the gravity of the situation."

Johnson's surprise speech from the White House came at the end of another tense day made worse by North Korea's implied threat that it would put on trial and then punish the crew of the *Pueblo*.

But, plainly, North Korea had all the guns in this battle. All the threats, insinuations, and implications amounted to little more than official rhetoric.

To the families of the crew, the news of the *Pueblo* capture was heart-rending.

In Japan, Linda Harris was sleeping soundly early on the morning of January 24. Linda and Tim Harris were on top of the world after four months of marriage. He had a wonderful future to look forward to in the Navy and she looked forward to sharing it with him. They had rented, for $100 a month, a lovely two-story shingled house in a residential district about five miles from the Emperor's summer palace and about ten miles from Yokosuka. The house had a typically tiny Japanese garden in the back with a good view of Mt. Fuji, and the Harrises were fortunate to have friendly, helpful Japanese neighbors next door. The Japanese couple were in their middle thirties and had two children. The two families communicated well even though the Japanese could hardly speak a word of English; while Tim was gone the Japanese had been especially kindly and solicitous. Tim and Linda had great plans to tour Japan when he returned from his mysterious mission aboard the *Pueblo*.

Linda had no idea what the ship or the mission was all about, which put her several steps behind the bar girls of Sasebo, and when the doorbell rang early on the morning of January 24 she thought it was her neighbor. It was a U.S. Navy officer and two Japanese policemen. The officer took his hat off, asked if he could come in, then said, "Is your husband Timothy Harris?"

Linda, puzzled, said that was correct. "Well," he said, "the ship your husband was on has been captured by North Korea and has been towed into Wonsan harbor."

Linda said: "You've got the wrong person."

"I'm afraid not, ma'am," he said. "You should turn on your radio. It's on there."

Linda Harris, normally self-possessed, became angry. "No one captures a U.S. warship," she said. "I don't believe you." The officer assured her it was true, gave her his name and phone number, and asked her to call him if she needed anything. Then he left, leaving Linda standing by the door open-mouthed and bewildered. She stood there for several minutes, then went to her neighbor's home. The Japanese woman, tears streaming down her face, met her at the door and led her inside. Her school-teacher husband was also crying. They had heard the news on the radio an hour before but had not wanted to intrude on Linda, thinking she had been notified.

Linda Harris went back to her home about an hour later, in time to see a bus pull up in front. Some men got out and began speaking loudly in Japanese through a megaphone. Linda was frightened and didn't know what was going on, but after a few minutes they left. Later, she found out they were what the Japanese call "Demos," for demonstrators, and that they were probably Communist.

The next day Linda received a mimeographed letter from E. H. Werdelman, assistant chief of staff for administration and personnel, Commander U.S. Naval Forces, Japan. It read:

The USS *Pueblo* to which your husband is assigned has been boarded by military forces of North Korea while the ship was oper- ating in international waters. The Department of Defense has an- nounced that the *Pueblo* is a Navy Intelligence Collection Auxiliary Ship. This is all that should be said about the mission of the ship or your husband's duties.

You may be assured that every effort is being made to effect the release of all persons in *Pueblo*. Your anxiety in this situation is under- stood and when further information is available you will be promptly notified.

If I can be of any assistance . . .

On January 25, Linda Harris received a telegram. It read:

To *Pueblo* wives and families.

Just want to tell all of you that I wish was with you during this critical and trying time. I received a phone call from Admiral Moorer today at 1:35 P.M. PST in which he stated "We all had his understanding and support and that everything possible is being done."

I have received so many messages, telegrams and phone calls from people everywhere wishing us well. Just keep being brave and strong girls, and I am confident everything will be alright.

Rose Bucher

Francis Ginther's wife, Janice, was in Pottsville, Pennsylvania, on the morning of January 24 giving her two-year-old daughter breakfast when the phone rang. It was a long-distance call from a friend in Maryland. The friend said, "Janice, have you heard from Frank lately?" Janice said that he was out to sea. "Oh, Janice, then you haven't heard the news," the friend said. "His ship has been captured." Janice became very dizzy and hung up the phone without answering. Then she turned on the radio and lay down on the couch. At about the same time, Ginther's father had just gotten to work at a dairy, where he drove a milk truck. One of his co-workers wanted to know what ship his son was on. When he told him it was the *Pueblo*, the man said, "Well, it's been captured." Without another word, Mr. Ginther turned and ran out the door. He doesn't remember driving the eight miles home. When he got there, he called the doctor for Janice.

In Cresswell, Oregon, in the house her husband had built by himself twenty-two years previously, Stella Hodges was alone on the morning of January 23 when the 9 A.M. news came on the radio. The first item on the broadcast was about the *Pueblo*'s capture. Mrs. Hodges sat still for a moment, thinking of her six-foot-three son, a champion wrestler in high school, the last of her six children still living at home. She called her daughter, who came immediately. Her husband, Jesse, arrived a few minutes later from work, breathless and shaken, and they tried to get more information.

They learned that one of the crewmen was critically injured, then they learned that he had died. They called the Navy and the Red Cross, but neither could help. Jesse Hodges had a terrible premonition that it was his son, who had been on active duty almost two years to the day, who had been killed.

On February 7 a chief petty officer drove the twenty miles from Eugene, Oregon, to tell Mr. and Mrs. Hodges that their son was dead.

On March 7 the wives and parents of the *Pueblo* crewmen received a form letter from Vice Admiral B. J. Semmes, Jr., Chief of Naval Personnel. It read:

Perhaps I have been remiss in not communicating with you further . . . . It is my impression that the local naval commands have been looking after your welfare during this period and I trust that this is so.

. . . It is obvious to you, I'm sure, that the North Koreans have calculated very carefully the courses of action open to the United States.

The U.S. Government has been patient. . . . We must realize that precipitate action could punish the North Koreans for their illegal and barbarous act, but put farther away the prospect for return of the men.

So the government must ask for your support.. . .

It must ask that you be patient. . . .

"All Americans resent the North Korean flagrant disregard for law and the precepts of common decency.

In due course the crew will be safely recovered.

Your Casualty Assistance Officer stands ready to help in any way he can, and I do too.

The puzzled, foolish rhetoric had disappeared. The United States was accepting reality. The crew of the *Pueblo* began to slip from public notice.

Twenty-four

THE PRESS CONFERENCE was the first in a succession of moves designed by the Koreans to humiliate the *Pueblo*'s men and rob them of their self-respect. The men were not in a mental or physical condition to resist. The Korean strategy, more importantly, was designed to humiliate the United States before the world, and the United States was equally incapable of doing anything about it. So in a quick succession of events the men reached a nadir, and the people of the United States could only wonder what tortures had forced them into cooperating. They would have been surprised to learn that a few simple things like fear, uncertainty, loneliness, and bewilderment, mixed with moderate physical punishment applied by a people crafty in the ways of pressuring captives, had worked wonders. No one hung by his thumbs, or was castrated or branded, or had his fingernails pulled out by the roots. There wasn't even any brainwashing as the word was understood by Americans.

On February 15 Tim Harris was taken to the interrogation room. The other officers were already there. Bucher was standing next to Super C, who announced that a petition of apology to the Democratic People's Republic of North Korea had been prepared. Bucher said he wanted everyone to sign the petition, which would ask forgiveness of the Korean people for the criminal acts of the *Pueblo*. The petition, written in English in longhand on plain white paper, was lying on a table.

Bucher began to read it while the Koreans tape-recorded the message and took films of him. It was dreary, damning reading:

We the whole crew of the USS *Pueblo* frankly admit and truly repent . . .

We deserve any punishment by the Korean people regardless if its severity for the crime we have committed. . . .

The Government of the Democratic People's Republic of Korea has treated us in such a humanitarian way that there is little difference between our present life and our life before our detention except for our guilty consciences as criminals. . . .

Our . . . grave criminal acts . . . our sincere deep apologies . . . beg your generosity . . . premeditated and prearranged acts of espionage . . . have mercy on us . . . the real facts of our crimes . . . we firmly pledge . . . please take mercy on us and our kin . . . give us a chance . . . we will never join in such criminal acts again. . . .

We openly admit to the world that we intruded. . . .

To commit these acts is a serious crime against the Korean people . . . .

These acts are a sin against God. . . .

We may expect such a severe punishment as may deprive us of even the possibility of revival. . . .

We write this . . . for the sake of our families . . . for our children . . . for the sake of ourselves . . . that you will show us great mercy. . . .

Our minds are united in our desire to open our hearts to the Korean people . . . make an earnest appeal . . . we beg . . .

Eighty-two men of the *Pueblo* are on their knees. . . .

We submit this letter of apology to the Government of the Democratic People's Republic of Korea, again entreating that it recognize the truth and honesty of our statements and forgive us generously and leniently. . . .

The officers signed the document. Then the enlisted men began to come in in groups of fifteen to twenty. Bucher told them what they were supposed to do. It was the first time Harris had seen the enlisted men since they had entered The Barn and he was shocked at their appearance. They looked at the officers out of the corners of their eyes, but there was no attempt at communication, not even by the flicker of an eyelid, and no expression. They appeared frightened and looked around nervously at the slightest noise.

Harris thought that Hammond looked the worst. He was unshaven and pale, and his body quivered. The men stood quietly at attention until told to sign. Then they were led out.

The next day the Koreans had another surprise ready.

The officers were taken to the room where the press conference had been held. Super C was waiting for them with his interpreter, a man the crew called Silver Lips. Of all the interpreters, Silver Lips was by far the best. A major, he was quiet, soft-spoken, somewhat shy, studious, and plainly intelligent. He was heavy through the shoulders and had a sloping forehead and black, slightly wavy hair. He was a hard worker. On occasion he was mean.

Super C said through Silver Lips that it had been decided that the officers would draft a letter to President Johnson. Then he handed Bucher the letter. The officers read it—and made a naïve, foolish mistake. They told Super C that the letter was poorly written, in terminology that no American would understand or believe, and President Johnson would know it had been dictated by the Koreans. The officers of the *Pueblo* were still suffering from the delusion that they could personally come to terms with the Koreans and they thought it would pay to cooperate. They thought a sincere effort would be effective and would help them obtain their freedom. Their judgment had been roughened by their experience and it played them for fools. Super C said: "Okay, you write it."

For the next two weeks the American officers and oceanographer Dunnie Tuck labored over the letter, negotiating each passage with Super C. After several pencil drafts, Bucher and Lieutenant Schumacher composed the final draft and submitted it to the colonel. He liked it. Several members of the crew— Law, Russell, Iredale, Goldman, Langenberg, Kell, McClintock, and Bouden—were called in and the officers discussed it with them. They agreed that it was okay. Elton A. Wood, a CT from Spokane, Washington, was called in to write the letter in ballpoint on plain white paper. Wood was considered to have excellent penmanship.

All the men were then brought in to sign it but they weren't allowed to read it. The American officers were pleased at their handiwork. They were still in their age of innocence.

The letter contained the same degrading semantics of Bucher's confession, except that this time it was in reasonably good English. The letter said the crew wanted the President of the United States to have the complete facts, and then it outlined those facts up to and including five listed intrusions into Korean waters. The Koreans had eliminated the one that put the *Pueblo* inland. The letter said the men were being treated well and fed well, and added: "In fact, the treatment we are receiving is clearly beyond our expectation."

In closing, the letter said: "We firmly believe, now that you have the facts, that you will take all the necessary steps for our expeditious return."

The North Koreans considered President Johnson an embodiment of all that they hated, and if it was their purpose to do him a bad turn, they were successful. Those close to the President said he was very unhappy with the letter.

Among the enlisted men, Stuart Russell had some idea of Bucher's frame of mind in his period. In early February Russell had been given the daily assignment to clean Bucher's room. On his first day on the job he walked in while a Korean officer was

standing over the captain. Bucher was at his desk writing. He
was plainly harried. Russell heard him tell the officer he
couldn't possibly finish what he was writing for three or four
hours. The officer told him to keep working and then left. Bucher
looked up and said, "Hi, Russell." Russell asked him when they
were going to get out of there. Bucher said: "About thirty days.
As soon as they're satisfied with my confession."

Two days later, Russell walked into Bucher's room and
found him slumped in his chair, looking haggard. Russell asked
the same question. Without looking up, Bucher said: "We're
never going to get out of here. We're going to be shot."

Russell, horrified, said: "They wouldn't dare."

Russell and Hayes, who served Bucher his meals, were the only
enlisted men to see Bucher. Russell thought he looked defeated
and felt sorry for him.

There was a surprise of a different nature coming. About
8:30 on the night of February 24 Chipmunk came into Tim
Harris's room and told him to put his hat on. Since this was out
of the established pattern, Harris was worried. He followed
Chipmunk into the hallway and found the other officers there
waiting in single file, in order of rank and with their heads
bowed. Without a word they were marched down the stairs and
out the front door. It was a clear and bitterly cold night, and
there was snow on the ground in places. Despite his heavy clothing, Harris was shivering as they marched down a dirt road,
turned left, then right, and continued for several minutes, the
only sound their own feet scuffing softly in the dirt. A terrible
fear crept into Harris as they walked, surrounded by guards and
led by two officers. "They're going to take us out and shoot us,"
he whispered half aloud, and he heard a guard close by in the
darkness grunt at him. He looked around desperately for some
opening to make a break for it, realized it was hopeless, and then
wanted desperately to talk to someone. Even that was impossible,
so he trudged along silently, hunched in his quilted jacket,
praying.

The men marched down a dip in the road and under some
kind of overpass and then into what looked, as best Harris could
tell, like a stadium. He could vaguely see a couple of buildings

that looked like barracks, and some bleachers, and then he stepped onto a track that ran around a field.

Chipmunk halted the officers and said, "Now you may exercise."

Harris chuckled in relief and waved his arms, touched his toes, and jumped up and down, mostly to keep warm but partly out of sheer joy. It was the greatest fright he had experienced since the early days of the capture.

After they had been there about five minutes, Harris heard more shuffling and saw two ghostly, silent columns come into the stadium. It was about half the rest of the men in their exercise period. The whole thing lasted fifteen minutes, and Harris was surprised how, although he had always been ready to stay up all night for frolic, he now felt so tired and winded. He was glad to get back in his little room and go to sleep.

Shortly after, the Koreans instituted regular morning exercise in the building. The officers were ordered to stand in an alcove of the main hallway, and the enlisted men were divided up at either end. Bucher picked Charlie Law to lead the exercises and he stood in the center. This was the beginning of Law's leadership of the enlisted men. Their spirits began to revive from this point, when they were able to see each other regularly and occasionally pass a word or two to the others. For the officers it was a great bonanza. Total isolation had begun to prey on them. Now their spirits took a great leap forward. The enlisted men thought the officers had been shot or taken to another place, and the men exchanged greetings softly as they passed in the hallway.

It was a pitiful reunion, but regardless of their individual likes and dislikes they were overjoyed to be participating together in something wholesome again. The exercise period in the morning lasted fifteen minutes; the Koreans held the exercises at night as well.

The Koreans also set up two ping-pong tables in the hall and allowed the officers to play for half an hour each day. Aside from the exercise, the ping-pong games gave the officers a chance to whisper to one another when they were sitting on the bench waiting to play, although one of the guards was always running up to Bucher and yelling "Goddamn" whenever he saw the cap-

tain's lips moving. The officers weren't supposed to talk except
to give the score of the game. Bucher's standard response was an
innocent look and the remark "I didn't say anything." The guard
would give him a hard, threatening look and walk away muttering. The guard couldn't understand a word of English anyway.

The officers speculated mostly on when the United States
would get them out, and wondered why it was taking so long.
They also discussed the letter to the President and still thought
it would have some effect. Bucher passed word that the colonel
had told him the United States had denied any *Pueblo* intrusion.
Bucher, incidentally, was easily the best ping-pong player.

After one morning exercise period, the customary pattern
was broken when one of the Korean officers told the crew to
remain in place. There was a ripple of excitement as Bucher
hurried to the center of the hall, a piece of paper fluttering in his
hand, waited for the shuffling of feet to cease, and then said in
a loud, firm voice:

"Gentlemen, I have great news!"

The men tensed, hardly able to contain themselves.

"Today we have received a telegram from the United States!"

The men prepared to let out a cheer.

"I have something here you really want to hear!"

A murmur broke out, despite the presence of the guards, who
walked down the ranks muttering, "Goddamn, goddamn."

Then Bucher said: "Gerald Hagenson's wife has had a
baby!"

The crew stood in stunned silence. Hagenson, his face blank,
said without emotion, "Yeah, great."

Even Fetch was shaken. "Is that all?" he said, puzzled.

It was a misfired attempt at morale building.

One night near the end of February, Super C had the officers
brought in for a talk, and Harris got his first real exposure to the
Korean mentality. Silver Lips was there with two Korean officers
the men called Imperialist and Snake. Super C discussed U.S.
reaction to the capture and used his lighter, a package of
cigarettes, an ashtray, and a pencil to represent the United States,
Korea, the crew, and the people of the United States. He pushed

USS *Pueblo*. (*Official Photograph U.S. Navy*)

Map showing the spot,
well outside the twelve-
mile limit, where the
North Koreans boarded
the USS *Pueblo*.
(*George Linyear*)

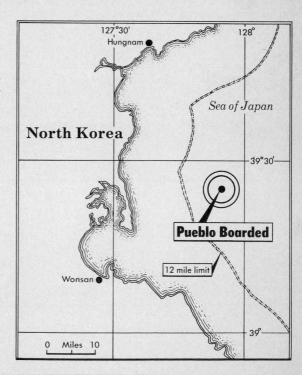

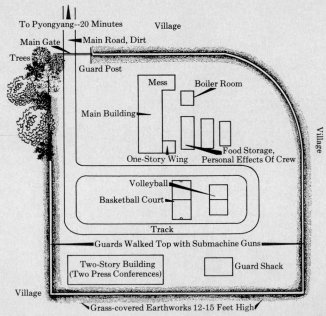

Diagram of the compound where the Pueblo crew was held from March 5, 1968, until their release in December. It was reconstructed from the memories of several crewmen. (George Linyear)

North Korean SO-1 Submarine Chaser
of the type used in capturing the USS *Pueblo*.
(*Official Photograph U.S. Navy*)

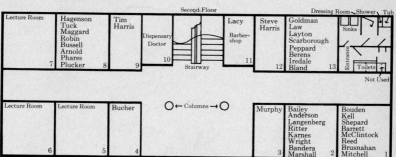

Second Floor

Lecture Room	Hagenson Tuck Maggard Robin Bussell Arnold Phares Plucker	Tim Harris	Dispensary Doctor	Stairway	Lacy Barber-shop	Steve Harris	Goldman Law Layton Scarborough Peppard Berens Iredale Bland	Dressing Room / Shower / Tub — Sinks / Entrance / Toilets — Not Used
7	8	9	10		11	12	13	

Lecture Room	Lecture Room	Bucher	○ ← Columns → ○	Murphy	Bailey Anderson Langenberg Ritter Karnes Wright Bandera Marshall	Bouden Kell Shepard Barrett McClintock Reed Brusnahan Mitchell
6	5	4		3	2	1

Diagram of the second floor of compound, showing the living
quarters of half the crew. (*George Linyear*)

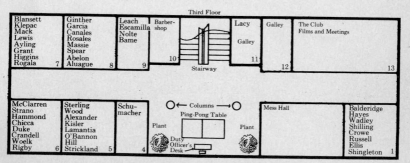

Third Floor

Blansett Klepac Mack Lewis Ayling Grant Higgins Rogala	Ginther Garcia Canales Rosales Massie Spear Abelon Aluague	Leach Escamilla Nolte Bame	Barber-shop	Stairway	Lacy Galley	Galley	The Club Films and Meetings
7	8	9	10		11	12	13

McClarren Strano Hammond Chicca Duke Crandell Woelk Rigby	Sterling Wood Alexander Kisler Lamantia O'Bannon Hill Strickland	Schu-macher	○ ← Columns → ○ Ping-Pong Table Plant Duty Officer's Desk Plant	Mess Hall	Balderidge Hayes Wadley Shilling Crowe Russell Ellis Shingleton
6	5	4			1

Diagram of the third floor of compound. (*George Linyear*)

Fireman Steven E. Woelk with a Korean doctor during his confinement in hospital.

Quartermaster
Charles B. Law.

Marine Sergeant
Robert J. Hammond.

Ensign Timothy L. Harris,
the junior officer of the Pueblo.

Photographer's Mate Lawrence W. Mack.

Communications Technician
Francis J. Ginther.

Communications Specialist
Victor D. Escamilla.

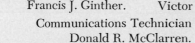

Communications Technician
Donald R. McClarren.

Communications Technician
Angelo S. Strano.

Picture taken towards the end of the imprisonment. Seated from left: Howard E. Bland, Donald R. Peppard, James D. Layton, and Monroe O. Goldman. Standing: Ronald L. Berens, Harry Iredale III, William W. Scarborough, and Charles B. Law. At first the Koreans believed the Pueblo men who said the extended finger was a Hawaiian good luck gesture. Late in the imprisonment, they learned the obscene meaning of the finger gestures and punished the men harshly. *(Wide World Photos)*

Above left, Commander Lloyd M. Bucher crosses the "Bridge of No Return" separating North and South Korea, following the crew's release by North Korea. *(Official Photograph U. S. Navy)*
Right, Steve Woelk crosses to freedom as Commander Bucher talks to U. S. Army men in the background. *(Official Photograph U. S. Navy)*

Coffin containing the body of Fireman Duane Hodges, killed during the capture of the USS *Pueblo*, is put aboard an ambulance by North Korean attendants as North Korean guards watch on the day of the crew's release. *(Official Photograph U. S. Navy)*

Crew members file across the bridge following their release by the North Koreans. *(Official Photograph U.S. Navy)*

The Aftermath: Navy Board of Inquiry.
(Official Photograph U.S. Navy)

them all together and said that was what had to happen before the crew would be released.

Harris noted that the Koreans always treated the government and the people of the United States as separate entities.

Super C said there were two conditions to be met before the crew would be released. The men had to make a sincere apology to the people of Korea and confess all their crimes, and the United States had to do the same. He read to the officers a statement by Dean Rusk in which Rusk denied that the *Pueblo* had intruded; Super C said these statements hurt the crew's chances of repatriation.

Then Super C went on to other subjects. He said that the cherished desire of the Korean people was unification with the South, and that U.S. troops were occupying South Korea illegally. He said that U.S. troops cut off the breasts of women and he used a cutting motion across his own breast to illustrate. He pounded the top of his head to show how U.S. troops drove nails into the skulls of women, and made a swimming motion to illustrate how women and children were thrown into oceans and lakes. He recounted biological experiments the Americans had allegedly tried on Korean prisoners of war and said the Americans were worse than the Nazis. He said the Koreans did not want war but would smash the Americans as they had before if the United States dared attack again. By now Super C was more riled than Harris had ever seen him and he pounded the table with his fist as he pointed to Imperialist and Snake as examples of men who had lost their parents in American bombing raids.

Harris listened in disbelief at first, and then laughed out loud, but the colonel was shouting so loudly that no one heard. Harris quickly shut up. He couldn't believe that someone as smart as the colonel could be so dumb, and wondered if Super C really believed that stuff. The harangue lasted for more than two hours, and Harris learned later that all the colonel had said came straight from Kim Il Sung. Harris later read the same statements endless times in the propaganda material. To the officers, this became Speech No. 59. They had difficulty keeping a straight face the first time. The many later times they were simply bored and thought about other things.

Harris felt himself finally coming back to life after the low point of his confession and the letter to the President. He had heard from Bucher about the death of Hodges, news which had shaken him because Imperialist had told him everyone had survived. Bucher had told him on February 25 that Hodges had died long before the *Pueblo* reached Wonsan. He also found out at the same time that some of the crewmen had been beaten, and that Woelk was more badly injured than he had thought.

Harris got another insight into Korean psychology shortly after the conference with the colonel. Harris was looking at a magazine called *Korea Today*. The cover showed several boys and girls about seven or eight years old in white shirts, red neckerchiefs, and short pants running up a hill.

Snake came into the room and saw Harris looking at the cover. He asked Harris what he thought the children were doing. Harris said they were playing games, just like little kids in the United States. Snake said they weren't; they were preparing to fight the U.S. imperialist aggressors and unify Korea. Then Harris noticed the little wooden guns.

Twenty-five

THE CREW WILL NEVER FORGET MARCH 5, 1968. In Charlie Law's room it started when Thumbs, a squatty little junior officer with bushy black hair who had very small thumbs, walked into the room in the morning and in a very officious manner told the men to bundle up all their belongings in a sheet, mark their room number on the sheet, and put it in the hall. Law asked Thumbs what was up. Thumbs, in the Koreans' usual secretive manner, said: "In ten hours you will know everything."

Jimmy Layton said they were going to Wonsan, get on the *Pueblo*, and sail home. Howard Bland said they were going to Panmunjom, where they would be released. They bet each other a beer. Law didn't want to guess, but he was pretty excited, as were the others, and considered it just possible that they were going home.

Thumbs was equally mysterious with Tim Harris. He came into his room and touched the radiator. He noted it was cold, something that Harris had been trying to tell him all along, and said the room would be fumigated.

He ordered Harris to take the sheet off his bed, put everything in the center, and tie it up. There were forty or fifty guards in the hall and much moving about as the beds and mattresses were removed from the rooms. About dusk, all were told to stand by their doors in the hallway. They were marched out and placed in buses, which had covered windows. Harris thought they were being taken to some kind of concentration camp with wooden barracks, barbed wire, and police dogs, but many thought they were going to be freed.

After about forty-five minutes the buses stopped and the men were ordered out. They marched past marble columns, up steps, and into a large, high-ceilinged hall, dominated by a huge picture in color of a somewhat bloodied Korean soldier. As they came in the door they were stopped next to a big wooden shelf filled with rubber-soled slippers and told to take their boots off and put the slippers on. In a whisper, Law asked Steve Robin what he thought it was all about. Robin said, "This is where the brainwashing starts." Law said the building looked like a courthouse to him and that they were going to be put on trial. The mystery was dispelled in a few minutes when the colonel and his staff, somewhat excited themselves, marched in. He told the crew this was their new home. "You might be able to watch movies and play volleyball," he said with Silver Lips translating. "But you must take care of your new building."

Bucher made a short speech. He said he had asked the colonel for a change of scenery for recreation and health purposes. But Bucher warned, "There is a thin difference between arrogance and pride. Do not abuse your privileges or they will be taken away."

The men were something less than thrilled but they were cheered when the colonel told them that they would be able to turn out the lights at night and that the windows wouldn't be covered. After six weeks of sleeping in rooms with the lights burning, it was no small privilege.

The officers were then called by name and led by a guard up two flights of stairs. Tim Harris was taken two doors to the right and put in a room across from Bucher. There were some improvements, Harris noted. The room was about the same size, the bed and mattress were the same, but now he had a low, circular table in pretty good shape, a small mirror, a chest of drawers, a cabinet with swinging doors, and a ceiling light with a globe on it. There was also a large green plant in one corner. Harris tested the radiator first thing and was overjoyed that it worked. Over the window was a shade, apparently made out of a target because there was a big, black bull's-eye in the center, but it went up and down. Harris worked it several times just for fun, although it was too dark to see anything out of the big, waist-high window. The bundle from the old room had already been delivered, and Harris had just started to smoke a cigarette when the colonel strode in, plainly pleased and excited.

"And how do you like your new surroundings?" the colonel said as Harris jumped to attention. Harris said it was fine. After looking around to see that everything was in order, the colonel went across the hall to Bucher's room and took him out for a tour of the building.

About fifteen minutes later a junior officer came into the room and told Harris he was going to see a movie, then led him up to the third floor and down a long hall to a large room with a lot of tables and benches. Harris on the way noted potted plants everywhere.

The men filed into a room, which quickly became known as The Club, and settled down for whatever was to come, thankful at least for the change in their boring routine.

The evening started off pleasantly enough. An officer the crew called Captain Queer because of his high voice and effeminate ways got up and announced: "Now we will have a movie." He stood in front of the white sheets that had been hung for the screen and began to explain the gist of the story they were going to see on the screen. He had been speaking about fifteen minutes when the crew got its first hint of a new disaster. An officer walked into the room obviously very angry and spoke briefly to Captain Queer. Then he turned and told the men in a loud, angry voice: "You have not taken care of your new quarters. You have already caused a fire and much trouble!"

The men sat stunned and silent, wondering what they had brought upon themselves now. The officer said a mattress in Room No. 5 had caught fire. It was Mike O'Bannon's room. After a lecture on the virtues of being careful, the men were told to rise and march in single file to Room No. 5. They were led past the mattress, which indeed had a hole in it a foot across. It belonged to Michael Alexander, and as the roommates reconstructed the crime later, it must have occurred while they were standing next to the window smoking before the movie call. The window was open because the room was hot, and the roommates speculated that an ash had blown back into the room and smoldered in the mattress. Despite their initial displeasure, the Koreans did not punish anyone, but they brought ashtrays the next day. The incident marked Room No. 5 as troublesome, and the officers brought up the incident again and again.

After this interlude the men were returned to The Club to see the movie, which was about a man and his daughter who were separated when the father joined Korean patriots fighting the Japanese in the late 1930's. The father was a composer, but the Japanese wouldn't let him compose his own music, so the father joined the guerrillas in the hills while the mother and daughter struggled through life. They lost track of one another, but in the meantime the father became a great hero because of his songs, and the daughter became a great singer. One night the composer heard his songs performed with great gusto by a woman and went backstage to congratulate her. Of course, the woman was his daughter.

Captain Nice did the narration into English, and after two and a half hours of bad photography and hackneyed plot the men thought it was like being back home watching late-night TV. They thought the movie was bad, but it was the best one they were to see.

Friday became movie night. The movies were a highlight despite the product, not only for the Americans but also for the Koreans. They could practice their psychology on their captives, totally unaware that what they regarded as gospel the Americans considered sometimes hilarious but usually boring. The crew made an effort not to laugh in the wrong places because it puzzled and infuriated the Koreans. The boy never fell in love with the girl. He fell in love with his tractor or thresher.

All the movies followed the same theme. They memorialized industrial, political, and farm heroes of the Democratic People's Republic of North Korea and damned the United States. Many were based on the Korean War and always showed the Americans in headlong retreat or committing atrocities on the innocent populace. For the Americans it was like watching Westerns with the Indians always winning.

When each movie was over the Koreans would ask the men if they got the gist of the plot and wanted to know what they thought of it. The Americans usually answered that the colors were nice or that the acting was wonderful.

Even the comedies had the same ax to grind. The Koreans made the mistake of asking the men one night what kind of movie they would like to see. Stuart Russell got up and said: "I would like to see another movie about that lovable little red tractor." The Koreans were so pleased with the response that they didn't notice that the men were choking with suppressed laughter.

But, despite such occasional fun, the situation seldom got to the point of being funny. Many of the crew were extremely nervous when called upon to answer questions during these Friday-night propaganda sessions. The threat of violence was there under the best of circumstances. Guards moved about to make sure no one went to sleep, and poor answers could bring punishment.

But the Americans finally learned how to handle the situation and occasionally turn it to their advantage.

One night a movie about the Korean War was shown. The villain was a thin-faced officer with a scraggly mustache named Major Kingster, who performed in the best tradition of the Nazi Gestapo agent of American films. Super C himself asked Commander Bucher what he thought of the film. Bucher gravely informed the colonel that he had a friend named Kingsley back in the States who was so embarrassed and ashamed of the similarity in names that he changed his to Yelsgnik. The colonel was extremely pleased and apparently never caught on that Yelsgnik was Kingsley spelled backward.

At least, the movies gave the men a chance to talk to one another, if only in fragmented whispers.

The morning of March 6, 1968, was another great event for the men. They could look out their windows. Charlie Law went to his window as soon as he woke up. The day promised to be bright and sunny as Law looked out over a level plain that stretched toward tall hills six or seven miles away. There was a row of trees a couple of miles away and railroad tracks running along the row. Otherwise, the men seemed to be in the middle of a barren wasteland. They were to learn later that they were surrounded by rice paddies. In the distance Law could see some dilapidated buildings of concrete construction, with tile roofs and with smoke rising from the chimneys. He deduced that they were the homes of peasants. The crew's compound was rather large. It was surrounded by an earthen wall twelve to fifteen feet high on which half a dozen Korean guards carrying submachine guns patrolled constantly. The guards were changed every two hours. The men were to discover that their building was on the edge of a large athletic field with a track around it. On the other side of the field from the main building was a long, two-story building and a guard shack. Behind their own building, which faced end-on to the field, were the boiler room, a generator, and three small auxiliary buildings. There was no barbed wire and apparently there were no police dogs—just the guards with submachine guns.

Within the first couple of weeks after the move to the new building, several things became clear to the crewmen. The Korrean administrative staff was headed by the colonel. His right-hand man was a junior colonel known as Odd Job. Odd Job was fat for a Korean; he had a thick neck and a cruel streak. He looked like the Oriental in *Goldfinger* who threw the metal-brimmed hat with such fatal effect.

Possum, Robot, and Specs were the political officers and handled all the lectures. They were also room daddies. That is, the rooms were divided among the three and they were charged with keeping the men in line and indoctrinating them in Communism.

The man they called Jack Warner was around frequently because he was in charge of taking pictures, and the Koreans were forever filming the crew's activities. He was probably the ugliest Korean of all, about fifty and dirty, with hair that stood straight up, and a thin, short body. He was also a bad dresser. Jack Warner was always motioning and waving his hands and talking unintelligibly while his chief assistant, Ensign Light Bulb, did most of the work.

The habitability officer, Skeezix, was in charge of the daily routine. He was responsible for keeping the building clean and making sure the men followed the rules. He was about forty, very skinny, with a thin face and sunken cheeks, and talked in sort of a squeal. He reminded the men of a standup comedian and they could never take him seriously, although he could cause them a lot of trouble.

Captain Queer, who shared the movie narration with Captain Nice, had a small build and beady eyes. He affected an intellectual pose and was usually seen walking about in deep thought, as though he were thinking about world problems and their solution. The men will never forget his movie performances. "Today we will enjoy another Korean feature film," he said regularly in his soft, high voice. And "Now we will give you the gist of the story if you will permit me."

Surprisingly, the Koreans provided a doctor full time, a chubby, cheerful, fat-faced fellow who painted everything with iodine whether it was needed or not. The men never trusted his medical ability and frequently suffered through their ills rather than go to him. Naturally, they called him Witch Doctor, and his two nurses Little Iodine and Flo. The nurses were a great disappointment to the crew. They were young but squatty, with thick legs, no makeup, stringy hair, and flat chests.

There were about a dozen junior officers who served as duty officers. They varied widely in cruelty and meanness, ranging from Fetch, who was eager to follow orders but would never hurt anyone, to King Kong, who harassed the crew whenever he thought he could get away with it.

The guards, enlistees in their late teens and early twenties, gave the men the most trouble by far. The men dreaded going to the head. The guards were adept at kicking the men in just the right place on the shin for maximum pain, although they frequently telegraphed their kicks by looking around first to see if a duty officer was in sight.

The longer the guards were on duty, the meaner they got as they learned how far they could go in beating the crew. Fortunately, they were rotated about once a month, and the men usually got about a week of relative peace while the new guards learned the ropes.

The first captain of the guards didn't last long. He was one of the few Koreans the men saw daily who was armed, but he was relieved quickly after he slapped Clifford Nolte hard a couple of times for a minor infraction. The men were in a period of relative peace, and their spiritual strength began to return. The Koreans had gotten much of what they wanted from the crew, and there were no more organized beatings. It was apparent that they were anxious to win their captives over.

The Koreans organized the men to take care of themselves as soon as they were in the new building. They were permitted to eat together. Charlie Law was made leader of the enlisted men on the second floor. Surprisingly, Sergeant Robert Hammond, the man who had resisted the Koreans the longest, was made leader of the third floor. For what it was worth, Hammond had earned the Koreans' respect. The floor leaders led the men in calisthenics, organized the cleanup of their respective floors, and organized any mass movement of the men. They got their orders each day from the duty officers and everything was conducted in a military fashion. The orders had to be given in Korean by Law and Hammond, which meant that Law had to be instructed frequently in the language and the crew had to learn a few key phrases.

The floor leaders were responsible for anything that went wrong and received punishment along with the culprit when there was an infraction. Anything the Koreans wanted the crew to do was transmitted through the floor leaders. The floor leaders, who had to consult Bucher on certain problems, were also the men's link with the officers. Through this link Bucher remained in firm control of the crew and continued to make any important decisions necessary. This liaison was unofficial, however. The Koreans did not want the men and the officers communicating and were constantly on guard against it.

There was no visiting between rooms, and no communication, except that which the men could sneak. No one could leave his room without knocking on the door first and asking permission of the guard, and then usually it was only to go to the head.

The officers were supposed to walk with their heads bowed whenever they left their rooms, but Bucher exaggerated the motion and walked bent over at the waist, a position that the other officers copied. The Koreans got tired of it finally and told Bucher to knock it off, so he walked with his head in a normal position and the Koreans let him get away with it.

Bucher was regaining his strength, and he found many little ways to resist. If there was a particularly obnoxious guard on duty and the officers were walking in file, they would do just the opposite of what the guard commanded.

They frequently elicited a string of "Goddamns" from the guard by marching in the wrong direction and coming up against a wall, where they continued marching in place while the guard screamed in rage. If the guard motioned for them to open a window farther, they closed it, pleading, while the enraged guard charged them, that they didn't understand. They raised the shades when they were told to lower them, and opened doors when they were told to close them. It was a little game to occupy their minds and provide a small token of resistance.

The daily routine was established. The officers got up at 6 A.M., exercised for fifteen minutes outside, then washed themselves and cleaned their rooms, using the buckets and rags provided by the Koreans. After breakfast they went back to their rooms with orders to read the propaganda material. Their normal procedure was to open a magazine, lay it in their laps, and then doze, on the alert nonetheless for the guards or duty officers who popped in frequently. Four or five mornings a week there was a lecture, sometimes lasting two or three hours. After lunch they were allowed outside for another hour of exercise.

The hour before dinner was set aside for "self-conscious criticism" of their daily lives. To the officers it was just another hour of sitting around. Dinner was at six and lasted twenty minutes.

The six officers sat together in the mess hall after marching there at the head of the enlisted men. For the first month, Korean women served the food. Later, the crewmen did the serving. The food was cooked on the first floor and put into big cans, which were carried upstairs to the mess hall and dished out into the dog-food platters. The food was usually turnip soup and rice. Sometimes it was hot and sometimes it wasn't. The men had to be on constant watch for rusty nails, animal teeth, stones, and all sorts of insects. Flies were found in the food so frequently that the men began to consider them part of their diet. Sometimes there was a piece of rotten fish which smelled so bad that even the Korean guards turned away from it when it was carried past them. The men called it sewer trout and figured it was perhaps carp.

The food was generally horrible and barely at a subsistence level, but despite the things they found in their food and its generally undelicious nature, the men gobbled everything in sight and were never satisfied. Hunger was a constant companion, unrelieved by the traditional Korean music that was sometimes played over the loudspeaker.

After dinner the officers were allowed to play cards from 8 to 10 P.M. and all day on Sunday. No religious services were allowed. The officers and men had to wash their own clothes. They were allowed baths every Friday.

Bucher and Schumacher were the only two officers who knew how to play bridge, but the others soon learned. While four would play a rubber of bridge, the other two played gin rummy. Bucher wanted to play for a tenth of a cent a point, but Steve Harris and Murphy wouldn't play for money. Bucher told them, "What the hell, you're going to get hostile-fire pay and it's tax free. You can afford it." But Harris and Murphy wouldn't do it, and while the others played for a tenth of a cent for a while, eventually they stopped keeping track. Bucher was by far the best player anyway, and he was running them broke.

The enlisted men followed much the same routine as the officers, which was strictly regulated. But to relieve the terrible boredom the men began to play word games of all sorts, make drawings on ther toilet paper, and invent crosswood puzzles and pass them from room to room on the sly. They discussed politics, sports, sex, and religion, and when they got into an argument they frequently wagered a steak dinner—payable at some indefinite date—on the answer.

Chuck Ayling invented a game patterned on Monopoly and utilizing a chessboard. Only prescribed activities were permitted and Monopoly and its variation weren't prescribed, so Ayling and Lawrence Mack hid the instructions in cigarette packages and referred to them when the guard wasn't looking. If the guard wondered why they were playing chess all the time with so few pieces on the board, he never did anything about it.

The men carved constantly after the Koreans gave them little pocket knives. Crosses were a favorite subject, and Earl Kisler and Charles Sterling made a carving of the *Pueblo* from a scrap of wood. Tim Harris, who had memorized about fifteen rock'n' roll songs, played an imaginary guitar for hours, singing under his breath with one eye on the door. He didn't want to be caught violating a rule, and he didn't want to be caught looking like a nut, strumming something that wasn't there and tapping his foot in time to music no one could hear.

On the night of March 17 Steve Woelk returned to his crewmates, a circumstance that caused much pleasure because the crew liked Woelk's bright, friendly personality. The Koreans made an occasion of it and he was stopped by Fetch as he came through the front door of the new building. Woelk's wounds were still open and draining and the rough ride had left him weak, but he was happy to see Bucher and the other officers coming down the stairs smiling, their hands extended. They all sat in a circle in the lobby while the officers questioned him on his treatment and his condition. Bucher explained to Woelk their schedule of living and then escorted him to Room No. 6, on the third floor, which he would share with McClarren, Strano, Hammond, Duke, Crandell, and his old nursemaid and friend, Rigby. The room was brightly lighted by Jack Warner, and the Koreans filmed the happy reunion.

The Koreans allowed him to remain in bed whenever he wanted and offered to have his meals served in his room, but Woelk declined. He didn't want to be left alone again. The second day back, a guard came up behind him and kicked him hard in the calf. Bucher found out about it and complained to the colonel. It was one of the few complaints the Koreans ever listened to. The guard was removed from the building. Woelk later got his first bath since the capture; despite continued problems with his wounds, he thought his troubles were over.

If things were going well for Woelk, they took a tragic turn for Angelo Strano, the mop-haired, self-assured technician from Hartford, Connecticut. Strano was half sleeping through a lecture when he heard his name called and jerked upright. The lecturer asked him if he had a brother in Vietnam. Strano said he had a brother, James, with the 1st Cavalry Division in Vietnam. The lecturer said James Strano, twenty, had been killed in action, and then went on with his lecture.

The next day, Specs, Strano's room daddy, took him into a room alone and asked him how he felt about his brother being dead. Strano, almost in tears, perceived that the Koreans were trying to use him and he mumbled: "It's a lousy world. Maybe he's better off dead." The Koreans never brought it up again.

Twenty-six

THE KOREANS WERE in a reasonable mood in March, a month of bitter winds and much snow near Pyongyang, but events soon changed that as the month neared an end.

The men in Room No. 5 on the third floor had been missing cigarettes; they were being stolen every time the men went outside. The roommates—O'Bannon, Sterling, Wood, Alexander, Kisler, Lamantia, Hill, and Strickland—considered it a serious matter worthy of complaint. They suspected a guard named Cheeks. They had found that it was almost useless to complain about anything since the Koreans would, after investigating, deny that anything was wrong and turn the affair against the men and accuse them of lying, a highly punishable offense. But this was serious and O'Bannon complained to Dracula, a duty officer, about the missing cigarettes. Dracula wrote it down, but when they didn't hear anything for a couple of days they figured it had gone the way of all complaints, and at least they wouldn't be punished.

But two days later the colonel himself strode into the room with several of his staff members and the men realized at once they had made a terrible mistake. The colonel was in a screaming rage.

"Who the hell you think you are!" he shouted at Sterling, the room leader. "My guards don't steal. You insult all Korean people. You will be punished!" Then he stalked out. The colonel called a mass meeting the next day in The Club.

When the men had assembled, most of them unaware of what had happened, the colonel repeated the circumstances and called by name those who had complained about the cigarettes. He was plainly in a foul mood, and as the culprits stood up shakily he repeated his accusations of the day before, pounding the table, strutting around in front of them, and calling them liars. He was putting on his biggest show in the new building to date, and he complained bitterly of the treatment the Koreans had received in return for lenient treatment of the prisoners.

Finally he stood stockstill and said in an ominous voice, "What should we do with these men who have lied and brought disgrace on themselves and their benefactors?"

Bucher, now wise in the ways of the colonel, jumped up and said: "I think these men have realized they are wrong and I think you should give them one more chance." Others among the crew asked to be heard, then supported the captain.

The colonel, unmoved, said, "I would like to hear those responsible confess their crime."

Sterling stood up, his head bowed, and admitted before the crew that he had stolen some cigarettes. He begged forgiveness. O'Bannon stood up and said he had lost cigarettes on the playground and thought he could get some more by lying. O'Bannon, his head bowed, begged forgiveness.

A ripple went through the crew. "You rats," someone said. "How awful," another said. "You ought to be beaten," a third said. The colonel was exceedingly pleased at the humiliation of Sterling and O'Bannon and at the reaction of the crew, and for the first time he smiled. The men thought they were going to be beaten or lose some of their meager privileges. Despite the fact that it was all a game between the crew and the colonel, it was a tense situation and the men were relieved when they were allowed to leave after three hours.

The next day Robot called Hammond and O'Bannon to his desk in the hallway and told Hammond he was in charge of O'Bannon and would be responsible for all his crimes. Then he looked at O'Bannon and said, "Which guard took the cigarettes?"

The incident had more repercussions. Apparently the Koreans felt it was time to crack down on the crew and show them who was boss. They raided all the rooms and confiscated forbidden articles. The men lost their wooden crosses, scraps of precious paper they had hidden away, games they had made up, anything that had not been specifically prescribed by the Koreans. The affair became known as the April Purge. It signaled a general tightening of restrictions.

There was another cross to bear for the crewmen. Letters they had been told to write in February to their families and U.S. government officials began popping up in the Pyongyang *Times* late in March, column after dreary column. They read much like the confessions the men had already written, but the Koreans allowed them to include personal messages at the end of letters to their families. Later, they would use the opportunity to express their true feelings; for the time being they weren't fully aware of Korean naïveté.

A typical letter was one by Commissaryman Harry Lewis to Senator Robert F. Kennedy, addressed to him at the Senate Office Building in Washington:

I have three suggestions to offer, that the United States Government:
(1) Admit the true mission of the Pueblo.
(2) Apologize to the government and people of the Democratic People's Republic of Korea.
(3) Give a firm guarantee that all espionage activities against the

Democratic People's Republic of Korea will end.

The Government of the Democratic People's Republic of Korea has been very lenient with us thus far. We are being treated well.

I would appreciate greatly any help you could give in putting my suggestions into effect.

Harry Lewis

The Koreans had the men make three copies of each letter and told them they would be sent by different routes so that the U.S. government, which the Koreans said was on the lookout for letters, would not be able to intercept them all. Later, families of the men began to get the letters and some tapes from all parts of the world. Tim Harris's wife, by then moved to Jacksonville, Florida, got a letter mailed via France and a letter from a man in Sweden who said he had a tape of her husband's voice and wanted to know if she wanted it. She wrote and asked him to send it.

Harris had a little bad luck to begin with on his letter to his wife. He submitted it to Captain Nice for approval, but Captain Nice returned it the next day. "You have written a love letter," he said, "and it is important that your wife know all the facts about your espionage activities. You should explain the details of your spy operation to her and tell her you have asked forgiveness of the Korean people and have written a letter to the President of the United States. Tell her you will have to apologize before you can be repatriated."

Harris mumbled something about why didn't they tell him they wanted a propaganda letter in the first place, and did as he was told.

Ron Berens was one of the few who refused at first to write pleas to government officials. He was taken from his room and severely beaten. He then agreed to write the letters. The Koreans were putting on an act of kindness as long as the men were willing to crawl. Anyone who stopped crawling was beaten.

Early in April the Koreans learned of another propaganda weapon supplied them by the people of the United States. Dr. Martin Luther King, Jr., was assassinated in Memphis, Tennessee, and it didn't take the Koreans long to transmit this news to the crew. The Koreans even solved the murder: they said President Johnson was behind it.

The Koreans talked to the two Negro members of the crew, Harry Lewis and Willie Bussell, separately from the others and showed them great sympathy. The Koreans had questioned Lewis and Bussell frequently about life in the United States, and seemed to be disappointed in their answers. They wanted to know why Lewis and Bussell didn't participate in the "Negro upsurge" and questioned them about the riots. The Koreans couldn't understand Lewis. He told them he owned a car for which he had paid $3,200 and they flatly refused to believe him. Nonetheless, the junior officers showed continued interest in the car and questioned Lewis at length about it. When the two Negroes failed to respond to the news of Dr. King's death with the proper dialogue, the Koreans dropped them. Thereafter, they were treated no better, and in some cases worse, than the rest of the crew.

In March and April the Koreans tried to indoctrinate the crew in the joys of communism and made what amounted to a half-hearted attempt at indoctrination outside of the regular lectures.

About the second week in April, Possum began to call members of Charlie Law's room aside for long interviews on life in in the United States, on the history of the United States, on the terrors of colonialism and capitalism, on President Johnson as an imperialist, and on many other typical Korean bogeymen. Law and the others quickly discovered the Korean idea of a capitalist in the United States. He was always portly and bald, he smoked a long cigar, and he had a gold watch chain hanging across his bloated belly. Law would usually agree that there was some truth to be found in the stereotype, but then thought back to the time when he weighed more than two hundred pounds under capitalism.

Robot was interested in Mike O'Bannon's views of the Vietnam War, figuring perhaps that he had a good subject to bait him with and perhaps use to work him into the position of agreeing with Communist views and aims. But the Koreans were so transparent in their motives and so naïve about politics that they were easy victims for the Americans until the Koreans got irritated and shut off the conversation with a threat. O'Bannon

washed his hands of Vietnam quickly by telling Robot that it was
a problem for the United Nations. The mention of the United
Nations was enough to infuriate any Korean, and Robot
responded by telling O'Bannon how the Korean People's Army
had won the Korean War against the United States and its UN
stool pigeons.

Mike wanted to know how come the United States had
pushed the Koreans clear back to China. Robot said it was a trap
laid by the Koreans and the United States fell into it. Both were
thoroughly heated up by now, half shouting at each other, and
O'Bannon said the Chinese had saved the Koreans their skins.
Robot denied that the Chinese had helped at all. When O'Bannon
laughed, Robot admitted the Koreans had gotten some food from
the Chinese. O'Bannon laughed again, and Robot, furious, stood
up and began pounding the desk.

"You fool!" Robot shouted. "I will have you shot for your
opinions!" O'Bannon shut up.

The Koreans, while continuing to engage in political discussions with the Americans, eventually gave up their campaign of
informal indoctrination and left it to the lectures and the propaganda magazines. They suspected that the Americans were not
really reading the material. On occasion, when they were being
tough, they would make the men read aloud to one another and
then ask them questions.

The weather began to get warm about the end of April, and
the men watched from their windows as the peasants flooded
the rice paddies which practically surrounded the compound.
Everything was getting green and the weather grew steadily
warmer, but about all spring meant to the men of the *Pueblo* was
that it gave the Koreans another opportunity to exhibit their
cruelty.

Tim Harris had noted that the Korean guards were
willing to go out of their way to kick a dog with the same gusto
that they kicked the prisoners, and one day he got an even better
lesson. There were women on the first floor, typists and stenog-
raphers apparently, although the men were never allowed downstairs and weren't sure there were even offices there. As the
weather got warmer the men could hear the women giggling at

the guards. One of the guards had found a birds' nest on the ground full of baby birds, and while the girls screeched and giggled, the guards threw the birds one by one in the windows. The girls threw them out again, and the game continued until the birds were dead.

The warm weather brought new problems for the crew. The Koreans began to serve what looked like chopped-up grass at every meal. It was tasteless, but it was green and the men were starved for green vegetables. But the grass had worms in it, and the men got the worms. The Koreans blamed the worms on the Americans, as they did the bedbugs the men were also plagued with. They said they had brought them from the ship. The men wanted to know if they had also brought the huge gray rats which began to appear, and the mosquitoes and flies which flew in great numbers through the screenless windows.

The weather turned Harris's attention to the big plant which stood in one corner of his room. If the Koreans treated birds, dogs, and men inhumanely, they were exceedingly solicitous about the plants, which were in every room and in the halls. The plant in Harris's room was in a porcelain pot a little smaller than a bucket. About four feet high, it had long branches, long, narrow leaves, and a woody stem. King Kong gave Harris full instructions on the care and feeding of the plant and cautioned him that he must give it a cup of water every day. The first thing King Kong did whenever he came into Harris's room was inspect the plant to see if it was being watered. This angered Harris. The Koreans were a good deal more concerned about the health of the plants than about the health of their captives. Finally, Harris began to urinate each day in the porcelain pot instead of watering it.

The plant was in remarkably good health and took its new treatment well for about a month. But slowly the limbs began to droop. Several leaves turned yellow. A couple near the bottom wilted. Harris kept pouring it on. It became a test of strength between himself and the plant, which stood for the whole Korean nation.

King Kong was getting worried. When he noted the leaves turning yellow, he brought in a cup of fertilizer and spread it around the base of the plant while Harris watched, assuring him that the plant had plenty of fertilizer. King Kong tested the dirt every day with his finger to be sure the soil was moist.

The plant came down to its last half-dozen leaves, and they were plainly in trouble. King Kong was sick with worry. He paced between the plant and the door one day, glancing at the plant from time to time. He turned to Harris and said, in a high, angry voice, "Why plant die? Why plant die?" Harris said it probably didn't get enough sun since his room wasn't on the sunny side of the building. King Kong asked, "How you water plant?" Harris said he used the water from his teapot. King Kong's face lighted up. "Ah," he said. "You should not do that. That is the trouble. All minerals boiled out of drinking water. Therefore bad for plant. Bring water from bathroom and water plant." Harris agreed that that might be the trouble, and for the next week he dutifully carried water from the bathroom to water the plant. Between the water and urine, the plant was now drowning. It was down to its last three leaves, and they were about to go. Harris felt as if he were on the verge of his greatest triumph. By now, Bucher was in on it, and nodded his approval each time he saw Harris carrying a cup of water from the bathroom.

When it became apparent that the new treatment was having no effect, King Kong ordered Harris to carry the plant to Bucher's room across the hall and set it in the sun. Harris had to carry it at arm's length because it smelled so bad, and he wondered why King Kong didn't smell it.

Once it was in Bucher's room King Kong asked the captain, "Why plant die?" Bucher scratched his chin thoughtfully and finally said, "Well, I think it needs pruning." King Kong, grasping any straw, said, "Okay, you prune." Then he left. Bucher and Harris looked at each other and pulled out their penknives. The three remaining leaves came off first. Then they began to trim off the branches. They whittled on the stem next. When they were finished, a six-inch bare stump remained. When King Kong came back and saw the stump, he was speechless. He stammered and rushed out the door, then returned in a minute with Snake, another duty officer. While King Kong stood by the door nearly prostrate, Snake screamed at Bucher. "Why you kill plant, huh, huh, huh?" he said over and over. Bucher said, "Goddamn it, I didn't kill the goddamn plant," and walked away. The Koreans left the stump in Bucher's room, and from time to time King Kong would come by and point it out to the other duty officers. Harris felt free again, for the moment.

April was special for one major reason—Easter. Commander Bucher, becoming more concerned each day about the quality and quantity of the food, thought he could euchre a feast of sorts out of the Koreans by selling them on the idea of celebrating Easter.

The April Purge movement had died down, and the Koreans were returning to one of their benevolent periods. Bucher thought it was time to get something out of them. The trouble was, no one knew which Sunday Easter fell on. Bucher spent hours trying to figure it out and finally came up with April 7. Then he went to the colonel and tried to explain to him the importance of the holiday to the Americans. The colonel was unimpressed, since it was a religious holiday, but finally agreed to do something.

When April 7 arrived, each member of the crew got one boiled egg, a tremendous windfall, which they savored with each bite. They didn't learn until much later that Bucher had missed Easter by a week and they had celebrated Palm Sunday. Easter went unnoticed.

By now the men were in good spirits. Morale was excellent because they could see and communicate with each other, and the exercise periods gave them an outlet.

The Koreans wouldn't let them play baseball for historical reasons. When the Japanese were occupying Korea, they made everyone play the game, and a great hatred was generated for the sport. The men were allowed to play volleyball and basketball and their own form of baseball, which was kickball. They laid out a diamond and used a volleyball, which was rolled toward the "batter." The rules were the same as for baseball, and the Koreans didn't seem to realize that it was no more than a variation of baseball. The guards especially were interested in the game. When the men were back in the building, they would look out the windows and see the guards trying to play the game during their recreation period.

The men wanted to play football, but they didn't have a football until Jimmy Layton devised one from a volleyball. The Koreans were unhappy with the way the volleyball was cut up and folded, but they offered no resistance until the first game, when they saw one side walk back and huddle. The officer on duty ran over to the huddle and said, "What you doing? You passing secrets?" He was certain that the men were plotting something and listened as they discussed buttonhooks and Z patterns. He stopped the game while Layton and Bucher argued with him, then reluctantly permitted the men to continue while he joined in each huddle. The huddle was a constant source of agitation to the Koreans, who couldn't understand what the men were talking about.

The men played one-hand touch, with first eight and then eleven men on a side. Layton usually quarterbacked one team and Bucher the other. Bucher, an ex-football player, was good, but Layton thought he was worn out and participated only to show the crew he had something left. His leg continued to bother him from where he had been kicked during the early days and he sometimes limped badly, but he remained as active as anyone in all the sports.

The Koreans were looking for an excuse to stop the football games and got their chance when Charles Sterling ran into another player while running a pass pattern and broke his nose. The Koreans said the game was too rough and took the ball away.

They also stopped the basketball games when Aluague broke his kneecap going in for a layup; the Americans began to hide their injuries, including one broken arm, so they wouldn't run out of allowable sports.

If nothing else, the recreation period allowed the men to exchange information and gave Bucher the opportunity to keep a grip on the crew and pass the word when he wanted something done. His word was considered final. His role was slowly changing from commander to leader.

The pleasant spring days of April stretched into the warm days of May without great event and without great pressure from the Koreans, who seemed to be content that things were going well. Near the end of May the Koreans called a mass meeting.

The colonel told the men they were going to be put to work. Until then, they had been responsible for keeping the entire building clean, with the exception of the first floor, and for keeping the trees and shrubs around the building watered. They also had to cut grass, a tiring enough chore since they had to get on their hands and knees and do it with their pocketknives. The Koreans seemed to lack the simplest tools, even lawnmowers. As soon as the grass started growing in the spring, the men received a short course on how to cut the grass properly by holding up tufts and sawing at them. The crew suspected that the tufts later ended up in their dinner plates. The men also had to weed the peach orchard.

The Koreans, however, felt that this wasn't enough and said the men should take on added chores; it would be good for their health and would justify their existence. The colonel was in a good mood and asked for suggestions. He asked how many could drive and was astounded when all put up their hands. Few Koreans could drive since few had cars.

A crewman said he could type and serve as a yeoman. "Ah, no," the colonel said, smiling and shaking his finger. "We can't have you working on our files." Larry Mack, the photographer's mate, stood up and said he could take pictures. "Ah, no," the colonel said, smiling and shaking his finger. "We can't have you going around our country and taking pictures." Another crewman suggested they could be lumberjacks and cut trees. Another thought they would make good farmers; perhaps the colonel would give them a farm to run. The colonel had reasons to say no to both suggestions. Someone suggested that they could work as mechanics, and the colonel seemed to like that idea. The Koreans were horrible mechanics. When their generator broke down they sent someone out to hit it with a large stick. If that didn't work they called in specialists from Pyongyang who were almost equally helpless. The colonel said he and his staff would digest their suggestions. The Koreans digested them so well that the Americans never heard of them again, and their duties remained basically the same throughout their imprisonment.

At the end of the meeting Bucher stood up and asked for permission to speak. The men half groaned. The meeting had already lasted six hours. But it soon became apparent that Bucher had something up his sleeve. Bucher began to explain the importance of May 30 to Americans. He spoke at length about the great holiday which honored America's war dead, then paused and said: "I thought the colonel would be interested in Memorial Day as a point of information." In fact, Bucher thought he might euchre something out of the Koreans, but it became apparent immediately that his "point of information" was a terrible error. The colonel lost his good humor and became furious.

"You mean," he shouted through Silver Lips, "that you want to participate in this so-called holiday? How dare you bring that up! You would honor the U.S. imperialist aggressors who came to kill Koreans. You insult us with that suggestion!"

Bucher realized his mistake and stood up again while the colonel was still speaking. "Well, if you feel that way, sir," he said, "I withdraw my point and apologize for bringing it up."

The crew went without a boiled egg on Memorial Day. Bucher, who loved to match wits with the colonel and who thought the colonel enjoyed the same game, had lost a round.

Twenty-seven

PYONGYANG OCCUPIES ONE OF THE FEW level places in North Korea. Its winters are bitter. Spring is dry and windy, but in June the weather begins to get hot and humid, with frequent rainstorms. It was a very uncomfortable month for the crew of the Pueblo. The bread became moldy and the butter rancid. Harry Lewis picked up a loaf of bread in the galley and saw that a rat had chewed through it from one end to the other. He looked through it as though it were a telescope. There was no fruit or meat, just sewer trout, chopped grass, heavy sticky rice, and an occasional turnip. Without vitamins and protein, the men's legs and arms began to swell. Some ankles doubled in size overnight.

The entire crew was struck by dysentery. Men collapsed in the hallways, doubled up by horrible cramps, and defecated in their pants where they lay. Sores wouldn't heal, and insect bites swelled and festered all over their bodies.

Huge boils covered their legs, thighs, and buttocks.

The lack of vitamins seemed to affect certain nerves, and some men had trouble walking. They had to go to the toilet constantly because their kidneys were affected. Huge scabs formed on the backs of their necks, cracked open, and became running sores. Nearly everyone had a rash on his groin, and Dale Rigby developed what the Korean doctor diagnosed as a fungus. The doctor gave the men little black pills for the dysentery and painted everything else with iodine or mercurochrome. The men didn't get much help from him and rarely went back.

Bucher complained to the colonel about the diet, but the Koreans didn't seem to understand the problem. Their solution was to increase the portion of rice for a couple of days. Some of the men began to worry that they wouldn't make it if conditions didn't improve.

Morale was high, nonetheless. The men began to take control of the situation as they learned how far they could push their captors. The men deliberately angered the guards and took their lumps for it. If a situation became serious, they played dumb and said they didn't understand the order. Some, like Ron Berens and Lee Hayes, simply refused to do certain things and got away with it. They fought the Koreans the way they fought the bugs, swatting at them constantly. The flies and mosquitoes had gotten impossible and the Koreans and the men held daily contests to see how many insects they could kill.

If you killed fifty flies in a day you became an Ace; two hundred and you became a Blue Max. The mosquitoes became so bad that the Koreans finally got nets for the men to sleep under.

One night a guard came into Don Bailey's room to inspect the nets and forgot to turn the light off when he left. Bailey, angered at being awakened, yelled, "Goddamn it, come back here and turn out the lights!" Then he cringed, horrified at what he had done. The guard rushed back into the room, looked around, and turned off the lights.

As the heat, humidity, insects, and food grew worse, tempers shortened and friction mounted. Every room had its conflicts as the men grew tired of hearing the same stories over and over and began to needle and harass one another. The men in Room No. 1 on the third floor had the best fights, and once they had such a brawl that the plaster was knocked off the ceiling of the room below. Stuart Russell fought with Lee Hayes over whether or not to leave the door open and Hayes punched Russell in the jaw and knocked him over a bed. Russell got up and Hayes knocked him down again. Russell got up a second time and John Shilling stepped in and broke up the fight.

On another occasion, Shingleton called Baldridge an old man. Baldridge took offense and the two slugged it out. Shingleton got a knot on the head and Baldridge got a black eye.

The plaster came off the wall during a fight over a word game. Russell, in bed with a badly infected foot, was serving as judge for the game; when he ruled against Shingleton on a word, Shingleton called him stupid. Russell hobbled off his bed, and the two wrestled on the floor until someone started thumping from below to complain about the noise and the plaster.

In Room No. 6 on the third floor, Hammond and Strano got into an argument over religion, and Strano threw a cup of water in Hammond's face. Hammond jumped him. They knocked the tea kettle off the table, and a guard came running in and demanded to know why they were fighting. Then he took them to the duty officer, who made each write a confession as punishment.

In Room No. 7 on the third floor, Blansett needled Mack and Rogala, and Ayling harassed Blansett, finally angering him into a fight one day. Blansett charged across the room after a biting remark from Ayling and tried to strangle him. Mack broke it up.

The men were still getting their daily slaps and kicks from the guards, who took every opportunity to humiliate them. One in particular began to earn a reputation. The Bear was a senior guard about twenty years old and much bigger than the average Korean. He had high cheekbones and a square chin. His eyes were narrow slits and his lips were thin and he never smiled or laughed without sending shivers down an American spine. His expression was normally sullen and hateful. He was feared by everyone.

His favorite trick was to go into a room and stare them all down to see them cringe, then slowly scan the room until his eyes lighted on a victim. He would call him into the hall. In a moment, the men in the room could hear their crewmate grunt and bounce against the wall. In a few minutes he would come back in bent over, holding his stomach, knots beginning to swell on his forehead. The Bear, like most of the Koreans who administered the beatings, was careful not to blacken an eye, break a nose, or inflict serious damage that would show up later. Thus the Koreans concentrated on the ribs, stomach, forehead and under the arms. Fortunately, the Bear didn't pack much of a punch, although it made him angry when he couldn't knock a man over and he would redouble his efforts.

The guards had become expert in administering beatings without getting into trouble themselves. Don Bailey was cleaning the alcove one day when he noticed the wall plate lying on the floor under an electrical outlet. Bailey picked it up, and the guard came over immediately and motioned for him to replace it on the wall. But there were no screws. Bailey looked around desperately for the screws while the guard stood over him shouting. When he tried to explain the problem to the guard, the Korean laughed and hit him in the forehead with his fist, knocking him down. As Bailey struggled to his feet, dazed and hurt, the guard brought up his knee and hit him in the jaw, knocking him down again. Then he pushed Bailey with his foot, waving him away.

Bailey crawled back to his bucket and rag and began cleaning the floor again, but he watched the guard out of the corner of his eye. The guard glanced around furtively, then reached in his pocket, pulled out the screws, and replaced the plate.

Bucher was ill part of the time in June. The nerves in his hip and leg pained him from where he had been kicked repeatedly by the Koreans, and he, too, was suffering from the poor food. On occasion, Stuart Russell served him his meals in his room and one day asked him what he thought about their situation. Bucher was in a depressed period and said he didn't care what happened to them then or what would happen if they got home.

But the men were getting used to their environment and began to adjust to it. Pete Langenberg gave Japanese and Russian language lessons to pass the time. Donald Peppard and Jimmy Shepard gave German lessons. Escamilla taught Spanish. Garcia lectured on Tautog, spoken by Filipinos. Steve Ellis, twenty-five, from Los Angeles, taught English. Harry Iredale taught math and even gave pop quizzes. His students were graded on their efforts. Sergeant Chicca by now had become fairly proficient in the Korean tongue and taught that, although many crewmen didn't want to learn as a form of resistance. Practically everyone learned how to play cards and chess.

Chicca carved a pair of dice from a piece of scrap wood he found in the recreation area outside, and Crandell got into Mc-Clarren for more than a thousand dollars before Crandell said to forget it.

Radioman Lee Hayes scavenged material for a radio and slipped it piece by piece to Angelo Strano. Hayes also drew a schematic for a crystal set and slipped that to Strano in the playground. The radio was designed to receive only, but the men were starved for news from the outside world and hoped they would be able at least to pick up a South Korean or Japanese station. Charlie Law somehow came up with six strands of good copper wire for the coil and stole a pencil from The Club to serve as an antenna stand. Someone else swiped a piece of a razor blade for use in the earphone, and Chicca carved an earphone from a piece of scrap wood. Hayes picked up a couple of nails from the playground for the voice coil in the speaker, and the men took the foil from a cigarette package for the diaphragm. They had the essentials but couldn't find any way to magnetize the nails. Strano coiled a piece of wire around a nail and gave it to Rigby, who took it to the galley and shorted it across the switch on a heater. The nails were of poor quality and wouldn't hold the magnetism for long, but Rigby kept trying. Law found out where the interpreters kept their earphones, and while he waited for the chance to steal one, Strano hid the radio parts under a floor board in his room.

Francis Ginther, meanwhile, found out about some of the secret material the Koreans had captured. The Koreans, apparently tiring of the intelligence game, had stored some of the classified materials in barrels on the roof of the building.

One hot day, Ginther was supervising the cleanup of the mess hall and was himself cleaning a window ledge when he heard a flutter. He looked up and saw a small bird perched on the swung-out window. The bird had a piece of paper about three inches square in its beak, and while Ginther looked at it curiously, the bird, frightened by something, flew off, the piece of paper fluttering down to rest on the window ledge. Ginther picked it up and glanced at it. The word "Secret" was stamped across it in big blue letters; it was part of a page from a classified publication. Ginther showed it to Wood and Alexander, hiding it carefully in the palm of his hand. But the guard saw the three of them together and ran over, demanding with grunts and motions to know what Ginther had. Ginther slipped the paper into his other hand and held out his empty one for the guard, but the guard wasn't fooled. He grabbed Ginther by the wrist and made him surrender the paper. Then the guard took it to Bloke, a duty officer who spoke English with a British accent.

Bloke came into the mess hall and said, "Mr. Ginther, where did you get this paper?"

Ginther was speechless. Finally he shrugged and said, "A little bird dropped it."

Bloke looked as though he were going to hit him and Ginther shrugged again and said, "I didn't think you'd believe it."

Bloke went to the window, looked out, came back, looked at Ginther again, and questioned Wood, Alexander, and O'Bannon. Then he went away. The next day on the playground he came over to Ginther and said, "You must not tell anyone about this paper, Mr. Ginther. You must not tell my superiors. It would cause a great deal of trouble." Ginther heard no more about it.

As the men sweated in the heat and humidity, fought among themselves and with the insects and rats, made up crossword puzzles and songs, played games, and dueled with the Koreans, they thought of only one thing for any length of time: home. They realized they had to be patient, but as the days, weeks, and months went past with excruciating slowness and they became haggard and weak from poor food and disease, they began to lose hope. They felt an inward gnawing: remorse at their own failures and the failures of their country; hate for their captors; irritation with one another and with their surroundings. They needed a spark to bring them together again and revive their spirits.

One hot night in June, the Koreans gave them that spark.

The crew filed into The Club as usual, dreading the boredom of another picture about a red tractor or an industrial hero, or the Americans losing again to the glorious Korean People's Army.

They got that, of course, but there was an added attraction, an old newsreel film which showed the North Korean soccer team arriving in London for the 1965 World Cup championship. The picture showed the North Korean team arriving at the stadium, waving and smiling from their bus, then filing off. Right in the middle of the crowd stood an old English gentleman, white mustache, bowler hat, umbrella and all, giving the North Koreans the biggest, stiffest finger the crewmen had ever seen. The Koreans bowed and smiled at the old gentleman and a barely suppressed ripple of laughter started in the back of the room, spread through the crew, and washed up against Captain Queer, their narrator. He turned, puzzled, but half-smiling at their reaction, and then went on with his narration.

The men were excited, as though they all had the same thought at the same time, and their excitement heightened with the next sequence of the newsreel, a documentary showing the return of two U.S. Army helicopter pilots after they had strayed into North Korea and had been captured. The pilots were returned after long negotiation, and crossed into freedom at Panmunjom. As they arrived in the custody of North Korean officers and with the usual frenzied picture taking by them, a U.S. naval officer turned to a camera and clearly and unmistakably stuck the middle finger of his right hand in the air. The North Koreans obviously didn't know what the gesture meant.

As the men marched back to their rooms after the movie, they whispered among themselves. "Did you see that?" Law said to Escamilla. "These guys don't know what the finger means."

The next day on the playground, the finger was discussed whenever possible and the word was circulated to use it. Dunnie

Tuck said that if the North Koreans ever questioned them on it, "Tell them it's the Hawaiian good-luck sign."

As Charlie Law dismissed the men after leading them in calisthenics, he raised the finger on his right hand and said, "Good luck to everyone!" The men solemnly raised their fingers back and said, "Good luck." Then they broke up laughing. The duty officers were pleased to see their charges in such good spirits.

Ron Berens soon got an opportunity to use the finger when the Koreans came to his room to take his picture for mailing to his home. He was sitting in a chair reading one of the Korean propaganda magazines, and he carefully bracketed his two middle fingers around it as the photographer snapped his picture. Thereafter, the finger became the men's major weapon. If it showed up in Korean news photographs, they could show the world the way it really was in North Korean detention. They would pay for the liberty later.

If June was bad, July was worse. The only bright spot was a heavy storm which knocked down two big propaganda billboards at the end of the playing field. One sign showed a Korean soldier standing over a cowering U.S. soldier, his bayonet poised. The men were happy the next morning to see it flat.

The heat and humidity got worse, along with the insects, the food, and the Koreans, who were in one of their repressive periods because of Bucher's Memorial Day blunder. Thus, July the Fourth went unnoticed except for one of those weird circumstances that could only happen in the bizarre world of the *Pueblo* crew.

About 4 A.M. on the Fourth, Chuck Ayling had a terrible urge to urinate, but the men were not supposed to go to the head between lights out and reveille. The morning before, Kisler had tried it and had been beaten in the hall. Ayling wanted to go, but he didn't want to risk the beating, so he searched desperately for an alternative. His eyes settled on the water bucket in the corner of the room that the men used for cleaning. He crept over to it silently and waited until he heard the guard go past the room to the other end of the hall.

The trick was to hit the side of the bucket and muffle the noise, but Ayling was unsophisticated in the matter. He hit the water. As the guard walked past the room again, he heard the noise and slammed open the door, shouting "Moya!"—the equivalent of "What's going on?" Ayling tried to shield what he was doing but only succeeded in wetting his leg as the guard strode over and indicated with loud grunts and wild motions that he wanted to know what Ayling was doing. Ayling tried to explain the situation and then decided he might just as well finish the job which he did while the guard stared at him in amazement. When he turned abruptly and left, Ayling thought he was home free. But it was just the beginning.

The next morning Snake, the duty officer, summoned Ayling and Blansett, the senior man in Ayling's room, to the desk in the alcove, and launched immediately into a tirade. He said that Ayling was like an animal, using the bedroom for a toilet. He said that he was a "sanitation criminal" and that the act gave him a bad impression of the Americans. Ayling and Blansett tried to explain that the men were being beaten in the hall whenever they went to the head at night. Snake ignored their argument completely, as though they had never said anything. Snake called all the senior men to his desk and continued his tirade, ignoring their explanations.

Blansett had been asleep, but Snake told him it was his fault, as senior man in the room. As leader of the third floor, Sergeant Hammond got most of the blame. "You responsible for Ayling," Snake said in an angry, high-pitched voice. "You pay too!" The conversation and the tirade went on and on around the desk between the wildly gesticulating crewmen and the desk-pounding Snake. The guards merely stood around smirking, waiting their turn.

After breakfast, Ayling was assigned to clean the head. Snake told him he wanted it spotless and kept a guard standing over him. Ayling accepted the whole thing as a farce and worked resignedly on his hands and knees, risking a boot in the rear every time he turned in the wrong direction.

Before lunch, the Koreans called a mass meeting of the crew, and Skeezix, the habitability officer, made a long speech criticizing Ayling. He said that Ayling's act was crude and animal-like and that he did it to provoke the Koreans. "These ceaseless provocations must stop!" he shouted, as though it were a meeting of the Military Armistice Commission. He noted that Ayling had once complained about the guards moving around in his room at night and making so much noise that he couldn't sleep. Skeezix said Ayling's complaint was a plot to keep the guards out of the room so he could insult the Koreans in his bucket. The men yawned. They had all done the same thing and had gotten away with it. Ayling was neither bored nor amused; he was frightened. The Koreans were unpredictable.

Skeezix said the entire room was responsible for Ayling's action and must assume the detail to clean the head every day. They were to lose all forms of entertainment and they had to turn in their decks of cards and their chess set.

As a final blow, Skeezix announced that Hammond's performance as floor leader had been unsatisfactory, and this was the final straw. "He will be relieved immediately," Skeezix said in a grand manner, unaware as the crew stifled a laugh that he had created a pun of sorts. Ginther replaced Hammond as floor leader; and in a solemn ceremony watched over by Snake, Hammond turned over to Ginther the ping-pong balls and paddles.

The Koreans thought it would be a tremendous disgrace to Hammond; he would lose face before the crew. They didn't like him anyway because he was still hard-nosed toward them and they had never forgiven him for holding out longer than the rest. As further punishment, Hammond had to clean the head with Ayling and his roommates each day. If the Koreans thought they were destroying Hammond with their action, they were dead wrong. He was the happiest man around. As for Ginther, he was crushed, even though he had charge of the ping-pong equipment.

The same day King Kong told Higgins, a roommate of Ayling's, "If I in your place, I would knock Ayling down many times. He has disgraced you and made you do work." King Kong was very emotional about the subject.

The incident heightened the tension between the Koreans and the Americans. Jimmy Shepard took a survey and discovered that from the day of capture until July 4 someone had been beaten or struck every day. Bucher increased the tension, inadvertently, on July 4.

The Koreans were making them march with their heads down again, and Bucher was leading the officers up the flight of stairs to the third floor, exaggerating the order by marching bowed from the waist. This apparently angered a new guard. Just before Bucher reached the top of the stairs, the guard kicked him flush in the stomach. The blow caught Bucher unaware. He reeled back down the stairs, just barely remaining on his feet, the wind knocked out of him. He took a moment to regain his composure and his breath, and then went back to his place at the head of the line. Without looking at the guard, he bowed from the waist again and the line marched past. A duty officer who witnessed the incident came up to Bucher and told him he was a "bad man." Bucher was furious and demanded to see the colonel. He told him he was fed up with the treatment he and his crew were receiving. The colonel was unresponsive, but the Koreans eased up briefly after the incident and the tension relaxed.

On July 16 the colonel conducted another mass meeting. He was in a good mood and explained to them the procedures on the physical examination each was to receive for the next three days. Then he said, "I have great news, something beyond your wildest dreams." While the crew stirred, the colonel went through his usual act. He walked back and forth, strutting, his big teeth gleaming in a face split by a wide smile, his hands on his hips, while the crew squirmed in anticipation. Finally he said, "This is such great news, I would like you to guess what it is. Can anybody guess?" Hammond stood up and said, "We're going home?" The smile disappeared and the colonel said, "Oh, no, you are hoping for too much." Anything else was an anticlimax, but the crew continued to guess for form's sake. Finally tiring of the game, the colonel said, "Today you are going to get mail."

The men put on their usual show. They applauded, and Bucher got up and said, "On behalf of the officers and men of the *Pueblo*, I would like to thank you."

Bucher had asked the colonel many times about mail from home; each time the colonel said the U.S. postal service was holding it up deliberately. Actually, the Koreans had been sorting the crewmen's mail for weeks on the first floor but had held it back for some unknown reason. Many crewmen got large bundles of letters, most of them innocuous. The letters were addressed to USS *Pueblo*, Central Post Office, Pyongyang, Korea, on instructions from the U.S. Navy, and dropped in the nearest mailbox.

None were received by the crewmen sealed; while the Koreans did not censor them, any letter that displeased them was simply thrown away. If a crewman complained that he was apparently missing a letter, the Koreans would blame it on the U.S. Post Office. If some terminology in a letter puzzled the Koreans, they would bring it upstairs and ask a crewman what it meant before delivering it.

The men received several letters addressed to the entire crew, including one from a man in California who complained that he had been separated from his daughter by the U.S. and British governments. He asked the crewmen to contact him when they were freed so he could find out how they managed it. Bucher read the letter to the crew at the colonel's request. The colonel said the man's plight was an example of how the American and British ruling classes treated their people. The crew put the man down as a nut.

Bucher, who had frequent conferences with the colonel to air his many complaints, discovered at a meeting just after the men received their first mail that the colonel wasn't pleased. He told Bucher that too many families were including too many mentions of God in their letters. "This is an issue between our two countries," he said. "There should be no third parties."

At that point, the letter writing was a one-way street. The men could write only when—and what—the Koreans told them.

July was notable for another, much less pleasant event. Soon after Steve Woelk returned from his forty-four-day sojourn in the hospital, he got tonsilitis. The doctor treated it, but by April the tonsils had become infected and Woelk had trouble eating. He began by hiding his ailment because he didn't want to go through another ordeal with Korean medicine, but during the three-day physical the crew took in the middle of July the doctor found his tonsils in bad shape.

Just before dinner on July 23 the duty officer came into Woelk's room and told him not to eat with the others and remain in his room. Woelk and his roommates had an idea why, and his roommates, in an attempt to cheer him up, kidded him about losing his tonsils. For one of the few times in his life, the normally responsive and cheerful Woelk didn't respond. "You just don't know what it's like," he said, half in tears, as his roommates left. For the first time since the hospital, Woelk was alone again, and he sat in his room shaking despite the muggy heat, all the old fears and terrors flooding over him. A nurse came to the room and took him to the doctor's office, gave him a blood test, and took his pulse.

The Koreans had brought in a specialist from Pyongyang for the operation. He came into the office wearing a gauze mask. He examined Woelk briefly, then told him to sit in a straight chair and lean his head back.

The nurse blindfolded him, handed him a pan, and swabbed his mouth. The doctor gave him a local anesthetic, tied a string around one tonsil, and began to operate. After several minutes Woelk heard a snap and felt the tonsil being pulled from his mouth. When he heard it drop in the pan, he became dizzy. He motioned to the doctor to stop while he recovered his composure. Tears were running down his cheeks, which the nurse wiped away, and then the doctor went back in for the other one. The operation lasted about half an hour but seemed much longer. When the nurse removed the blindfold, the doctor, smiling, showed Woelk his tonsils. He seemed quite proud. The Koreans allowed Woelk to remain in bed the next day.

The dizzying, humid weather of July dragged on and conditions continued to worsen. Every man was ordered to kill 50 flies a day. Radioman Lee Hayes contracted hepatitis. His skin turned yellow, and for a time there was fear that he might die. All the men thought they might die if someone didn't rescue them or if the Koreans didn't improve conditions. But suddenly, and without explanation, the food began to improve about the first of August. The men were fed a lot of butter and potatoes and some canned pork. The quality of the soup improved, and they began to get apples. The apples were a great treat and much coveted by the men, although they were obviously from the bottom of the barrel, green and wormy and small.

The men didn't know the reason for the improvement, but they gobbled everything in sight, and practically overnight their condition began to improve. Bucher and the other officers got the idea of what it was all about the first week in August when the colonel called them in for a meeting.

The colonel said that the Johnson Administration was playing politics with the *Pueblo* crew as the presidential election approached, and the crew must do something to bring its plight to the attention of the world.

"You must rally the American people to your support and force the U.S. government to apologize," the colonel said, going into his act. "You must think among yourselves what you can do to help yourselves."

The *Pueblo* officers knew one thing: whatever the colonel was trying to draw out of them was already well planned. It was their job to guess what it was, in order to save a lot of conversation. They also knew that, whatever it was, it was a lot of nonsense and would be of no benefit to the crew. The colonel said, "You may discuss now."

The officers kicked the problem around while the colonel paced the floor. They suggested to each other another letter to the President, a visit to Panmunjom, a phone call to the U.S. negotiator at Panmunjom, another press conference.

Bucher asked the colonel what he thought would be effective, probing to find out what the colonel really had on his mind. The colonel said, "I am here to offer advice. Ask me questions and I will try to help you." Silver Lips interpreted as all six officers threw out suggestion after suggestion, watching the colonel's expression for a clue. It was a little game. The colonel knocked down their ideas one at a time, but Tim Harris noticed that his eyes flickered for a second when someone mentioned an international press conference. The meeting was recessed for one day while the enlisted men were called in in groups and subjected to the same routine. Meanwhile, Bucher and the other officers discussed the problem and decided that the colonel wanted a press conference, but they hadn't hit on exactly the right way to present the idea.

The next day the officers suggested an international press conference again, but the colonel said the issue was between the United States and Korea. The officers suggested that American correspondents be allowed to attend, but the colonel said the United States would never allow its reporters to come to Korea; he was plainly interested, however, and he stroked his chin thoughtfully as the officers then suggested a press conference which would include the enlisted men. After a moment his eyes lighted up and he said, "That is it! Word has come to me that your enlisted men wanted a press conference. I think you have hit on the answer!" He strutted, pleased, while the officers congratulated themselves on figuring out what he had wanted them to do all along.

The colonel wanted them to think it was their idea, as he always did; the officers had caught on to the trick early in their detention. The colonel always had an answer for everything until he had painted them into a corner. Then he congratulated them on thinking up the solution.

It was too late for heroics, the officers thought, so they just might as well go along; the colonel was going to win anyway. There followed many hours of discussion and paperwork as the officers and the colonel worked out the details of the press conference. The officers had to write out all the questions they thought they would be asked, and the answers, and they had to pick out the participating enlisted men. Bucher suggested a cross-section of the crew after checking the rooms for the best speakers. After much discussion it was decided that no more than twenty-five men would participate. Bucher submitted a list to the colonel, who rejected the troublemakers, using a phony excuse on each. Meanwhile, the colonel began to rewrite the questions and answers, wearing the officers down to the point where they were willing to agree to anything just to be rid of the chore. The colonel warned them that the press conference must not appear rehearsed, then told them all to go and study the questions and answers carefully.

The food was great, and the colonel was in excellent spirits. He called the press conference for August 12 and said he would tell them the site soon, but for several days the crew had seen great activity at a long, two-story building across the field from their own building. When the colonel finally announced that it would be held in the building across the field, Bucher stood up and said, "Well, colonel, that is a great surprise."

The weather was clear and warm on August 12. The enlisted men, spruced up for the occasion, were marched across the field and into the building, where the same gang of reporters who had attended the officers' press conference awaited them. The participating crewmen were nervous, but the press conference went off like clockwork in two hours. Robot moderated again, and Silver Lips translated from English to Korean. It made no difference what the men said in answer to questions. The Koreans weren't taking any chances. Silver Lips had the answers on cards and read them off. The men who did not participate had to watch the conference on TV, and had been warned by Bucher not to change expression under any circumstances. Korean duty officers had been assigned to the TV group in The Club and were to report on any laughter in the wrong places.

A picture taken at this press conference was circulated in the United States and raised speculation that the crew was dead because the picture had obviously been cropped and pieced together. In fact, Jack Warner and his crew had just fouled up the photography.

At any rate, soda pop and cookies were furnished, and the officers had a chance to mingle with the men during intermission with no interference, a rare treat.

The Koreans had lined off the volleyball and basketball courts, and after the press conference the men were allowed to play while the reporters came onto the field and mingled with them, asking questions and taking pictures. The men were busy dodging reporters and posing in front of the cameras. They wanted to be sure their extended middle fingers got the proper exposure.

The colonel thought it was a good press conference. He told Bucher it would do the crew much good and would gain much support from the people of the United States. The press conference did do the crew much good, but not in the way the colonel intended.

Bucher had ended the meeting himself and put the crew's self-control to a horrible test even as he helped their morale. He stood to say a final few words, then put his finger in the air and said, "Good luck, everyone."

Twenty-eight

THE AMERICAN PUBLIC was afflicted by the same kind of schizophrenia that beset the government. It was at first outraged at the seizure of the ship and then at the failure of the United States to retaliate. But, at the same time, there was fear that an overt act would result in the death of the crew or in a war. There were other momentous events to occupy public attention. The assassinations of Dr. Martin Luther King, Jr., and Senator Robert F. Kennedy, the moon race, the Vietnam War, and the 1968 presidential election quickly pushed the *Pueblo* to the inside pages of the newspapers. There was a childish faith that the United States, with all its power, was doing things the public didn't know about in regard to the *Pueblo* and that the crew would be freed rather quickly.

The United States actually had only one thing going for it— the secret meetings at Panmunjom between military representatives of the United States and North Korea. All other diplomatic efforts had failed, and the government's great campaign to muster world opinion against the North Koreans and force them to free the men, while it may have been an artistic success, was a failure in fact. Eventually, the public began to sense that there was little going on behind the scenes and that the United States was trying to wait out the situation. Scattered but growing signs of disaffection began to appear, the main one being centered on Mrs. Rose Bucher, wife of the *Pueblo*'s imprisoned skipper. An attractive, somewhat shy and introverted person, Mrs. Bucher had been the typical Navy wife, who moved in the shadow of her husband's booming personality.

With the principals in North Korea out of reach, the press

turned its attention to the next best thing—Mrs. Bucher. She responded, apparently in a sincere attempt to satisfy the press's demands, by sending through the press messages to relatives of other *Pueblo* crewmen. Unfortunately, she was soon branded as a publicity seeker and a rift quickly developed between her and the U.S. government as her demands for action increased.

Mrs. Bucher had learned about the *Pueblo*'s capture from a TV broadcast early on the morning of January 23, three hours before a phone call from the Navy had informed her officially.

Thereafter, she was subjected to constant questioning from the press after each new development; she worried all the time that she would say something that would jeopardize the crew. In fact, the North Koreans were enjoying the situation as news filtered back to them of her criticism of the U.S. government. During the frequent lectures to the crewmen, North Korean officers would sometimes include news of "Madame Rose." Some officials in Washington accused her of aiding the Koreans and hurting the crew by creating unfavorable publicity and thus lengthening the time the crew would spend as captives.

Her first real confrontation with the Navy came in late March, when she requested the home addresses of the immediate families of the crewmen. She had about a dozen, and had wired and written the families to cheer them up. When she asked the Navy for the others, she received a letter from Vice Admiral B. J. Semmes, Jr., chief of naval personnel, which refused the request and said:

"We believe we should protect the privacy of families placed in this position and thereby give them a measure of protection from news media or agitators."

The Navy and the State Department were careful, however, to keep her informed, especially when rumors of the crew's release began to pop up, as they frequently did.

But when a news broadcast said the North Koreans had announced that the crew would be "severely punished" for its crimes, she began a long duel with official Washington by calling President Johnson at the White House. Her call was refused, but an hour later she received a phone call from an officer in the

Navy morale service who told her she should try to remain calm. She made another request for the addresses and soon received a letter which said:

> We have given your request for the mailing list of the next of kin of the *Pueblo* a lot of thought.
> We have found that it is difficult and not particularly useful to correspond with individuals who are not in sympathy with the Administration or who are looking for a target on whom to vent their frustrations. You might inadvertently encourage that type of correspondence.

Mrs. Bucher was plainly on the outs with the government, but she was not alone. Others began to join her cause.

Meanwhile, Mrs. Bucher made a trip to Chicago to interview a pilot who had once been a prisoner of North Korea. Captain Carleton V. Voltz and Captain Ben W. Stutts had strayed over the border between South and North Korea on May 17, 1963, and had been shot down. Exactly one year later they were released at Panmunjom, looking relatively fit and well fed. They had been debriefed by the military and then they had faded back into obscurity, their story never made public.

Stutts had later been killed in the crash of a military plane, but Voltz was alive and living in Chicago when Mrs. Bucher flew there to talk with him. She wanted to know what it was really like in a Korean prison camp. One thing that had puzzled her was her husband's quick and abject confession, and she wanted to get some idea of what the Koreans had done to him to obtain it.

According to a story written afterward by Joseph Albright of *Newsday*, Voltz told Mrs. Bucher: "To be blunt, they torture you."

Voltz, a commercial airline pliot, told Mrs. Bucher: "The main way was to cut off the blood supply to your limbs. They used a fishline . . . and they would tie it around your ankles as tight as they could while they forced you to kneel on a cement floor. Then they would force your hands up behind your back into a position that is higher than you could hold them yourself, then tie your wrists. They would tie the same cord around your neck so that if you let your hands come down you would choke yourself.

"Another method was to tie me in a chair with my face six inches away from an exposed light bulb and then leave me this way all night. The bugs would get you. Sometimes they would take a small length of cord, tie knots in it, then make it into a loop. They would put it around my forehead and tighten it by twisting a stick in the loop."

Voltz told Mrs. Bucher the Koreans were always careful not to inflict permanent damage, and he got good food. Their purpose seemed to be to extract any scrap of information, no matter how small. "I would lie," Voltz said. "I would say one thing and then they would check it out, then come back and work on me some more, until I said something else." At the end of four months, Voltz said, a North Korean doctor halted the practice because his physical condition began to deteriorate. The next four months were spent in endless indoctrination lectures on the slums of the United States and the glories of the Democratic People's Republic of Korea. The last four months he was left alone.

According to Albright's article, one expert on North Korea told him of the *Pueblo*, "I doubt that there was physical torture because they want to get the maximum propaganda value out of this when [the crewmen] are released."

Albright, speculating on what the United States might do to obtain the release of the *Pueblo* crewmen, pointed out the method used to get Stutts and Voltz freed. As in the case of the *Pueblo*, the North Koreans had demanded an admission of spying and an apology. Finally, on May 16, 1964, Major General Cecil E. Combs, senior representative of the Military Armistice Commission, signed a formal document publicly admitting that Stutts and Voltz had been captured in North Korea "while committing military acts of espionage" on the orders of the Eighth Army. The document included a guarantee that the United States "will not commit such criminal acts . . . in the future."

The day after the pilots had been freed, the United States said it hadn't meant a word of it. "Such an admission is, of course, meaningless," a spokesman for the United States said.

Albright asked an American diplomat why the United States didn't use those tactics again, and reported in his article that the diplomat told him: "There is a feeling in the higher levels of government that the method used to obtain the release of the helicopter pilots was a mistake.

"The feeling is that this was not an honorable course for a nation of the stature of the United States to pursue."

Honorable or not, Albright wrote, an apology may ultimately be the only course that works.

After the article appeared, Mrs. Bucher exchanged letters with President Johnson. She questioned him on a report she had heard that the White House had cleared Commander Bucher of "any possible misconduct." In a long reply, President Johnson said of Bucher:

> On present information, we have every reason to believe that he handled himself to the best of his ability.
> . . . Your husband's reputation among those comrades who know him best is high and strong. Knowing him so, and being moved by patriotism and fortitude of your own letter, I renew my promise of perseverance and success to you both.

As the days dragged on for Mrs. Bucher and others concerned with the crew of the *Pueblo*, support began to appear. So did red, white, and blue automobile bumper stickers, bearing the slogan "Remember the *Pueblo!*" In Portsmouth, Virginia, across the Elizabeth River from Norfolk, site of a large Navy complex, the Admiral McKee Navy Wives Club began a letter-writing campaign on behalf of the *Pueblo* crew.

An organization called the National Committee for Responsible Patriotism, with headquarters in New York, announced it would collect a million signatures and deliver them to President Johnson. San Diego, because it was the site of a large Navy complex and because Mrs. Bucher lived near there, became a center of agitation. Committees of volunteers formed there and elsewhere across the nation to distribute bumper stickers. The San Diego *Union* began running a box on its editorial page counting the days since the *Pueblo*'s capture.

In San Diego also, a remarkable fourteen-year-old girl with long blond hair began a grass-roots campaign of her own. Marcee Rethwish of El Cajon, California, saved her baby-sitting money and collected donations for ten big billboards to be placed in and around San Diego which said: "Please remember our men on the

USS *Pueblo*. Pray for them every day."

To note the hundredth day of their imprisonment, she hired a pavilion in Balboa Park and organized a "Bring Back the *Pueblo*" prayer session; it was attended by Mrs. Bucher, several other *Pueblo* wives, and fifteen hundred other people. She organized a second prayer session on the two hundredth day. The San Diego *Union* carried an editorial about Marcee entitled "A Child Leads." Marcee also compiled a fifteen-foot telegram to President Johnson with more than a thousand signatures, urging a speedy return of the crewmen. The billboards, as well as Marcee's other patriotic efforts, were noted by Congressman Lionel Van Deerlin of California. The Congressional Record carried a speech he made in which he recounted how she had ordered campaign-style buttons for eight cents each which said, "Support Our Men in Vietnam," and sold them for twenty-five cents, using the profit for billboards supporting the men in Vietnam. "I believe a lot of our problems would vanish if more Americans shared Marcee's gumption," Van Deerlin said.

Marcee's efforts typified the whole movement—spontaneous, fervent, determined, and basically ignored by the vast bulk of the American public and by Washington. It seemed as if bands, parades, and patriotic causes had gone out of style.

Nonetheless, Mrs. Bucher continued to be a rallying point, and her efforts went on unabated. She was receiving encouraging letters from all over the world, sometimes as many as four hundred a day, and she wrote many herself, including one to Major General Pak Chung Kuk, the chief North Korean negotiator at Panmunjom. He refused to accept it from Admiral John V. Smith, who was chief negotiator for the United States in the first sixteen secret *Pueblo* meetings.

Politically, the *Pueblo* was a hot subject, with the presidential election coming, but, to their credit, the candidates never made it a major issue, perhaps for fear that it would damage the crew's chances of an early release. Senate Democratic Leader Mike Mansfield proposed that the United States send a special mission to interview the captured crewmen after asking the North Koreans to accept the mission on good faith, the idea being to "ascertain the facts" so the United States would not be negotiating "in the dark." In other words, maybe the *Pueblo* did intrude.

In July, Senator Stephen M. Young, an Ohio Democrat, predicted that North Korea would return the crew in August in return for an apology and a large indemnity payment. The State Department said in a statement of reply, "We just don't know where Senator Young came by or obtained such information. We find it questionable."

And General Curtis LeMay, candidate for vice president on the American Independent party ticket with presidential candidate George C. Wallace, said, "If Governor Wallace and I are elected, we will get them back for you." LeMay said he thought the United States ought to try to get the *Pueblo* men back through diplomatic methods for "a couple of days" and then start applying pressure on North Korea.

In Washington, the mother of Radioman Lee Hayes of Columbus, Ohio, went with a Remember the *Pueblo* committee to picket the State Department and demand that the United States use force if necessary to free the men.

She and the Rev. Paul Lindstrom, the so-called committee coordinator for the Chicago area, charged that the administration had been "vacillating and incompetent" in the handling of the *Pueblo* affair. Mrs. Hayes, who was turned down in her request for an interview with Dean Rusk, said that if her son was faced with a "slow death over fifteen or twenty years" in captivity, she would rather see him die in an attempt by the United States to free the captives.

Meanwhile, reports had circulated that Bucher had committed suicide, and the State Department quickly tried to run them down. In response to a U.S. inquiry at Panmunjom, the North Koreans said, "There has been no change in the condition of the crew." On July 11 the House Armed Services subcommittee approved a bill to pay each member of the crew of the *Pueblo* an extra $65 a month in hostile-fire pay, retroactive to January.

It had been determined early by Mrs. Bucher that the Navy actually had nothing to do with the release of the crew: this was in the hands of the State Department. The Navy answered her questions about the *Pueblo* as best it could, but then put her in touch with the State Department. A political adviser for the Bureau of East Asian and Pacific Affairs wrote and offered his assistance, then told her briefly what was being done to free the crewmen. But on later phone calls he became more brusque and finally told her, "Mrs. Bucher, you're harassing me. I don't know why I even bother to talk to you."

Mrs. Bucher told the press later that he also said, "If you were my wife and I were Pete Bucher, I'd like you to get yourself into a nice rocking chair by a quiet lake and stop asking questions." He told her the government would handle it.

On July 24 Mrs. Bucher met with Rusk in Washington for a briefing that lasted more than an hour. During that time, according to press accounts, Rusk explained to Mrs. Bucher why no help had been sent to the *Pueblo* on the day of the capture, and assured her that the Central Intelligence Agency had not been involved in the mission. Rusk was apparently too vague to suit Mrs. Bucher at the meeting and she complained that he answered most of her questions with a question. When she returned to San Diego, Mrs. Bucher wrote and thanked Rusk for seeing her, but it was apparent that the State Department wanted nothing more to do with her or anyone associated with the cause.

There were other developments. In September, Robert J. Donovan of the Los Angeles Times–Washington Post News Service reported on a four-phase plan for processing the crew once it had been released, with the twin objectives of determining through interrogation to what degree the *Pueblo*'s capture compromised national security, and whether any crewman should be prosecuted or disciplined for his behavior during imprisonment. The State Department, Donovan wrote, had already assigned two men who held strategic intelligence security clearance to take part in the questioning.

As an example of the meticulous planning for the safeguarding of national secrets, Donovan wrote, someone with the proper clearance would be present at all times when any *Pueblo* crewman from a sensitive area of the ship was receiving medical care under anesthesia. If disclosures were made by the man under anesthesia, the security man was to make a special report immediately, including the identity of all those within hearing. Special communications facilities were to be provided for the rapid transmission of debriefing material to top officials in Washington, Donovan said.

There was another item of interest. The Navy announced on September 27 that the *Pueblo* crewmen would be accorded all their legal rights when they were released and cited a directive issued in June by Paul H. Nitze, deputy defense secretary, which said, "Particular care must be taken to insure that their rights and privileges are in no way compromised or diluted."

While the picketing, the petitions, the predicting, and the protests went on, the secret meetings continued at Panmunjom, and Major General Gilbert H. Woodward, a native of Suffolk, Virginia, took over from Admiral Smith as chief negotiator for the United States. Before he left for South Korea, his father, Richard L. Woodward, advised him, "Go ahead and apologize, and then say we didn't mean a word of it." General Woodward dismissed the idea. "This country can't indulge in lies," he said.

Hugh Haynie, the nationally syndicated cartoonist of the Louisville *Courier-Journal*, perhaps best expressed the mood of the country. He drew a cartoon of an admiral, an anguished look on his face, standing under a portrait of Captain James Lawrence, who also had a horrified look on his face. The caption read: "You gave up the WHAT?!!"

Twenty-nine

THE AMERICANS CONSIDERED THEIR CAPTORS naïve at best, stupid at worst, and cruel always, a rather narrow scale. The Koreans were arrogant and overbearing, and while a few among them had redeeming qualities, the Americans found conversation with them unrewarding and one-sided and always ending with the Americans finishing second in a two-man race unless they had something going for them that the Koreans didn't understand.

In the latter part of August, the colonel called a meeting of the officers and suggested that they write a letter as a group to some public figure in the United States and plead for assistance. The officers sat around the colonel's desk in a little group and discussed whom they might write to. The colonel said, "You should discuss among yourselves who should write and I will give you advice."

Bucher set the tone of the discussion. He said, "How about Bill Bailey? He is an influential minister in the South." The colonel nodded his head sagely.

The other officers caught the spirit immediately. Someone suggested Jimmy Hoffa. The colonel, his arms folded in front of him, said, "That is good." They got another nod when someone said Billy Sol Estes and someone else suggested Jimmy Brown. The game went on for two hours, the names becoming more ridiculous until finally Bucher said, "How about John Dillinger?" Tim Harris began to laugh so hard that the colonel became worried. Bucher explained that Dillinger was a preacher from Florida who baptized people and had drowned three of them. This floored Harris and the others and the laughter was so loud that the colonel didn't know what to make of it. He half grinned, and the officers could almost read his mind. He was afraid he had just lost face, but the thought was so horrible to him that he was afraid to pursue it. The session ended and the whole thing was forgotten.

As the days dragged on following the press conference, the Koreans returned to their repressive measures. The food worsened again, and the men were beaten constantly in the halls by the guards. As more and more complaints filtered in to Bucher, he complained bitterly to the colonel, who either ignored the complaints or said the men were lying. In desperation, Bucher went on a hunger strike and refused to eat for five days. He got his point across. The Koreans customarily assigned one duty officer to watch both floors, but because of Bucher's overt resistance they added a duty officer to the regular complement so that both floors would be protected at all times. The beatings went on, but at a reduced rate for a while.

The crewmen by now had pretty well divided themselves into groups according to an individual's feelings. There was lingering remorse because of what some considered their betrayal of their country. They had given in too easily, some thought, and it made them angry. The finger gave them a chance to recover their self-respect. A small group of men like Kisler, Hayes, Berens, Chicca and Hammond disobeyed and frustrated the Koreans whenever they thought they could get away with it. There were the whiners, also, those men who thought they had been betrayed by their country and spent a lot of their time moaning about the injustice of it all. Many of the older men were passive in their attitude, accepting their fate and determined to wait the situation out, meanwhile attempting to keep themselves and the younger, more hard-nosed men out of trouble.

There was one man who got his principles and the realities confused. He said one day to a crewman who was relating to his roommates the circumstances of his latest questioning: "How can you go along with them one minute, and then come in here and laugh at them behind their back?"

The man replied, "Well, that's how you play the game."

There was only one crewman the others thought crawled for their captors too much. He attempted to ingratiate himself with the Koreans almost from the start, and the other men were careful not to say anything damaging when he was around for fear that he would squeal.

The man eventually discovered that he was doing himself no good with either side. The Koreans thought he was weak and picked on him more than the others, and his roommates harassed him constantly. But later, when the chips were down, he stood up with the rest and talked back.

Essentially, the crew was resistance-minded but strangely unresponsive to the occasional escape plan that cropped up. The men in Layton's room had discussed a plan that would have gotten them out of the compound, but there were too many problems involved in reaching safety, and the plan became little more than conversation, although Berens stole a knife and hid it in case the men decided to try. Escape from the compound would have been relatively easy, but after that the men would have been on foot in rough, unfamiliar country with no idea of the best way to go. Some of them determined that if they lived through the next winter they would try to escape in the spring.

Thus, they were reduced to getting word to the American public. Late in August, Law's room committed its greatest coup, again capitalizing on the Koreans' lack of savvy and their intense ignorance about everything but their own little world. Bloke came into Law's room one morning and told him they were going to take pictures of the crewmen in the room for distribution to their families.

The men had not been enthusiastic about writing letters home because the Koreans dictated so much propaganda to them, so their captors decided they would let the men write what they wanted, as long as it wasn't damaging to them. Pictures would be inserted in each letter. Two photographers showed up shortly thereafter and began to take shots of the crewmen playing cards and reading. After half an hour, Law suggested that they take a group picture of the eight roommates, and Bloke agreed that it was a good idea. The men lined up in two ranks of four each, and while the photographers busily snapped shots from all angles, Bland, Layton, and Goldman, in the front row, and Law in the back row, stuck out their fingers.

The group picture was inserted in a letter each roommate wrote to his family. Law happened to send his letter to his uncle in the state of Washington. The uncle was puzzled by the fingers, and after a while he released the picture to the local paper, which released it to the national wire services.

The picture created a sensation. Newspapers called on deaf-mute printers from their composing rooms to decipher the signals. Several printers said that the men were clearly spelling out the word "Help," and it was so reported. The people of the United States were puzzled and concerned, and simply wondered what was up.

The Associated Press caught on, however. When it moved the picture over its national net, the caption included this caution: "Your attention is called to the possible obscene nature of the fingers in this picture." Then a couple of national magazines printed the picture and clearly stated what the men meant. The free press, usually a blessing, had inadvertently blown the whistle on the men by tipping off the Koreans and the men would pay for it.

The crewmen, heartened by their success, daily grew more bold. The Korean duty officers, trying to satisfy their vast curiosity about the United States, got into long arguments with the men over the relative values of the two forms of government. The arguments usually ended with a discussion of sex, a subject that would often bring a blush of embarrassment to the officer's olive brown face and a giggle to the interpreter's lips. Possum, the short, cagy room daddy of Jimmy Layton's room who always made out he knew everything about a crewman, told Layton that U.S. sailors were always looking for sex and cited this as an example of decadent democracy. Layton thought he was jealous because it was plain that Possum never had the chance to indulge. Possum said there were no prostitutes in North Korea. He said that rich American businessmen had more than one wife; Possum told Layton he had learned all this from questioning U.S. prisoners from the Korean War. But if Possum and the others professed to be offended by American sexual mores, their curiosity on the subject was insatiable. Layton felt that if they had questioned the Americans as closely on military matters as they did on American women, the entire U.S. Navy's communications system would have been in jeopardy.

Don Bailey argued with Possum constantly over Communism and told him it was stupid.

"I used to wonder," Bailey said to Possum one day, "how the Communist countries could be in such bad shape. Now that I'm here, I understand." They hadn't gotten to the sexual part of the conversation yet, so Possum, instead of becoming insulted and threatening Bailey with punishment, said, "You should read the materials again and again and think it over. You say those things because you don't understand." Possum finally admitted that he attended church in the old days when the Japanese ran the country. "Things much better now," he said. Bailey said he didn't understand that, because he figured things couldn't be much worse.

In this same period, Charlie Law was going blind. He became aware of it about the time the Koreans were still worrying about the *Pueblo*'s intrusions and did not feel that the six intrusions they had plotted were sufficient. They worked with Law, Murphy, and Leach, and came up with eleven more intrusions for a total of seventeen. The Americans were encouraged in these exaggerations by Bucher, who told them to come up with as many as they could to show the world the foolishness of the situation. "But don't plot the ship inland again," he warned, "or we'll have to face charges of running the ship aground when we get home." Law's eyes began to bother him while he was working on the charts. He had double vision and everything began to look blurred. His eyesight had been 20/13 and 20/14, which is excellent, but now he was having trouble reading anything and he was worried.

He had not told anyone because he didn't want to expose himself to Korean medicine, but about the first of September Bucher noticed that, as Law was initialing the intrusion chart he had worked on, he had trouble finding the place to sign. Bucher asked him if he could see the buttons on his jacket, and Law said he couldn't. Bucher turned to the colonel, who was there for the signing, and told him Law's eyes needed immediate attention. The next day a specialist arrived from Pyongyang and examined Law. The doctor, an Army officer about forty years old, with a businesslike manner, told Law he had a serious infection of the optic nerves and he had to be treated immediately. By now, Law was virtually blind. He could see only by looking out of the corners of his eyes, and then not well.

The doctor told him to lie on a couch and roll his eyes back. Without further word, he stuck a three-inch needle into the lower part of each eyeball. Law could hear it crunch and he cried out with the pain. He got the shots on six successive days, along with vitamin pills, and then seven more shots. The doctor told him he thought the disease was caused by poor nutrition. The treatment improved Law's eyesight by clearing up the double vision and blurring, but total blank spots remained in the center of each eye, and Law could see only by using his peripheral vision.

Law thought this was convenient at times. He could look right at the colonel and not see him. The doctor told Law it was unlikely that the blank spots would ever disappear. The optic nerves had been scarred and not even glasses would help the condition.

While Law was suffering with his eyes, the men were preparing for another grand event, perhaps the capstone of their lives in captivity. The colonel called in the officers one day, went through his old guessing-game routine, and then announced that the crew should prepare for a great event.

"The Democratic People's Republic of Korea," he said grandly, "has arranged for an international press conference in order to bring your cause before the world. You should begin to prepare yourself."

The press conference, set for September 12, would include about a dozen of the enlisted men and all the officers. Bucher was well aware of the importance of the event to the colonel, who warned them that they should do nothing to foul it up. The food had improved immensely again and the crew was getting away with just about anything, a signal that the Koreans wanted full cooperation. Bucher understood that if things went badly the crew would see no end to repressive measures and circulated word to the crew to be careful. "Put them down if you can," he said, "but don't get caught." The quarters were cleaned thoroughly, and the men got new shirts and their suits were cleaned.

For days they watched out their windows as Korean technicians swarmed over the two-story building across the field, stringing wires and carrying in equipment. There was no doubt that this would be a big and important affair. Even the colonel was nervous as the day approached, and Bucher sensed that the colonel's reputation and career were on the line.

The men even had to rehearse. They were marched across the field and coached on how to file in and sit down. They had to study their questions and answers at great length as before, and the colonel and his staff roamed the hallways and held conferences with the American officers constantly, impressing on them the need to put on a good showing, for their sake.

"This will be a big step toward your freedom," he said one day, strutting and posing. "You must do everything to make it a success." The officers agreed among themselves that it was a big step, but it was more likely to aid the colonel's career than theirs.

The press conference was scheduled to begin at 9 A.M., and early on the morning of September 12 an area next to the barracks began to fill up with small Russian- and Japanese-made autos driven by Korean Army chauffeurs. Although the colonel tried to tell the Americans that the foreign writers had been brought to North Korea for the occasion, they knew they had come for the twentieth-anniversary celebration of the founding of the Democratic People's Republic of Korea, which was September 11. The crew had been allowed to watch the big parade in Pyongyang on television the day before.

As reporters from Russia, East Germany, Poland, Bulgaria, Mongolia, France, Italy, India, Japan, Spain, the United Arab Republic, and several African nations straggled across the playground to the press conference building, the participating officers and men dressed up in their refurbished clothing. The men wore white shirts and dark-blue Nehru jackets; the officers, light colored suits over regular dress shirts buttoned at the collar. At the last minute, the colonel came by their rooms and delivered a brief warning that everything should go well. The look on his face and the tenor of his voice made them think that while a good performance would not result in their freedom, a poor performance could make things desperately bad for them in captivity. They became worried and nervous.

About 60 correspondents were already in their seats as the crew marched across the field, including a chubby American with glasses and a pointed nose named Lionel Martin who said he was a correspondent for the New York *National Guardian,* a leftist newspaper. The American officers understood later that he lived in Cuba and supplied material to papers throughout the world.

The room was hot and crowded. Lights and cameras were stuck into every corner of the room when the crewmen arrived. They were seated in wooden chairs behind little stands, each of which held cigarettes and a microphone, and they stared around nervously at the jostling, laughing crowd, many of whom were military men dressed in civilian clothing.

Robot was the moderator again. The Koreans had stationed interpreters by each national group, and as Robot began to speak, a babble of voices arose in the room as the interpreters translated into a dozen languages.

"We now declare the press conference open," Robot said as Captain Queer translated into English. Captain Queer was way out of his class in this league. The job was too strong for him and the pressure got to him immediately. He stumbled and stammered, sweating and coughing to cover his inadequacy as Robot rambled through the standard opening.

Robot named all of the foreign news agencies represented at the conference, then said: "Twenty delegates selected from the *Pueblo* crew are taking part in this press conference. Commanding Officer Lloyd Mark Bucher is going to introduce each of the twenty delegates."

Bucher stood and introduced his men, then made a brief opening statement: "Before the general questioning begins, on behalf of the entire crew body, I would like to greet all of the reporters and correspondents present. Thank you for taking the time to attend. We sincerely hope that the reporters present will report our answers accurately and sympathetically."

Robot took over again and noted that the questions had been submitted in advance and they could proceed.

The Koreans had planned this part of the program so well that the men didn't have to be called by name. As Robot read the questions off the cards, crewmen would jump up without being asked and answer. Then there was a fifteen-minute wait while the room filled with chatter as the questions and answers were translated into a dozen languages.

The situation began to deteriorate. An African reporter fell asleep in the first few minutes, lulled by the heat and the boredom. A Bulgarian, chagrined because he wasn't being allowed to ask questions from the floor, said loudly in English, "I wonder how much longer this shit's going to last." Captain Queer looked at him horrified.

A dark-complexioned, thin little correspondent from India in the back of the room kept popping up and shouting, "I can't hear." Captain Queer coughed and sweated and looked around desperately. They had forgotten to give him a microphone, and the room was so cluttered with people and tangled wires that there was no hope of his getting one. Several of the reporters were plainly angry and showed it by their expressions and by the fact that they stopped paying attention. They smoked, dozed, talked to their neighbors, or gazed out the window as Robot tried to talk over the babble of voices. The crewmen were in stitches as everyone tried to talk at the same time. They began to ad lib their answers. Ralph McClintock composed a beautiful answer when he was asked, "What wishes do you want to make to Johnson, the U.S. government and your families, and to the press of the American public?"

McClintock arose on cue, grinning, and said: "Oh, how I long to walk down the quiet shaded streets of my home town, to swim again in the surf of Old Cape Cod, and to indulge in the sumptuous feast of one of Mom's famous apple pies. . . .

"I swear on my life that if I am ever allowed to return to my beloved home and family I will never commit such a naughty crime again."

The crewmen in The Club watching the show on TV had to use every restraint to keep from breaking up.

The men participating in the press conference were having the time of their lives. They leaned back and smoked, enjoying the confusion and chatting with their fellow crewmen while Robot tried to keep the conference under control.

Finally, Robot called for an intermission and the crewmen were allowed to go into a room by themselves and eat cookies and apples and drink soda pop. They exchanged information and laughed at the Koreans, their nervousness now dispelled. Still, they hoped they wouldn't be blamed for what they considered a total disaster. The colonel, in civilian clothing, was watching the conference on TV in the other building, and during the intermission he sent word that it was running too long and that Robot should cut off several questions.

The crewmen had hardly returned to their chairs when Robot stood up and said, "We now bring this press conference to an end. It is time for the crew of the *Pueblo* to eat their lunch." Turmoil ensued.

Lionel Martin jumped up and said: "I have one more thing to ask." Cameramen and reporters holding microphones rushed in a group toward him to get the story. The reporter from India stood on his chair and shouted, "Well, I have several things to ask the crew members of the *Pueblo*."

But Lionel Martin had gotten the jump, and as the reporters

pushed and shoved, tripping and falling over the immense tangle
of wires, Martin shouted above the din, "I can see from the statements of the crew members that they really did commit espionage
and intrusions. . . . When I get back to the United States," he
shouted, waving his arms, "I will tell the American people about
this." Then he went down in a tangle of squirming reporters,
still waving his arms. The crewmen were laughing openly. Robot
had given up and rested his chin on his hand, a resigned expression
on his face. Tim Harris, watching him, wondered what a Korean
court-martial was like. The reporter from India gave up, got
down off his chair, and dived into the pile around Martin.

Bucher then turned farce into catastrophe.

He jumped up and started to make a speech, unrehearsed,
and the room fell into an uproar. The reporters and cameramen
abandoned Lionel Martin and rushed to engulf Bucher, thereby
drowning out practically everything he had to say. A small Japanese reporter tried to crawl through the crowd, his microphone
extended, and disappeared in a forest of legs. The reporters
climbed onto the desks and knocked over and trampled one
another as they swarmed around Bucher, shouting and shoving
and calling out for Bucher to repeat himself.

Robot had lost control completely and the crewmen were in
hysterics. Even the Korean duty officers in The Club were
glancing at the crewmen with embarrassed grins as Robot pounded
his gavel and shouted above the noise. Bucher didn't let anything
stop him. He spoke for fifteen minutes, declaring that the men
had suffered enough and that they should be released at least by
Christmas.

When Bucher was finished and sat down to a round of applause from the crew, Robot, sweat pouring down his face and
with one eye on the door for the colonel, ended the press conference. The crewmen were limp with laughter as they marched
back to their building. The day wasn't over, however.

The men were told to go to their rooms. Tim Harris took
advantage of the informality of the day to walk across the hall
and into Bucher's room. The captain, in good spirits and still
laughing, greeted him and then posed with him for some photographers who entered the room. In a few moments the room was

crowded as a herd of reporters and cameramen descended on Bucher. Out of the corner of his eye, Harris saw the colonel, in civilian clothing and holding a handkerchief over his face, mingling with the crowd outside the door. Harris nudged Bucher and warned him that the colonel was incognito in the hall. The captain put on his best smile and stuck out his hand as Lionel Martin pushed his way through the jabbering crowd and into the room.

"Is it really true," Martin said, his pudgy cheeks quivering and his pencil poised over his notebook, "that you intruded sixteen times?" Bucher said the number was seventeen, "but it might be more before we get home again." Martin shook his head in disgust and wrote furiously in his notebook.

"And what slogan would you like me to take to the people of the United States?" Martin asked. "It should be a great rallying call!" Bucher raised his arm in the air and shouted, "Remember the *Pueblo*, sir! Home for Christmas!" Martin went away satisfied. While Bucher posed for more pictures, Tim Harris wandered back to his room, certain the fun was over. He noticed that the colonel had disappeared. "Boy, are we going to get it tonight, after this," he thought.

The reporters were allowed to eat lunch with the crew. The tables were loaded with beef, pork, good fish, fruit, fresh vegetables, and cookies. The men stuffed themselves and surreptitiously stuffed their pockets, answering questions through puffed cheeks. Charlie Law overheard one correspondent whisper to another: "These look like a bunch of kids. They don't look like spies to me."

Bucher and the other officers agreed that the press conference was an unqualified disaster and they shuddered at the possible consequences. After the reporters had left, the officers became worried and paced the floor trying to think up stories to tell the colonel to get the crew off the hook. But they didn't see the colonel for several days and didn't hear any reaction for about a week. Finally, Odd Job called them in and asked them what they thought of the press conference.

Bucher, trying to feel him out, said he thought they were very convincing. Odd Job eyed him uncertainly and finally said that the colonel though it had turned out okay and would get results. The officers breathed a great sigh of relief. At dinner that evening they wondered how, by any stretch of the imagination, even the naïve Koreans could consider the press conference a success.

Several days later the colonel called Bucher in to discuss some minor point, and Bucher noticed that he was more active than usual. He strutted around, hands on hips, and talked ponderously and at great length. Finally, Bucher noticed another star on his collar and said, "Congratulations, general. I see you have been promoted." The colonel glanced down at his collar and said, "Oh, yes, but I do not deserve it." Thus Super C became the Glorious General. He was extremely pleased that Bucher had noticed.

Thirty

THE FLIES HAD BECOME almost overwhelming. They poured through the screenless windows in such numbers that the men considering closing the windows and sweltering. The men on the third floor alone killed more than nine hundred in one day as, urged on by the Koreans, they swatted their way through the swarms.

A new guard had arrived and flies were his specialty. He was about twenty and weighed no more than a hundred pounds. His face was roundish, he had very bushy eyebrows for a Korean, and his ears stuck out. The crew thought he had something wrong upstairs. He was always grinning, even when he was beating them. He walked stooped over from the weight of his gun and he reminded the men of Dopey in Walt Disney's version of *Snow White and the Seven Dwarfs*. He was constantly going from room to room, pointing at the swarms of flies and shouting, "Kill, kill," the only English word he knew. The crewmen naturally called him The Fly. They were a little afraid of him because they didn't know how far he would go.

The Fly had hardly been on duty a day before the men in Mike O'Bannon's room began to miss cigarettes and apples.

Apples, even though they were green and wormy, were a great luxury to the crewmen. Losing them was a serious matter. The men had been in the habit of sticking them in their pockets at meal time and hiding them in their room for later eating, and they hated to give up the practice. They tried complaining once and discovered that the Koreans only turned their complaint against them, so they began to discuss means of halting the thievery without getting themselves in trouble. They were pretty certain that The Fly was the thief.

Someone suggested threading hairs through their cigarettes and leaving them out for The Fly. Someone else thought they could load the middle of a cigarette with matchheads, but the ideas were dismissed as being too tame. One of the Pueblo officers had told O'Bannon on the playground that he had also missed a couple of apples. He had punctured one around the stem with a needle and soaked it in salt water, then left it out for The Fly. The men thought that too tame. Finally, one suggested that they load up an apple with urine. The idea caught on immediately. The roommates began to lay their plans carefully.

The next day at lunch, Sterling took the best apple on the plate at his table and brought it back to the room. It was a beauty as Korean apples go—big and plump, with a nice red and yellow color. Sterling shined it up on his sleeve and showed it around to his roommates proudly, then hid it away carefully so the plan wouldn't collapse prematurely. After dinner, they went to work.

They first had to choose the man who would supply the urine, finally settling on Sterling because he had not urinated in several hours. They thought his medicine would be stronger than the others could supply. He hid a small bottle in the palm of his hand and took it to the head, where he filled it while his roommates carefully punched holes around the stem of the apple with a needle.

When Sterling returned to the room, one man listened at the door for the guard, while the others doctored the apple by pouring a few drops from the bottle into the needle holes. The apple was placed on the nightstand to soak. About an hour later the men noted with satisfaction that the urine had all soaked in, and another portion was added. The process was repeated several

times during the evening and again the next morning until the
bottle was nearly empty. The apple began to smell pretty bad
and the men washed it, then added the last drops to it. Just before
lunch, they rubbed out the pinholes with a wet match, and
Sterling, a wide grin on his face, rubbed and polished it with a
rag for ten minutes while his roommates crowded around, giving
instructions.

Then the apple, still bearing a faint odor but looking plump
and delicious, was placed bright and shining on a nightstand. The
men looked over their shoulders with satisfaction at their handiwork as they left the room for lunch. They had considerable
trouble keeping a straight face as they passed The Fly in the hall.

They returned to their room eagerly after lunch, expecting
the apple to be gone, but there it was in all its shining glory
exactly where they had left it. They were greatly disappointed
and a little worried. They suspected that the Koreans had somehow gotten onto their plot and were laying a trap for them.
Nonetheless, they left the apple where it was when they went to
the playground that afternoon. During exercises they told everyone. They whispered the story to Bucher while he was playing
volleyball and he began to laugh. He thought it was the greatest
and made them promise to get word to his room as soon as the
apple disappeared. He also cautioned them not to forget and eat
it themselves.

When they returned from the playground, the apple was gone.
The men were jubilant and patted one another on the back for a
job well done. Then they celebrated. Lamantia and O'Bannon
had saved their apples from lunch, and they cut them up for the
whole room to share. During the cleaning period they passed
the word that the apple had disappeared, and contrived to get the
news to the second floor as well. It was the main topic of conversation that night at dinner. If the Koreans had cared to notice,
they would have seen an unusual number of crewmen smiling
to themselves while they ate. Next to receiving mail in July, it
was the biggest morale lifter the men had gotten since their
captivity began.

The men waited anxiously the next day for The Fly to come
on duty, but he didn't show. He didn't show the next day or the

next, and the men were afraid to ask where he was. Finally, on the fourth day, he returned to duty. The men thought he looked a little peaked. They never lost another apple.

Despite an occasional triumph, the situation was no better. The food dropped off immediately after the press conference, and the Koreans began to put the heat on them again. They wanted the men to write a letter to *Newsweek* magazine asking for help in obtaining their release, and they wanted them to write another petition to the Korean government confessing their criminal acts and pleading for leniency. Most of the men, bored with the whole thing by now, went along with it. But some resisted. O'Bannon and his roommates told Robot flatly that they wouldn't write the letter to *Newsweek*. Robot didn't seem to be annoyed and let the matter drop. A few days later he came back and told them that every room but theirs had written a letter and that they had better do the same. The men discussed it among themselves, then handed Robot the letter. They had written it after his first visit, knowing they would have to do it sooner or later anyway. Everyone in the room had signed it but Kisler. He was adamant. Robot ordered him to an interrogation room. Robot, his "face" at stake, lost his composure and beat Kisler badly with his sandal and a stick, knocking him out of a chair several times. After an hour and a half, Kisler, one eye swollen shut and an outline of sandal treads showing plainly on his puffed face, came back to the room. "Well," he said through swollen lips, "you can add my name to the list."

Ron Berens, whom the Koreans disliked because he was always resisting and frequently fell asleep during the lectures, was beaten badly for the same reason.

Bucher also had his troubles. He was bothered constantly by the nerves in his leg and by a bad tooth, which the Koreans tried to treat without much success. Early in October Bucher got a bad case of diarrhea and suffered from chills and fever. Even the Koreans were concerned with his condition as it became more serious, and one day a guard found him collapsed in the hall. The guard called Charlie Law, who picked him up in his arms and carried him to his room. Law, half blind and afflicted with huge boils on his legs, made the guard go get the doctor. Bucher revived, however, and gradually recovered.

By now the Koreans were beginning to have suspicions about the finger gesture, but they didn't have the courage to press their fears just then. They were getting too many clues that the finger didn't mean what the Americans said it meant, and if it was something disreputable, they had been victimized in the worst way. The loss of face was too horrible to contemplate without further proof. Thus, the Koreans began to question individual crewmen in an offhand way. Possum asked Berens many probing questions about the finger gesture. He wanted to know how the custom originated, who used it and how frequently, and many other questions that Possum thought would seem innocent to Berens. Berens coolly made up answers as Possum went along, and continued to use the finger whenever he got the chance. Specs also questioned several men along the same lines. Bucher became worried. He passed the word on the playground for the men to be careful.

Also by now, the men were getting a real message of sorts out to their families and friends through their letters. They wanted to be sure no one was swallowing the Korean propaganda about humane treatment and American guilt. Tim Harris wrote a long letter to his wife, and at the end told her to be sure to say hello to Tom Swift, the fictional character. Chuck Ayling asked his father to say hello to three relatives, all of whom had been dead for at least five years. Commander Bucher wrote his wife: ". . . Don't lose touch with Fred and Cynthyssa Krociescheit." Others followed much the same procedure, and parents and wives all over the country opened letters and read them with emotion, followed by deep puzzlement until they figured out the strange connotations.

Despite everything, there were a few touches of humor. King Kong, a little stupider and a little meaner than the rest of the duty officers, came into Charlie Law's room one day and began asking questions about the United States. During a mild argument with Law he stood up and said, "You Americans can't imitate birds and animals the way Koreans can. I can even imitate the wind. Would you like to hear me imitate the wind?"

Law, curious, thought he would.

King Kong took a deep breath, and while the crewmen waited expectantly, he said, "Wind, windd, wiinnnddd."

Harry Iredale bit the inside of his mouth trying to keep from laughing, and the sight of his sucked-in cheeks broke the others up. They fell down laughing. King Kong turned as red as a Korean can and stared at them speechlessly while the crewmen half choked trying to regain their composure.

The men were amazed at how naïve even King Kong could be. They finally gave up and just laughed until the tears rolled down their cheeks. King Kong, realizing he had lost face, was too mortified to respond. He turned and left. The men in that room didn't see him again for days.

Events began to move faster as the middle of October approached. The weather began to get chilly, which meant that even the few vegetables and the meager amount of fruit the crew had been getting would disappear. The men didn't think they could stand a poorer diet and felt themselves growing weaker as the days passed. Now they faced another winter in their prison. They felt certain that some among them would never get through it.

But, just as their spirits reached a low ebb, hopeful signs began to appear. The Koreans started to treat them decently again, and the food improved slightly. Odd Job called the officers in for a conference one night and told them that their confessions were not complete and that they would have to rewrite them. Most of the enlisted men had not written confessions at all, and Odd Job said they would have to do so. The crewmen began to write and tape-record their confessions, while the room daddies—Specs, Possum, and Robot—went from room to room explaining that the Koreans had had to beat the crewmen in the past because they hadn't cooperated. The American officers began to sense that something was up but were reluctant to transmit their feeling to the crew for fear of raising false hopes.

But even the enlisted men began to get a feeling of excitement, and the Korean duty officers dropped sly hints that the men might be going home. The crew walked around half in a daze, wondering what was going on and hoping for the best. Then the general told Bucher the crew might be home before the end of the month. Since the general seldom told Bucher anything that turned out wrong, Bucher transmitted the news to the crew, with the warning that he knew nothing concrete and they should not expect too much.

As a further sign, the Koreans opened the Gypsy Tea Room across the field in the building where the international press conference had been held. The officers and men were taken one by one to the building, where they were interviewed by three civilians, who plied them with cookies and beer and asked them questions. The civilians were all smiles and very friendly. They asked the men what they thought of Korea and Koreans, what they were going to do when they got back home, as well as other personal questions, and asked them if they would accept a visit from "a friend" when they returned to the States. This last was obviously a rather stupid and transparent probe for weaknesses in the crew, a half-hearted attempt at subversion. The crewmen responded with ingratiating answers while they drank the beer, gobbled the cookies, and smoked one cigarette after another. Four or five of the men staggered back drunk from their meeting.

Not all of the interviews were pleasant. The smiling Koreans, their teeth gleaming as one of them poured him a beer, asked Don Bailey what he was going to tell the people back home about Korea. Bailey picked up his beer and said, "Waal, that's the easiest question I've been asked. I'll just tell them the truth and I won't have to exaggerate for them to get the message!" Then he started to take a sip of his beer. A Korean, his smile gone, reached out and took the beer right out of Bailey's hands. "That is all. You may go," he said. It was the shortest Tea Room interview on record.

On a cool night in the third week in October, the men received another hopeful sign. They were told they would go into Pyongyang to see a play. Tim Harris figured that the Koreans wouldn't be treating them so well if something wasn't up, and the men were excited as they marched out of the building and boarded four buses at the main entrance. It was also the crew's first journey away from their building since they had entered it on March 5, and they watched through the windows as the buses bounced up a dirt road, stopped briefly at a military check-point, and then turned onto the main road into Pyongyang. There was heavy truck traffic on the road but virtually no civilian cars as the buses drove down the tree-lined boulevard and past block after block of drab two-story combination stores and apartment buildings. There were few lights other than the mercury-vapor street lamps and several neon signs showing the profile of Kim Il Sung in red.

In contrast to their earlier ride through Pyongyang, the men saw many civilians in the streets. The buses were stopped at an-other checkpoint at the bridge over the Taedong River, and Tim Harris saw a guard approach two old women carrying bundles on their backs and ask for their papers. The government kept the populace on constant guard against South Korean infiltrators. Har-ris was delighted to see new faces and he appreciated more keenly than ever what personal freedom meant.

The buses went down a brightly lighted street with a big island in the middle. There were trees and benches in the island, and Harris caught an occasional glimpse of Koreans sitting on the benches despite the chill air. The buses pulled up in front of a big building, its eaves curled upward in Oriental fashion, and the men were hurried off the buses, past the few curious civilians strolling by, and into the playhouse. The playhouse apparently had been recently built; it was well decorated and furnished. The men were taken to the balcony, which was otherwise unoccupied, and sat in well-cushioned, comfortable seats. Except for the bal-cony, the playhouse was filled with Korean military men.

The play celebrated the twentieth anniversary of the found-ing of the Democratic People's Republic of Korea. It was en-tirely in Korean, but the duty officers scattered among the crew explained the plot as the play progressed. For a change, the crew was not at all bored. The play was colorful and bright, with a lot of singing and dancing, and the crew enjoyed the change.

There was only one incident, a minor one. A crewman who had kidney trouble was afraid to ask permission to go to the head. He tried to outlast the hour-and-a-half program, but didn't quite make it and went in his pants. Fortunately, the Koreans never found out.

The men went back to their prison expecting news of their release, but all they got was news of another trip, this one to a museum in Sinchon, a city about forty miles southwest of Pyongyang.

Several days later they were marched out of the building about 10 P.M. and taken by buses to the train station in Pyongyang. The Koreans always moved the men at night to keep them out of sight of the civilian population, a precaution the crew regretted because the darkness limited their view, but their disappointment was softened on this trip by a pleasant return to the train station in Pyongyang. Rigid security remained, but the visit was far different from the one they had made after their capture. For one thing, the quarters on the train were excellent. The men slept on benches with mattresses, and the cars were warm. The train spent most of the time in the station, then moved out in the middle of the night and arrived in Sinchon about 6 A.M. When the men filed off the train they saw the general's entire staff waiting. The general's car was also there, but he was nowhere to be seen. As usual, he was in the background making sure nothing went wrong.

The men were taken by bus into the country, and after fifteen minutes they pulled up in front of a plain stone building on a hill. Curious, the men were led inside, where a young, thin woman with stringy hair waited to guide them through the museum. The men discovered immediately that the museum was not educational, except in the psychology of North Korea. They were first led to a glass case containing a lock of hair. While the crew looked for something significant, the woman said in poor English, "This lock of hair belonged to a patriotic hero of the war who was brutally murdered by the U.S. imperialist aggressors."

The men blinked at one another and moved to the next glass case, which contained rosary beads.

"These beads," the woman explained, "belonged to American missionaries of the nineteenth century. The number of beads signified to American intelligence the number of Korean troops in the Army." The men blinked again and someone muttered, "Come on, honey, show us the real stuff."

The next glass contained what looked like a woman's ordinary purse. The guide said simply, "That is a spy bag used by the Americans." There was an old, rusty knife in the next case. "It was used to chop off the head of a patriotic Korean soldier," the woman said. The name of the Korean soldier was on the case.

There was a big glass case full of old shoes. The men guessed before the woman explained. They were from the feet of innocent victims of U.S. imperialist aggression. The Koreans, as usual, were taking pictures of the whole affair. Practically the whole crew, disgusted but somewhat amused by now, posed with their middle fingers extended for the cameras.

There were more cases of hair "from the patriotic . . ." and several pictures of dead Korean soldiers "executed by the U.S. imperialists." There was a picture of a pile of captured U.S. rifles, "weapons used against our people." More ominously, there were pictures of captured U.S. Army men, walking with their hands up and their heads down.

The guide led the men downstairs into a sort of dungeon and told them that the Americans had "burned nine hundred Koreans to death in here." Bucher asked if the nine hundred had been burned all at once, and the woman said they had. He noted that the crew crowded the dungeon pretty badly and wondered how all those people got in there at one time. The woman pointed to the ceiling and said, "If you look closely, you can still see the skins of the victims." The crew thought it looked like moldy rock. The whole thing had become too much by now, and Bucher stood next to the guide again, egging her on. "Did that really happen?" he said. When she affirmed the circumstances, he said, "Unbelievable!"

Upstairs again, the guide pointed out a large picture of an American military policeman, with a mean look on his face. The face was heavily shadowed by the visor of his cap, which made it appear as though he were wearing a mask. Bucher asked if MP's always wore those masks, and the woman said, "Of course." Bucher decided to quit because the crew were about to break up. The men were led from the building and back onto the buses, then driven a short way up a hill to two huge mounds of earth. "This is where the people of Sinchon, massacred by the U.S. imperialist aggressors, are buried," the crewmen were told. They were taken to another hill nearby, where they saw two brick buildings. The guide told them that Korean mothers had been placed in one building by the Americans and their babies in another, and burned. She pointed out "claw marks" on the walls, but the crewmen couldn't quite make them out as such.

The crewmen had ample time on the trip back to Pyongyang to ponder the strange, unreal world they and the Koreans were living in together. Tim Harris thought that if you could make people go for that museum you could make them go for anything and he began to understand a little bit about his captors.

The men understood something else shortly after they returned to their quarters outside Pyongyang: they were not going home at the end of the month. The Korean hints that they were to be released came as a result of a misunderstanding at Panmunjom.

Major General Gilbert H. Woodward had learned a good deal since taking over the *Pueblo* negotiations from Admiral Smith on the first of May. The fleshy-faced, slow-talking Woodward had once taught a course in Far East history, but he discovered there was a lot he did not know about the Koreans. Smith had gotten the negotiations to the point where the Americans knew what the Koreans were willing to accept, and he had submitted a counterproposal, which said essentially that the United States was willing to admit what it was guilty of and would allow a third party to investigate and negotiate the release of the crewmen. The Koreans wanted a full apology and an admission by the United States that all the charges made by the North Koreans were true. They were never willing to compromise.

Woodward had learned in many sessions, varying from half an hour to four hours, that his opponent, Major General Pak Chung Kuk, had no leeway in his negotiations, and that everything had to be explained carefully to him. If there was any doubt, General Woodward would write it out.

But at a meeting early in October there was a misunderstanding nonetheless. General Woodward told Pak that the United States was willing to give North Korea a receipt for the men. Pak interpreted the offer as an indication that the United States was ready to sign an apology, and so reported to Pyongyang. While Pak awaited word from his superiors, rumors grew from the meeting and spread to the compound outside Pyongyang that the crew was going to be released.

And the Koreans, always anxious to get one up on somebody else, let it leak to the crew. The misunderstanding was cleared up at the next meeting at Panmunjom and the crew remained where it was. The general himself told Bucher and the other officers that the release had fallen through because the United States would sign a receipt but not an apology.

The crewmen naturally were crushed, and the Koreans didn't make it easy for them. When it became plain that the Americans were going to stay longer, their captors returned to their old routine of poor food and beatings in the hall, the monotony broken only by news of the presidential election in the United States. The Koreans told the crew the day after the election that Nixon had been elected President, and even gave them the Electoral College count. Later, duty officers circulated through the rooms asking questions about the President-elect.

The Koreans were also looking for something to make another federal case out of, and they got the chance early in the second week of November. Two small holes appeared in a piece of paper covering a window in the head. A tiny strip had been torn off the bottom of the paper, and there was another small hole in the middle, as though someone had stuck his little finger through it.

The Koreans demanded to know who had committed the crime and sent Charlie Law around to each room to find the culprit.

Law made four trips, and on the fourth one Escamilla told him that if he couldn't find out who did it he would volunteer. Escamilla figured that Law would get the whole thing laid on him and thought that there couldn't be much to it anyway. On the fifth trip, the weary Law told Escamilla, "You don't have to, but I can't find anyone else." Escamilla said that he would do it, that it was better than another mass meeting.

In a few minutes a duty officer came and took Escamilla to the second floor, where Escamilla discovered that he was only volunteering for part of the damage. A seaman, Robert W. Hill, twenty, of Ellwood City, Tennessee, had volunteered for the small round hole. Escamilla quickly made up a story and told the Koreans he had torn the small strip off the window accidentally with a wash basin. Hill said he had made his hole in the paper on purpose so he could look outside. A guard came over and hit Escamilla in the face, knocking his glasses off. Escamilla picked up his glasses and put them in his pocket. Then he said in resignation, "I did it on purpose so I could look outside."

He and Hill were taken back to the third floor, and Escamilla was told to stand facing the wall with his arms up. Hill was taken into The Club, and Escamilla could hear him being beaten. When Escamilla's arms began to tire, he lowered them slightly and the guard hit him in the ribs.

At one point the guard walked away and Escamilla lowered his arms, but something told him to put them up again and he did so just in time. The guard had tried to trick him, and he rushed back to catch him with his arms down. Disappointed, the guard hit him in the stomach anyway. Escamilla doubled up and said, "Damn!" and the guard hit him again and knocked him down, then kicked him. After an hour and a half, a duty officer came and asked him if he was sorry for what he had done. Escamilla said he was, and he was taken back to his room.

By the third week in November the crewmen were worried. Their treatment had worsened and they began to receive ominous signs that the Koreans were disturbed. In fact, the Koreans were very disturbed.

Robot, Possum, and Specs began questioning Law and his roommates about the finger gesture, feeling their way along and trying to trap the Americans into an admission of some sort. Law began to get the feeling that the crew was in real trouble, the worst since the capture, and the Koreans were so unpredictable and illogical that he feared the worst. His fears were confirmed partially in the head one day when Bucher whispered to him that the Koreans appeared to be onto the finger gesture. "We finally got to them," Bucher said, "but we're going to pay for it." Law was certain that the punishment would be physical and severe, but the Koreans were in no hurry. Bucher discovered that they had possession of a copy of the picture taken in Law's room which showed four of the eight men with their fingers extended. The Koreans would not let him read the caption, but he feared the worst—an explanation by an American of the finger gesture.

Slowly, almost imperceptibly, the old fears returned, the fear of death, or torture, or both. The knifelike chill of a Korean winter was beginning to descend on the men again and they, in their weak condition, were prepared for neither the winter nor the anger of the Koreans.

Thirty-one

IN THE SMALL COAL-MINING TOWN of Norton, Virginia, high in the Cumberland mountain range of the Appalachian plateau in the southwestern part of the state, three men sat in an office discussing plans for a remarkable trip they wanted to make.

Carl McAfee, thirty-nine, a tall, blond ex-Navyman who has to watch his weight, had eager associates in his strange plan to help the crew of the *Pueblo*. Hugh Cline, his law partner, had been associated with him in a previous venture into international politics. Charlie Daniels, a successful plumbing and heating contractor and a balding veteran of two wars, was an ebullient adventurer who considered the whole world his playground. They were dissatisfied with the progress of the negotiations and thought that private discussions with the Russians and North Koreans would bring the crew's release.

McAfee in particular had an important ingredient to give the project; he had dealt with the Russians before on their home ground and he knew his way around.

The story began in 1959, when McAfee, fresh out of the Navy, rented an office in Norton over the shoe-repair shop of a man named Oliver Powers. McAfee didn't have much business then and used to pass the time of day with Oliver, who told McAfee that his son flew airplanes over Russia for a living.

"Oliver," McAfee would reply, "no one flies airplanes over

Russia except Russians!"

But one day Oliver rushed into McAfee's office, a shoe still in his hand, and shouted, "My boy! They shot down my boy!"

On May 1, 1960, the Russians had indeed shot down Francis Gary Powers over Russia. Powers, in the employ of the CIA at $30,000 a year, was flying a U-2 intelligence plane when he was downed and captured. The incident wrecked a planned summit meeting in Paris between Premier Khrushchev and President Eisenhower and caused a hundred red faces in the State Department, caught in a lie when it tried to cover up the incident. The affair also put Norton, Oliver Powers, and Pound, Virginia, fourteen miles from Norton and the home of the Powers family, in the international spotlight.

Once in the spotlight, Oliver Powers determined to stay there. He raised hell with everyone about "My Boy," so called because his other six children were girls. He badgered the State Department and the Russian Embassy, demanding to be allowed to go to Russia to see his son, without success; and through it all he depended on McAfee to guide and counsel him.

Powers wanted McAfee to represent his son at the trial in Moscow in August of 1960 despite the fact that some of the most important lawyers in the country were willing to pay for the privilege just for the publicity value. Eventually, McAfee became one of several lawyers representing Francis Gary Powers and flew to Moscow with Oliver Powers in August for the trial.

McAfee made one important contact then, a Russian lawyer named Greeniov who also represented Powers, and with whom McAfee had long conversations about Russian and American law. Greeniov told McAfee once, "Russian lawyers are like lawyers anywhere; they do the best they can for their clients."

The Russians had Francis Gary Powers cold, however, and there was not much doubt about the outcome of the trial. His attorneys tried to get him off on a plea for clemency, even taking pictures of his home in Pound to illustrate his humble beginnings as a member of the working class, but after a three-day trial Powers was found guilty of espionage and sentenced to two years at hard labor and eight years in a work camp. Powers was lucky. The Russians could have shot him. Powers later was freed in a dramatic exchange for Colonel Rudolph Abel, a Russian convicted of spying in the United States and sentenced to thirty years in the federal penitentiary at Atlanta. Powers returned to the United States and became a test pilot for an aircraft company in California.

The State Department had wanted McAfee involved in the Powers case because he was obscure and they didn't think high-powered lawyers were the best thing for Powers. They even told McAfee to act a little stupid. Thus, McAfee was no stranger to the State Department, and when he got in touch with James T. Leonard, South Korean country director for the State Department, and Winthrop G. Brown, deputy assistant secretary for East Asian and Pacific Affairs, on the matter of the *Pueblo* crew, he received sympathetic treatment.

There was another man ready to join this bold, imaginative group. Robert W. Ayling was a mechanical engineer with Westinghouse Electric in Staunton, Virginia, a city of about twenty-two thousand in the Blue Ridge Mountains a couple of hundred miles northeast of Norton. The Ayling family is a close one, and Robert Ayling was depressed and concerned about his son, Chuck, wasting away in a North Korean prison camp. He knew very little about the condition and care of the crew, and, like McAfee, he couldn't understand why the United States wasn't making more progress toward the crew's release. By late October there had been twenty-five meetings at Panmunjom and the two countries appeared stalemated. The North Koreans demanded an official apology for the "intrusions," and admission that the *Pueblo* was engaged in espionage activities off Korea, and a promise that there would be no further espionage activities off Korea. The United States would admit nothing and had proposed that the crew be placed in the custody of a neutral nation. If investigation showed that the intrusion occurred, the United States would apologize and punish those responsible.

This was essentially the situation almost from the beginning of negotiations, and neither side showed signs of budging.

Ayling was less concerned with the semantics of the situation than he was with the fact that the crew was still imprisoned. He and his wife had been conducting a letter-writing campaign on

behalf of the *Pueblo* crew without much visible effect, and now
he wanted to do something more positive. He wanted to see his
son in the prison camp outside Pyongyang. A member of Lions
International, Ayling appealed to his club for help. Dave Evans, a
Texan and president of Lions International, responded. He told
Ayling that Lions International would help in any way it could,
and pointed out to Ayling that a prominent member of the club,
Charlie Daniels, lives in Virginia and was interested in helping
the *Pueblo* crew. Ayling got in touch with Daniels, and the
scheme was activated.

The State Department had been besieged by people wanting
to go on a mission of one sort or another on behalf of the crew,
but for one reason or another it rejected each until it came to
McAfee, Ayling, Daniels, and Cline. The State Department
thought the chance of the group's success was enhanced because
a member of a crewman's family was involved, and was interested
in the participation of Lions International, which would provide
some financial support.

Publicly, the State Department officials provided nothing but
sympathy and warned that the group had little chance of even
seeing the right people. Privately, they told McAfee and Ayling
they would do everything they could to help them, without
getting involved overtly. The State Department made it plain,
however, that by law no private party had the authority to
negotiate on the matter.

It was a long shot, but anything was conceivable as the group
prepared to plunge into the strange, tangled world of international
politics.

It was decided that the group would work through Greeniov
in securing aid from the Russians, but McAffee was diverted by
the Russians to the chairman of the Moscow bar association. He
was out of the country, so McAfee wrote to the vice chairman,
a man named A. Korobov. The best McAfee could get from him
was a promise that he would receive McAfee when he arrived in
Moscow. Getting to Russia still wasn't easy, despite the effective
contacts. The Russians didn't want to get involved. Apparently
they were afraid of some sort of embarrassment in front of their
Communist colleagues, and they no doubt wondered about such

a wild scheme in the first place. McAfee stated plainly that he wanted to go to Pyongyang to see the crew. He was told that this was impossible but that no one would stand in the way of his trying.

Charlie Daniels nearly blew the whole thing at the start.

Late in November the men went to the Soviet embassy in Washington to get their passports validated. The timing was unfortunate. The embassy had been bombed a couple of months previously, and when McAfee and Daniels bustled through the door, eight of the nine people in the lobby took off. McAfee and Daniels heard doors slamming and bolts being thrown. The only Russian still in the lobby was in a bullet-proof cage, and he looked as though he were trying to escape. McAfee looked around and saw the cause of the commotion. Charlie Daniels, dressed in a heavy coat and wearing a fur hat, was striding about the lobby, his hands in his pockets, looking for all the world like a Chicago gangster. McAfee told him to take his hands out of his pockets.

After many travails and wanderings through the diplomatic maze, the adventurous four got the necessary clearance to Moscow, and on December 1 they drove from Staunton to Washington to pick up their visas from the Soviet embassy. On the way they listened to the broadcast of the Baltimore Colts–Atlanta Falcons football game in Baltimore. McAfee, a Colt fan, was delighted with the outcome, an easy Baltimore victory. Back in Staunton, Ayling's wife, June, was trying to call President-elect Richard Nixon and Vice-President-elect Spiro Agnew. The Aylings wanted them at least to know of the trip, and hoped that Nixon would privately seek Soviet aid for them.

The four picked up their visas without a hitch, then telephoned their travel agency in New York. The agency had arranged travel and accommodations, including tickets all the way to Pyongyang. When they got to New York, they learned that Nixon had replied to their plea for assistance, saying that he couldn't become involved in the *Pueblo* affair until after his inauguration. Despite this disappointment the four men boarded the Air France flight full of optimism, although they didn't have the slightest idea of what they were up against. To them, it had become a simple mission—to take a father to see his son.

There was only one hitch as they boarded the plane to Paris. They were well over the allowed weight for baggage. They blamed this on Charlie Daniels, who insisted on bringing along three cases of Wise County apples "for the boys in prison." After some discussion with the manager, at which time they pleaded their humanitarian cause, the group settled on a compromise charge of $50 for the excess baggage.

On December 3, about 4:30 in the afternoon, they arrived in Moscow after brief stops in Paris and Warsaw. It was cold and a light snow was falling as they trudged from their plane to the bus, which took them to the rather bare main terminal building at Domodedovo Airport.

They were passing through customs smoothly until the Russians came across Charlie Daniels's apples.

"What are these?" a Russian asked.

"Apples," Daniels replied.

The Russians were stunned and looked at one another. They opened all three cases. The apples were individually wrapped. The Russians unwrapped them, and finally agreed that they were apples but plainly suspected a plot. McAfee said the apples were for Brezhnev and Kosygin, but the customs officials were unmoved and called in a woman fruit and vegetable inspector, who looked them over and said they were apples. The Russians then hoisted the apples onto their shoulders and took them and McAfee off to another room. While his companion waited nervously, the Russians questioned McAfee some more and made several phone calls. Finally they allowed the four Americans and the Wise County apples through. McAfee cursed the grinning Charlie Daniels all the way to the hotel.

The Hotel National was built in 1905. McAfee figured it hadn't been repaired since, but it was ornate, the service was reasonably good, and Daniels and McAfee had the pleasure of being placed in Room 107, the best in the house. Lenin had slept in that room for several weeks after the Soviet government moved from St. Petersburg to Moscow in 1918. Daniels felt honored. McAfee figured it was an easy room to bug. He was convinced that the Russians thought he was a CIA agent.

The group was in Russia under the auspices of Intourist, the semigovernmental tourist agency. Payment entitled the Americans to accommodations at the Hotel National, meals, the services of an Intourist guide for six hours a day, and a car and driver for three hours. It became obvious to McAfee and his comrades that they had received a special guide. Alla Levitina was about twenty-five, stocky, with broad, pleasant features, brunette hair, and a strong sense of humor. She was extremely intelligent and spoke English well. She guided the men to their first meeting with a Soviet official on December 4. Mr. Koborov was a small, white-haired man of about sixty who chain-smoked and listened attentively as Alla translated McAfee's review of the *Pueblo* situation. He appeared sympathetic to the intentions of the Americans, but after a long discussion he could offer no help. He told McAfee that the Americans should approach the North Korean embassy directly. They decided to do that immediately.

The embassy of the Democratic People's Republic of Korea is on a Moscow side street. It has a side courtyard and high iron fence. When the four Americans and their guide found the gate open, they walked right in. Several North Koreans were washing a car despite the subfreezing temperature, and Alla went up to a relatively tall, well-dressed Korean in a fur hat who appeared to be supervising the car-wash detail. The Korean listened while Alla explained that they wanted to see the North Korean ambassador.

At that, a small, wild-haired Korean popped out of the guard-house and began asking questions. When Alla asked the name of the North Korean ambassador, the tall one said, "Don't you read *Pravda?* You can find it there." He turned away, saying, "Take your friends and leave our territory!" The Americans had been totally rebuffed on their first effort and they began to sense what they were up against. They were thoroughly discouraged as they went back to the hotel.

As instructed, they went to the U.S. embassy and related the incidents of the day. The personnel were interested and asked a lot of questions, but offered little encouragement or assistance. On a suggestion from Alla, they composed and sent a cablegram to Kim Il Sung and a letter to Kosygin. The next three days were spent in sightseeing, during which time Charlie Daniels passed out a few of his apples to some Russians waiting in line at the Kremlin. The Americans were awaiting replies to their messages, and some break in the impasse.

To help matters along, they composed a letter to the North Korean ambassador and sent Charlie Daniels with it to the embassy. They figured that if anyone could get into the embassy, Charlie could. Wearing a big fur hat, and with the letter tucked into the pocket of his huge fur coat, Daniels walked through the five-below-zero weather to the embassy, strode through the iron gate and up to the embassy door, and knocked.

A Korean opened the door slightly and peeped out. When Daniels waved the envelope containing the letter, the Korean stepped aside and pointed to a man sitting behind a desk in the lobby. Daniels walked up to him, holding out the letter. The Korean took it, smiling and nodding. He plainly thought Charlie was a Russian. Then Charlie made a mistake. In a Southwest Virginia drawl, he asked the Korean's name. The smile left the Korean's face immediately. He jumped up, thrust the letter back into Charlie's hand, and threw him out, more or less.

On December 9, Alla reported to her charges that the Soviet government did not want to become involved with private parties in the *Pueblo* affair and could not assist the group in obtaining an interview at the North Korean embassy. The Americans regarded her word as official. They had gotten nothing but a cold shoulder, but they were going to make one last try. They called the North Korean embassy and told the person who answered the phone that they would be there at 3 P.M. to talk with them about getting visas to North Korea. Then they called a newspaper friend, who agreed to alert the Western press in Moscow. At the very least, McAfee thought, they would embarrass the North Koreans by showing the world how shabbily they treated visitors. They hid the fact of press coverage from Alla; and when they pulled up in front of the embassy, several cars carrying newspapermen pulled up behind them. Alla recognized them immediately and was furious. As McAfee's party jumped out of the car, Alla called after them, "You are undesirable persons."

While photographers took pictures, the Americans walked into the courtyard and up to the front door. Amazingly, they were admitted into the lobby, where a huge picture of Kim Il

Sung looked down on them. The tall Korean who had been so rude to them previously in the courtyard stood waiting. He was joined by the wild-haired Korean, who looked nervously through the window at the large group of reporters outside while McAfee explained to the tall one, who spoke English, their mission. He heard McAfee out, asked in harsh tones why the Americans had brought the press, and then ordered them out. The fourth time he told them to leave, the Americans left. It was another failure, but at least they had gotten inside the door. And, obviously, they had made the Koreans angry.

Alla was shaken by the affair. When they arrived at the hotel she left them abruptly. Three hours later she came back with a bewildering proposal. She suggested that the Americans go to Outer Mongolia, 3,800 miles east of Moscow, where the North Koreans had an embassy in Ulan Bator, the capital. The Americans were suspicious, but when she said there was a good chance that they could accomplish something there, they decided they couldn't afford to discard any possibility, although they feared that the Russians had just been playing a game with them, hoping the Americans wouldn't cause any trouble. But after the incident at the North Korean embassy that afternoon, which apparently was embarrassing to the Soviets, the Americans guessed that the Russians were now anxious to get rid of them.

Alla said she would accompany them to Outer Mongolia and had brought along with her details on the two flights a week from Moscow to Ulan Bator. McAfee told her to make the arrangements for the trip and the visas, although he viewed the idea with some trepidation. Nonetheless, on December 10 the Americans went to the Outer Mongolian embassy and had their pictures taken for their visas. The Mongolians were polite and receptive and said arrangements could be made for the trip in two days.

But the Americans began to get cold feet, and a visit to the U.S. embassy strengthened their convictions. The personnel there, while interested in the turn of events, agreed that it might be a Russian trick to get them out of the way now that they had become embarrassing.

The Americans felt that any chance of success had to be pursued as hard and as quickly as possible. The U.S. and North

Korean negotiators at Panmunjom had not met since the twenty-fifth meeting on October 31. The Americans decided to ignore the invitation to Outer Mongolia, leave Russia, and start over again in East Berlin, where Alla had indicated in the past they might accomplish something.

Their decision came just in time. Pandemonium of a sort had broken loose while they made leisurely preparations to fly to Germany. The North Koreans had held a press conference criticizing the American "intrusion" into their embassy, of all the ironies, and the Russians were so chagrined that they apparently ordered Alla to get the Americans out of Russia as soon as possible. She booked them on an early-afternoon flight on December 11 and hustled them off to the airport, hardly giving them time to pack. Robert Ayling, unhappy with Alla's abrupt change in manner, told her he was disappointed in her. Her eyes filled with tears and she said she was sorry she couldn't help him see his son. She wished the Americans luck. A few hours later the Americans landed at Schöfeld Airport in East Berlin and passed through the Wall to West Berlin.

They had hardly gotten settled in the Hilton Hotel there when things began to pick up. Bill Brown, a correspondent with NBC, had learned of the men's sudden departure from Moscow and had tracked them down. He phoned McAfee and told him that through a Lebanese friend of his he had learned that the man to contact at the North Korean Embassy in East Berlin was the press secretary, Tscho Chull. Brown said that Chull posed as a former newspaperman but that he was actually high up in North Korean government circles. Brown volunteered the services of a cabdriver friend of his named Richard Helfreich.

Helfreich had an Austrian passport, which allowed him to move in and out of East Berlin with little effort. Brown said McAfee should go to the North Korean embassy with Helfreich on the morning of December 12. The situation had suddenly changed for the better, but the Americans were still suspicious. A Lebanese friend, a mysterious cabdriver, and urgent phone calls—all the ingredients of a bad spy movie.

Despite their skepticism, the Americans began to sense that something was up. Early in the morning McAfee left for East

Berlin with his knowledgeable but discreet cabdriver. Helfreich negotiated the Wall swiftly and delivered McAfee to the embassy, where McAfee was allowed to enter after he had handed the man at the door a slip of paper with Tscho Chull's name on it. In a few minutes, McAfee for the first time met a friendly Korean. Tscho Chull was in his early thirties, with unruly black hair and brown eyes, and, like most Koreans, he was short. Chull greeted McAfee cordially and said he had been waiting for him for three days. When McAfee looked surprised, Chull shrugged and said in broken English, "I hear from Moscow."

The two of them chatted like old friends. They discussed the weather, McAfee's trip, and each other's families. They even showed each other pictures of their families, and Chull asked McAfee what it was like where he lived. Then McAfee outlined the purpose of the trip, which Chull apparently already knew in detail.

McAfee said it would be a grand gesture on the part of the Koreans to allow Ayling to see his son and other members of the crew, and would perhaps even help the Koreans, who McAfee said were beginning to lose face with the world because they were prolonging the incident. Chull appeared to be interested. After five hours of discussion, McAfee left convinced that he was making headway. Chull promised to see him again shortly.

McAfee's visit created a stir in the State Department. When he called James Leonard in Washington and told him he had at least gotten into the Korean embassy and had talked with someone for five hours, Leonard said, "Well, I'll be damned." He told McAfee to call in the future over the U.S. embassy's "safe" line. Shortly thereafter, the Americans received a visit at the Hilton from William Dyess of the Eastern Affairs section of the embassy, who wanted McAfee to come to the embassy for a conference. By now, the press had caught up with the group and had staked out the hotel. Consequently the Americans left singly on the afternoon of December 13 to meet with Dyess and David Klein, the embassy political officer. As it turned out, the conference was a one-way street. The diplomats picked their brains for every scrap of information, examining every turn of phrase and inflection, but offering little service in return except to keep the embassy informed of developments.

On December 14 McAfee returned to East Berlin and a second meeting with Chull which lasted an hour. This time the two went so far as to discuss travel arrangements and visas to Pyongyang. Chull also told McAfee to bring Robert Ayling along on the next visit to the embassy. McAfee considered that Chull might be stalling and leading him on, but he couldn't figure out why he should bother, so he came back to West Berlin optimistic that they were making progress.

In the prison camp outside Pyongyang, Thumbs came into Chuck Ayling's room after dinner one night and asked him what his father did for a living and how much money he made. Ayling, puzzled, said his father worked for Westinghouse, but he didn't know how much money he made.

"How many factories your father own?" Thumbs asked.

"He doesn't own any factories," Ayling replied.

"Not even one?"

"No, not even one."

Thumbs left, obviously unbelieving.

Early in the afternoon of December 16, McAfee and Ayling went through the Wall with Helfreich to the North Korean embassy. After a fifteen-minute wait, Chull came in and greeted Ayling, obviously very much interested in him. At one time McAfee had considered taking Mrs. Ayling along as well, but the State Department warned that the North Koreans would be unimpressed by a mother's tears or any family plea. They would be impressed only by what the people of the United States thought, McAfee was told.

In the conversation with Ayling, Chull expressed surprise that the people of the United States were not in a constant uproar over the *Pueblo* affair. He said that in his country the *Pueblo* was the major topic of conversation. Ayling explained that the people of the United States were concerned with many things, but he assured Chull that they were solidly behind all efforts to free the crew of the *Pueblo*, and that many organizations had sprung up to support the cause. Chull appeared impressed, but when Ayling stated that he would like to go and see his son, Chull said,

"Not possible." After a moment of silence, Ayling realized that they were at the end of a long road. Quite abruptly, they had gotten the final word. He took a picture of his family from his wallet and showed it to Chull, pointing out his son. Chull looked at it with a sympathetic expression on his face and said, "Would like to release crew." Ayling repeated his request to go to North Korea, and Chull turned away. "Not possible," he said again. Ayling asked to see the North Korean ambassador, Ro Su Ek, and Chull said, "Not possible." As a last shot, Ayling went over all the arguments on why the Koreans should release the crew, pointing out that the best thing they could do would be to release the crew before Christmas. "Time is growing short," Ayling said. Chull said he would like to see the crew released but his country would have to have an apology. It would not be necessary for the Americans to come to the embassy again, Chull said, and showed them to the door.

McAfee and Ayling left, discouraged, and went to the U.S. embassy, where they related the events of the day while the diplomats took notes and discussed the situation. "It is apparent," a member of the embassy staff said finally, "that the Koreans are not going to budge." There was one more surprise still waiting for the Americans, who were convinced now that their game was up.

When they returned to the hotel, Helfreich told them he had arranged an appointment for them with a friend in Room 628. Mystified, but willing to grab at anything, McAfee and Ayling trailed along wearily to Room 628 and walked in. Sitting in the chair waiting for them was a man who struck them as the last player in the bad spy plot.

Herr Josef Frotz had thinning, sandy hair and bright blue eyes and weighed at least three hundred pounds. He overflowed the big armchair, and Ayling couldn't decide whether he looked like Sidney Greenstreet or Goldfinger. Great rolls of fat draped over his collar, and his whole body jiggled as he hoisted himself slowly out of his chair to greet the Americans. Then he got down to business.

"I can obtain the release of the *Pueblo* crew," he said in English, "if the price is right." He explained that he had "connections" in Moscow through his brother, the Catholic bishop of Cologne, and that he knew all of the important leaders of the Soviet government. He had arranged the release of people from behind the Iron Curtain before, he said. "I have an Irish passport, but I operate a plastics business in Cologne, and thus can move about as I please. I will tell you in two weeks how much it will cost. You may put the money in escrow and I will collect when the crew is released."

McAfee and Ayling listened wordlessly, too amazed to comment, and then said they would think the proposition over. They left and immediately informed the U.S. embassy about Herr Frotz. In return, the embassy told McAfee that the North Koreans had suddenly requested a meeting at Panmunjom after ignoring the situation since October 31, they said the embassy staff would check out Herr Frotz and assume that problem. David Klein told McAfee that he was surprised at the progress the group had made and congratulated him. "We don't know what this sudden meeting at Panmunjom means," Klein said, "but it perhaps explains why Chull decided it wasn't necessary to see you again." Relieved, and hopeful that they had contributed to the crew's possible release, the Americans made plans to go home.

Thirty-two

THE BEAR HAD BEEN AWAY on another assignment, but now he stood at the doorway to the mess hall, a sullen expression on his face, shifting his gaze slowly from table to table. The men could feel the atmosphere change as the word passed by nudge and whisper from man to man: "The Bear is back."

Charlie Law looked out of the corners of his damaged eyes at The Bear and shrugged. "They brought their hatchet man back," he whispered to Layton. Law had no illusions about what it meant. They were going to get it, and soon. Winter winds were sweeping the plains around Pyongyang as the first week in December neared an end, and already the crew could see patches of ice forming around the edges of the rice paddies. About fifteen members of the crew had trouble walking because, it was said, the poor nutrition had affected the nerves in their legs. The insects had long since gone, but the infections, the chills, and the fever continued. Bucher was especially ill and there were days when he could hardly make it to the mess hall.

The stocky, strong Law had dropped from 205 pounds to 160. Don Bailey, thin to begin with, was now emaciated. He had dropped from 140 to 102 pounds and he felt weak and tired all the time. Steve Woelk's ordeal had cost him 55 pounds. Engineman John Higgins, twenty-three, of St. Joseph, Missouri, who had walked off the *Pueblo* nearly eleven months previously standing six feet seven and weighing 280 pounds, was now down to 210.

But, even worse, the men were dispirited. The approach of another winter was a deadening weight, and they saw no sign, no hope of a break in the impasse between the United States and North Korea. They were caught in the middle—useful pawns in a useless game that neither side could win. Only the crew of the *Pueblo* could lose. It would have been different had the countries been at war. That would have been something to cling to, that the war would end eventually and the men would be freed. But there was no war and some of the men began to believe that they could live their lives out in their prison. Only the presence of their comrades kept some from losing touch with reality. In their world, they sometimes couldn't be sure what was reality and what wasn't.

Bucher and Law were like rocks in the middle of a stream, accepting the onrushing water and withstanding it without flinching, serving as guides for the other men. But Bucher grew sicker each day, and Law was groping through the halls, half blind, and weakening. Even the stubborn Hammond was coming to the end of his endurance.

At the end of the first week in December the Koreans' frustration and hatred began to spill over onto the helpless crew.

On December 7 the men in Law's room were taken to a lecture room and ordered to sit down. In a few minutes the eight men from Stuart Russell's room filed in. Robot began questioning each about the finger gesture, but it was plain this time that his was no idle curiosity. Robot wanted to know who had used the gesture and five crewmen raised their hands. He pointed at Russell, who had his hand raised, and asked him why he had done it. The usually easygoing Russell was frightened. So were the others. Russell said: "I just wanted the folks back home to know we were okay." He sat down shakily. Robot laughed without humor and continued to question each one. The Koreans no longer had any doubt about what the gesture meant. Now they were trying to determine if its use was organized, and, if so, who had organized it.

The mood of the Koreans was made plain to Law and the others in his room the following morning. A guard had been sent to get David Ritter, across the hall from Law's room, for some minor infraction, but the guard came to Law's room instead and ordered Harry Iredale, similar in build to Ritter, into the hall. The guard closed the door and Iredale's roommates could hear the guard jabbering at him just outside the door. It sounded to Law as though the guard were telling Iredale in Korean to put his head down. Iredale, frightened, said he didn't understand. Then the crewmen heard him grunt and his body thud against the wall.

The sound was repeated for several minutes, punctuated by groans. After about ten minutes the guard opened the door and shoved Iredale into the room. Iredale, holding his jaw, staggered to his chair and fell into it. The back of his clothing was covered with plaster from where he had bounced off the wall.

Later, the men figured out what had happened. Bloke, the duty officer, had ordered Ritter to write something, but Ritter told him he couldn't because Bloke had taken the pencils and paper away. Bloke, furious because he had lost face, left the room and sent the guard to beat Ritter. Iredale and Ritter were both short and both wore glasses, and the guard had picked the wrong man. Law and the others thought it was the worst beating a crewman had received since the early days of imprisonment.

About 9 a.m. the next day a guard came and took Goldman, Layton, Bland, and Berens from Law's room. Of the four, Goldman, Layton, and Bland had used the finger in the picture. Law, the fourth man who had used his finger, felt there was something ominous in the way the men had been escorted from the room.

He felt certain it had something to do with the picture and wondered why he hadn't been included, although Berens was a logical choice for any beating the Koreans wanted to administer. A strong Catholic and a good sailor, Berens was a tough youngster from Kansas, an ex-oilfield roustabout who hated Communism and the Koreans. In his quiet way he had resisted the Koreans with every means and had taken their harassment and beatings without flinching.

About noon Law went to the head, where he saw Bland. Bland's face was swollen and red and one eye was nearly closed. He whispered to Law that he had been badly beaten by The Bear. The news shook Law and he was shaken even more when Jimmy Layton, his face also swollen, came back to the room about 1 P.M. Rattled and hurt, Layton sat down and turned his face away from the others. In a few minutes Berens came back, his face puffy. He was limping from where The Bear had kicked him repeatedly in the leg. He was followed shortly by Chief Goldman, who had been beaten the worst of all. The Koreans had a special hatred for Goldman, a Navy veteran who had served on a minesweeper that laid mines in Wonsan harbor during the Korean War, and when the guard shoved him into the room his roommates could see what Korean hatred meant. Goldman's ear was torn and his lip split wide open. It was still bleeding.

Possum had been supervising the whole thing and had lost his composure when the men refused to admit what the finger gesture meant. While The Bear worked on Goldman, Possum beat Berens about the face with a rubber-soled slipper. Even when some of the others gave in and confessed what the gesture meant, Berens held out and was beaten until he fell down. Possum asked over and over again, "What does CIA use gesture for?" But Berens would admit to nothing.

The Koreans concentrated on Law's room to begin because they suspected Law was behind the gesture and they wanted someone to squeal on him. But the rest of the crew soon became involved.

On December 10, after lunch, the general called a mass meeting and told the men they had not been sincere and they would be punished for it. In addition, they must confess to everything they had done while in captivity and they must tell of everything they knew others had done. He warned them that they had only one more chance to be sincere. He was in a foul, uncompromising mood.

Tables were set up in the alcove and the enlisted men were immediately put to writing their confessions. There was to be absolute silence. The officers were allowed to write theirs in their rooms. Tim Harris, like the other officers, was unaware that some of the crewmen had been beaten and that they all faced imminent danger. He wrote one page on the night of December 10 and confessed that he had used the finger gesture in a picture that had been sent to his wife. Robot came in and glanced at it, then handed it back. "Not enough," he said. "You write more. You must tell everything." The door was left open and Harris got his first indication that the situation was serious when he discovered that the crew was not going to eat in the mess hall. A guard left his dinner on a tray outside the door. The food was worse than usual. Harris was supposed to continue writing his confession after dinner, but he didn't do anything and went to bed at 10 P.M. as usual. He had just dozed off when a guard came in, snapped on the light, and told Harris to get up and continue writing. He remained up the rest of the night, writing anything that came to mind. Breakfast was left at his door. When Harris went to get the tray, he could see Bucher across the hall sitting at his desk staring dejectedly into space.

Early on the morning of December 11, a Wednesday, ominous sounds began to sift through the hallways. The Koreans were moving furniture around, and the crewmen sat in their chairs listening silently to the scraping and bumping, glancing occasionally at one another as the Koreans bustled through the hallways. The Korean officers were brusque and efficient, their manner completely changed, and the men caught an occasional glimpse of The Bear striding past their doors, the sullen look on his face tempered only slightly by what the men regarded as a smirk. The duty officers went from room to room issuing instructions that the men were to remain in their chairs at all times unless otherwise instructed. Their heads were to be bowed and their bodies bent over, with their hands clenched on their thighs. It was

a painful, humiliating position, and the men had trouble maintaining it. The light was to remain on at all times. In the afternoon,
the Koreans began moving the men, emptying some rooms and
putting the men from those rooms in with others. They created
six twelve-man rooms and one four-man room, with the officers
remaining isolated. The Koreans needed the extra space for interrogation, and whatever else they had in mind.

On the morning of December 12, Hell Week began. Tim
Harris was sitting stiff in his chair when he heard a commotion
and looked up in time to see Odd Job and Silver Lips rush through
the door to Bucher's room.

Bucher was sitting at his desk writing when he heard them
coming and half stood to face them, surprise on his face. Odd Job
hit him in the jaw with his fist. Bucher managed to roll with the
punch, but Silver Lips caught him flush and knocked him onto the
desk, then pulled him upright and hit him again. The Koreans
were furious, and Tim Harris, stunned and terrified at the sight,
was aware of a growing turmoil all around him. While Odd Job
continued to strike Bucher, Silver Lips shouted that he was to
blame for everything. "You CIA man!" he shouted over and over,
and he pushed the dazed and shaken Bucher into his chair. Then
the two officers left the room.

Meanwhile, Charlie Law's confession had been rejected. He
had been told to confess to everything since the *Pueblo* had left
Bremerton, but mainly he was told to confess his crimes and the
crimes of others during the imprisonment. Law wrote twenty-
five pages, but Robot brought them back. "We already know
what you have written," he said. "We want to know what you
have not confessed previously." Law made up things to confess.
He said that he had told the crew to open the windows to waste
heat, that he had thumbed his nose at the officers behind their
backs, that he had urinated out the window—anything that came
to mind.

Law had escaped virtually unscathed through all the long
days of harassment and punishment in detention, but now the
Koreans zeroed in on him and his room, certain that Law was
a key man in what they thought was the organized resistance
of the crew. On the afternoon of December 12 they began ques-

tioning the men in his room one by one, using all their cunning and determination to trap the men into telling on one another and admitting that Law was the ringleader. Law was taken down the hall to Room No. 5, where Odd Job and an interpreter waited behind a desk, and as soon as he sat down in the chair in front of the desk they began to question him.

"Who behind the finger gesture?" Odd Job demanded.

Law, still not thinking the situation was serious, said he had instigated the use of the gesture as a sign of defiance. At the worst, he thought, he would get punched a couple of times and lectured and he thought he might as well get it over with. Since he was a logical suspect, the Koreans would believe him and it might save a lot of trouble for the others. He believed he could fake his way through it. Then, when Odd Job demanded to know the name of the CIA agent, Law paused, then threw up his hands and said, "There's no point going on with this. I am."

Odd Job disregarded the answer.

"It was your captain, wasn't it?" Odd Job shouted.

"No, it was me," Law said.

Odd Job shook his fist and shouted, "You're lying! It was Schumacher and he worked it through you!"

Law shrugged and kept repeating that it was he, and not Bucher or Schumacher. The two dueled for half an hour, and then Odd Job suddenly dropped the discussion of the finger gesture. His manner became more confidential and he leaned forward and said quietly, "Why you afraid of Bucher?"

Law decided to play along with him and see where the thread would lead. "I'm afraid of him because he can make it real rough for me." Odd Job leaned back and asked, "Why you afraid of Schumacher?"

"He went to college and uses big words," Law answered. The answers made as much sense as the questions, but it was part of the game and Law had no choice but to play it. He was still unconcerned about the outcome and he wanted to get it over with. He was getting hungry.

Law said he wasn't afraid of Steve or Tim Harris, but he was afraid of Gene Lacy because Lacy could beat him up. "Ah, so Lacy is CIA agent?" Odd Job said, his eyes lighting. "No, I am the agent," Law said again.

"So you are the one." Odd Job's face took on a thoughtful look and he stroked his chin. "What school you go to?" he shot. Law said he didn't remember.

"What kind of training you get? How you send Morse code with fingers?"

Law held up his hands and said, "Left hand means 'daw.' Right hand means 'dit.' "

Odd Job nodded and said, "Now tell me about secret words."

Law shook his head. "What do you mean?"

"Like mountain means 'Fight Koreans.' "

Law said, "Yeah. We have secret words." Odd Job handed Law a pencil and paper and told him to write down ten secret words. Law put the word "mountain" at the top of the list, then added words as they popped into his mind. Odd Job snatched the paper as soon as Law finished. He read the word "mountain" at the top of the list and raised his eyebrows.

"Is this so?"

"Oh yes. I'm surprised you knew."

A satisfied look on his face, Odd Job said, "We know everything."

Law wasn't sure whether Odd Job was that stupid or just playing with him. He decided it was both. Odd Job, his face hard, went back to the subject of Bucher and kept insisting that Law was getting his instructions from him. Law continued to deny it and saw that Odd Job was heating up more and more. Law had been there for more than an hour and his back was beginning to ache. When he flexed his arms once, Odd Job stood up and hit his fists on the table. "You son of a bitch!" he shouted, suddenly furious. He strode from the room and came back shortly, The Bear and another guard following him.

He ordered Law to get on his knees and sit back on his heels. The Bear was carrying a two-by-two stick about five feet long; he laid it down and hit Law below the right ear with his fist. Law swayed with the punch, but it hurt and The Bear grabbed him by the hair and hit him three or four times, then stepped back and kicked him flush in the stomach. Law, dizzy, grunted and doubled over. When he straightened up again, The Bear smashed him across the shoulders with the two-by-two. Pain flashed through Law's body, and as he fell forward he looked up at Odd Jobb and blurted, "Shit on you!"

Odd Job stepped forward and shouted, "Goddamn you! Goddamn you!" He motioned to The Bear, who gripped the two-by-two in both hands and beat Law across the back with it until it broke in two, one half flying across the room. The Bear jabbed Law in the ear with the broken piece. Tears came to Law's eyes, and for the first time he was very frightened. The Bear hit Law with one of the halves until it broke, then beat him with the other until that one broke. He stood there breathing heavily, holding the four pieces of wood in his hands, and kicked Law in the stomach again, knocking him over. Law lay on his side, sobbing and gasping for breath.

The Bear walked away and Odd Job told Law to get back in the chair. Law couldn't stand but managed to pull himself into the chair, where he sat with his head down, tears running down his cheeks.

"You ready to tell truth now?" Odd Job said.

Law thought he was going to be crippled, and all the anger, all the frustration, all the fear, welled up in him and spilled out.

"You son of a bitch!" he shouted at Odd Job. "Every goddamn thing I told you was a lie, you bastard!" The Bear stepped forward and smashed him on the side of the head with his fist, knocking him from the chair. As Law struggled to his knees, a guard came in with a four-by-four post. "God," Law said, "you can't hit me with that!"

The guard swung from his heels and hit Law across the back with the post, knocking him, sobbing, onto his face. Odd Job looked down at Law's semi-conscious form and said, "You have five minutes to tell the truth." Then everyone left the room.

Law lay on the floor, his senses slowly returning, his body overwhelmed with pain. His back was like fire, and he could feel the knots swelling on his forehead. He felt nauseated but choked back the urge to vomit. They wanted him to tell the truth, but he didn't know what the truth was.

After about fifteen minutes Odd Job returned with The Bear and told Law to get to his feet and follow them. Law wondered if he was going to be killed as he struggled first to his knees, then staggered to his feet and reeled after them. He was taken to Bucher's room next door.

Bucher was kneeling in the center of the room, his arms hanging loosely at his side, his body quivering. Silver Lips, standing over him, looked like a wild man. His hair was messed, his uniform in disarray, and he was pointing at Bucher and shouting, "Spy! Spy!" Bucher was dazed and sobbing.

"Aren't you a paid spy?" Silver Lips shouted.

"Yes! Yes!" Bucher sobbed.

"Aren't you going to tell us the instructions you passed to Law?"

"Yes! Yes!"

Silver Lips turned on Law and shouted, "What instructions he give you?"

Law, still dazed and shaken, said, "Pardon me?"

Silver Lips hit him in the jaw. "Pardon me! Pardon me!" he shouted as he punched him. Two guards moved in and hit him then, knocking him against the wall and beating him like a punching bag. Law crossed his arms and tried to protect himself, and a guard kneed him in the groin, doubling him over, nauseating him again. Then the guard dragged him back to the interrogation room.

Silver Lips demanded to know Law's escape plan. "I don't have any," Law mumbled. Silver Lips made him get on his knees again and a guard hit him several times in the side of the head, trying to knock him over. He couldn't, so he kicked Law in the stomach, driving the breath out of him and knocking him to the floor, writhing. Law curled up to protect himself and the guard kicked him in the thigh and rear, then dragged him back to the chair.

Silver Lips, his arms folded, said, "Escape plan."

Law, barely able to think, bowed his head in his hands and mumbled, "All right. Bucher made up the plan. Chicca and Schumacher planned it." He paused for breath and the guard hit him again.

"Hammond and Chicca were the scouts. Five more were in on it. We were going to sneak out the windows and capture the guards outside and steal a truck. I was to drive the truck. We were going to Panmunjom." Law looked up and saw that Silver Lips was leaning forward, listening intently. He was eating it up.

"You using crossword puzzles to pass message?" Silver Lips asked. "I don't know about that," Law said, and a guard hit him on the side of the head. "Yes," Law said. "We were passing the puzzles back and forth. They were messages on the plan." Silver Lips stepped back, apparently satisfied. It was after 6 P.M. Law had been beaten for five hours. He was told to sit in a corner of a room and write his confession, but he could hardly see and his mind was reeling. He wrote anything that came to mind in big, scrawling letters to fill space. The Koreans were impressed by quantity and Law covered fifty pages recounting his crimes. About 10 P.M. Odd Job came in and took his confession, glanced at it, and handed it back. "We know this," he said. "We want other serious crimes." He walked away and Law wearily went back to work, writing through the night. Whenever he stopped, a guard hit him. About 6 A.M. on December 13 a duty officer came by and took the confession and a guard brought Law some soup and a slice of bread, which he ate hungrily. It was his first meal in nearly twenty hours. Then he sat there until about 10 A.M., when Odd Job came back and said, "You are starting to become sincere."

Law said, "I've confessed to everything." But Odd Job wanted to know more about the CIA and CIC (Combat Information Center). Law wrote a description of the CIA based on the plot of a James Bond movie he had seen, then wrote several pages about the CIC, which he didn't know too much about. About 3 P.M. Odd Job came back and Law handed him 150 pages, but Odd Job didn't buy the story on the CIC. Law shrugged and said, "That's all I know." Odd Job made him get on his knees again and a guard began hitting him in the head with his fist. Law sagged, unfeeling and uncaring, and finally slumped to the floor. He was completely whipped.

He was dragged into the chair again, and Odd Job began lecturing him on repenting. While he was talking, Law heard someone cry out next door and recognized Chief Goldman's voice. After twenty minutes Odd Job tired of the lecture and allowed

Law to go to the head. As he was returning, his head bowed to his chest, he caught a glimpse of Harry Iredale hurtling through a door just ahead and into the hallway. Iredale was dragged back into the room as Law went past.

While Law was enduring his ordeal in Room No. 5, Tim Harris was sitting across the hall in Room No. 9, listening to the thumps and groans and turmoil around him. The noise was constant throughout the night, and Harris wondered when his turn would come. He didn't have long to wait. The Koreans had brought in a new group of young guards, and when one of them entered during the early-morning hours of December 13, Harris jumped from his chair and snapped to attention.

The guard walked straight toward him and hit him in the mouth with his fist. Harris ducked the blow partially, which infuriated the guard. He grabbed Harris by the throat, dragged him across the room, and knocked his head against the wall. Harris saw stars and gasped for breath. He thought the guard was going to choke him to death, but just then Fetch strode into the room and demanded to know what was going on.

The guard released his grip, and Harris sagged to the floor, gasping. The guard apparently told Fetch that Harris was trying to communicate with Bucher across the hall by tapping with a pencil because Fetch questioned Harris closely about Bucher, then sent the guard from the room. He told Harris to write his confession. About 5 A.M. the same guard came in, and when Harris jumped to attention the guard hit him in the face and began choking him again. Harris was sure the guard wanted to kill him, but again Fetch stepped into the room and sent the guard away, shaking his finger at him as he left. He told Harris to keep writing, and Harris was certain that Fetch was keeping watch on his room to see that he wasn't hurt too badly.

Hell Week started with the beatings of the men in Law's room and the terror quickly spread to the entire crew, with varying degrees of intensity. The Koreans concentrated on one or two rooms at a time, while the rest of the men sat rigidly in their chairs awaiting their turns, meanwhile being struck for the slightest movement from their uncomfortable positions.

In Room No. 6 on the third floor the situation had suddenly

become intolerable for the unpredictable Hammond. One after another, Strano, McClarren, Chicca, Duke, Crandell, Hammond, Rigby, and even Steve Woelk had been called to the doorway and punched, for no particular reason. Through the long hours Hammond had heard groans and cries from the other rooms as well and waited his turn to be beaten. He thought the talks in Panmunjom had fallen through, and now he couldn't see any end to their ordeal. On the first night of Hell Week he had been dragged from his bed because he had moved while sleeping. He was punched, then forced to stand rigidly beside his bed for what seemed like hours. Fear, fatigue, humiliation, and degradation led Hammond to a foolish act that even shocked the Koreans. He determined to commit suicide, hoping such an act would bring an end to the terror, or at least alert the world to the crew's plight if news of his death should leak out.

On the second night of Hell Week, Hammond secreted a small mirror in the palm of his hand and took it to the head with him, where he tried to break it on his knee. He only succeeded in making his knee sore. He wrapped it in a towel, laid it on a chair, and managed to break it in three pieces.

About 4 A.M. the guard took McClarren to the head, and in the guard's absence Hammond tried to cut his left wrist with a broken piece of the mirror. He could do no more than scratch the skin, so he began ripping and jabbing at the vein in his wrist, finally tearing a hole in it. It bled for several minutes, then stopped, and Hammond placed a jagged edge of mirror against the vein and rolled over on it.

The bleeding started again at a fast rate, and when Hammond felt his sheet becoming soaked he became frightened and tried to stop the bleeding with his thumb. It bled for nearly half an hour and was still bleeding when Hammond, weakened and exhausted, fell asleep, the wrist tucked under his body.

At 6 A.M. the guard told everyone to get up, and Hammond staggered to his feet with the others, still holding his wrist. His sheet was bloodsoaked, but the guard didn't notice at first, and Hammond began to make his bed. Then the guard saw the bloodstains on the sheet. He stared dumbly, plainly shocked, and grunted for Hammond to hold out his hands. His arms were caked with dried blood, and fresh blood continued to ooze through the cut in his wrist. The guard, shaking his head, took Hammond from the room and to the duty officer's desk. King Kong was on duty, and when he saw the bloodstained Hammond he knew immediately what he had tried to do. He stared at Hammond with a shocked expression on his face and threw up his arms.

"Hammondo, why? why?" he said. "Why you do this to us?"

Hammond didn't need further invitation. All the frustration of nearly eleven months poured out in a steady stream of invective and complaint while King Kong, for once, stood silently. Hammond raved for nearly fifteen minutes and shook his bloody fist at him, daring King Kong to shoot him.

Hammond said he was fed up with the beatings, and the next time someone laid a finger on him he was going to punch him back. Hammond had the advantage. The Koreans plainly didn't want anyone dead, and Hammond had proved his toughness beyond doubt since the start of the imprisonment. King Kong was shaken. When Hammond's tirade had run its course, King Kong asked meekly if he wanted to be taken to the doctor. Hammond said he didn't, and the guard took him to the head, where he washed off the blood.

Even The Bear was solicitous, but disappointed in Hammond. He cornered Hammond and said, "Hammondo, I am ashamed of you." Shaking his head, The Bear said, "I thought you good soldier. Thought you better man than this." Hammond said, "You touch me and you'll find out what kind of man I am." Hammond thought he had taken some of the fun out of The Bear's life.

Odd Job was waiting when Hammond was returned to his room and gave his a long lecture on his crime. "Because of you," Odd Job said, "your roommates will have to keep their heads bowed longer than the others." He asked Hammond if he had eaten breakfast that morning, and when Hammond said he had, Odd Job asked: "If you want to die, why you eat?" Hammond said he ate because he was hungry.

"If you do not become good guy," Odd Job warned, "we will put you in storage building by yourself."

The Koreans never touched Hammond again.

The other crewmen considered Hammond's success and

wondered whether they had not made a mistake during their long imprisonment. Perhaps they should have fought back with more determination instead of standing like human punching bags and taking it. No one had ever struck back at the Koreans. Instead, it had become a game to see how much one could take without flinching. There had never been much doubt in the men's minds that overt resistance to physical punishment could have resulted in death, or at least a severe beating, but they now wondered how far they could actually have pushed their captors. Hell Week was a bad time to find out, because the Koreans were in no mood to tolerate resistance, despite Hammond's success.

In Room No. 1 on the third floor, Hell Week started with The Bear peeping around the edge of the door. Bradley Crowe, aged twenty, of Island Pond, Vermont, saw him, and The Bear rushed into the room and kicked Crowe in the shins and chest. Baldridge, the veteran hospital corpsman and the senior man in the room, immediately protested the action to the general. Baldridge, who had not taken part in any previous resistance, stood his ground. "I am responsible for the men in my room. If they misbehave, it is my fault. Therefore, you should beat me instead." The general dismissed him. "Everyone is going to be punished," he said.

The men in Room No. 1 became victims of a peculiar circumstance at the beginning of Hell Week, when the doors to all the rooms were still closed. On the first day the door blew open, and Steve Ellis got up and closed it. The Bear rushed in immediately and hit Ellis in the forehead and kicked him in the shins while the others cowered in terror. Ellis kept saying, "I don't understand, I don't understand," while The Bear beat him about the forehead, raising huge knots.

The Bear had hardly left before the wind blew the door open again, and Kenneth Wadley, without thinking, got up and closed it. The Bear was back immediately, and Wadley said in fright, "Me no touchee door, wind do." The Bear smacked him across the face with his open hand and hit him on the forehead. The Bear had a special thing for Wadley and enjoyed tormenting him.

The crewmen in Room No. 1 decided they had had enough of the door and found out from the duty officer how to say "Wind

blew door open" in Korean. Thus, when the door swung open
again the next day, Lee Hayes was prepared when he went to
close it. The Bear came in immediately, and Hayes made his little
speech in Korean. The Bear ignored it and punched him in the
forehead. The Bear appeared especially infuriated with Hayes's
speech and chopped him in the throat with the edge of his hand.
While Hayes stood gasping for breath, The Bear kicked him, then
ordered him to stand at attention and remove his glasses. Hayes
pulled his glasses off, and The Bear, a wild look in his eyes,
knocked him across the bed. He was preparing to beat him some
more when Corporal Bob, a guard older than the others, came
into the room and told The Bear to leave. Bob's intervention
came too late for the slightly built Hayes, who staggered back to
his chair, his jaw broken.

Thus it went, in room after room, day and night. Their eyes
blackened, knots swelling on their faces, and their bodies aching
from the awkward position, the men sat in their rooms waiting
for the next punch, the next kick, not knowing and no longer
caring how long the torment would last. Some thought it was
the prelude to their trial and execution, and lost hope. The Bear
moved ceaselessly from room to room, administering punishment
with his fists, feet, and boards, usually expressionless but sometimes with a clear look of satisfaction on his face. Only Corporal
Bob and Fetch among the Koreans seemed to care. Once Fetch,
witnessing a beating being administered by Odd Job, turned away
mumbling, "Brutal, brutal."

Meanwhile, the confessions the crewmen had written began
to have their effect. The Koreans searched each room and had
remarkable success turning up the bits of paper, the pieces of
pencil, the carvings and writings the crewmen had hidden away
during the long months of detention.

Mike O'Bannon had hidden inside his cigarette lighter a North
Korean postage stamp, a small button with a Korean insignia on
it, and a little pill the Koreans dispensed for diarrhea, and something told him he should get rid of the material. When Hell
Week began, O'Bannon flushed the items down the toilet. Three
days later, Dracula, a junior officer, came and took O'Bannon to
an interrogation room.

He told Mike that he had not been sincere and had not con-fessed everything, and began to search him while O'Bannon protested his innocence. "I have confessed to everything. Where have I lied?" O'Bannon asked. "You know what," Dracula said. "I do not have to tell you. We have learned from other con-fessions you have not been sincere."

He searched the lining of O'Bannon's coat, and found a chap-stick, which he pulled apart and looked at, then pulled O'Bannon's lighter apart, bending it out of shape in the process. He found nothing incriminating and was very disappointed. When O'Ban-non returned to his room, he questioned his roommates about the lighter in an effort to find out who had told on him.

The crewmen didn't take the confessions seriously at first but soon discovered that they were being used by the Koreans to great effect in ferreting out the crew's little secrets. In addition, the Koreans wanted the crew to confess certain specific things, and in the course of Hell Week they forced the men to confess to eight different escape plans, most of them desperately made up out of whole cloth or from bits and pieces of relatively idle con-versation about possible escape methods the crew had indulged in over the long months.

Jimmy Layton was a special target, for some reason. Early in Hell Week, Possum took him aside and began talking to him in a confidential tone: "Layton, have you noticed that you have not been beaten?" Possum asked.

Layton said he hadn't noticed, because just a couple of days previously a guard had beaten him in the hall while he was going to the head, and had picked him up by his ears. "They're still sore," Layton said, rubbing them.

Possum was thoughtful, and then said, "That was a mistake. You should not have been beaten, because you have been sincere with us." Layton was puzzled, and Possum leaned over close to him and said, "We have only one question for you. Who is CIA agent?"

Layton was stunned. "Holy smokes," he blurted. "You took me for a patsy." He wondered what in his behavior made the Koreans think he would tell even if he knew. Possum then took a different tack.

"We have read your confession, but you have not told us what we want to know," he said. "There are six, maybe seven things we want to know."

When Layton looked puzzled and shrugged, Possum leaned forward and said, "Don't you want me to hint you?" Layton said, "By all means."

"Okay," Possum said, the confidential tone returning. "Number one, we want to know the escape plan. Number two, I will not hint you. You will have to figure it out." That was enough for Layton. He said he would figure out the rest.

Thursday and Friday the beatings and the cries continued, night and day. About 1 A.M. Saturday morning Fetch got Charlie Law and took him to Room No. 9 on the third floor and told him he could go to sleep. Law, thankful for the respite, fell into bed, having long since lost count of the number of hours since he had last been able to rest. Even then, he slept only lightly. His leg had stiffened and he could hardly walk to the room, and as he lay in bed his whole body ached and throbbed. He saw three other forms in beds nearby, and recognized Peppard, Layton, and Goldman. Peppard, his hand badly swollen from being hit repeatedly with a stick, groaned with pain most of the night and the others were restless, although any movement brought a shout and a kick from the guard.

The men were aroused at 6 A.M. as usual, and after they had made their beds and cleaned the room, breakfast was brought in. Then they had to sit rigidly in their chairs through the day and into the night, the monotony broken only by meals and the frequent kicks they received whenever they made the slightest movement. Law was shocked by the appearance of the others. Their faces were swollen and haggard, and their clothing was spotted with dried blood. They avoided looking at one another as much as possible.

On December 17, while the men of the *Pueblo* sat in their rooms, thoroughly terrorized and exhausted and expecting their torment to go on forever, events began to move rapidly elsewhere. The North Koreans and Americans were meeting at Panmunjom for the first time since October 31. The session lasted for more than four hours.

At the meeting General Woodward and General Pak worked out the details of an amazing document that would lead in a few days to the release of the *Pueblo* crew. While Jimmy Lee, a native-born Korean and a naturalized citizen of the United States, translated for General Woodward, General Pak wrote out the statement he wanted General Woodward to sign. It began:

To the Government of the Democratic People's Republic of Korea:

The Government of the United States of America, acknowledging the validity of the confessions of the crew of the USS *Pueblo* and of the documents of evidence produced by the representative of the government of the Democratic People's Republic of Korea to the effect that the ship, which was seized by the self-defense measures of the naval vessels of the Korean People's Army in the territorial waters . . .
Shoulders full responsibility . . .
. . . Gives firm assurance . . .
. . . Requests that the government of the Democratic People's Republic of Korea deal leniently . . .
These crewmen have confessed . . .

The document that General Woodward was to sign sounded remarkably like any one of a thousand confessions that the crewmen had composed and signed. There were two major differences. The end of the document read:

Simultaneously with the signing of the document, the undersigned acknowledges receipt of 82 former crewmembers of the *Pueblo* and one corpse.

Although he planned to sign it, General Woodward told his counterpart that the confession, written in its entirety by General Pak, was false and had no meaning; the United States would immediately repudiate it upon release of the crew. General Pak had no interest in what the United States would say after it signed the statement. He was much more interested in the table that would be used for the public meeting and the formal signing, after the details of the release had been worked out. He wanted the round table replaced with a square one, to show absolute equality. General Woodward couldn't have cared less.

The crewmen had no knowledge of these developments, of course, and sat in their rooms through the long day of December 17 listening to the sounds of men being beaten.

About noon on December 19 the beatings suddenly stopped. While the men wondered at the unaccustomed silence, they heard furniture being moved. The Koreans were putting desks and chairs in the alcove again, and shortly after lunch the men were taken to the alcove, where they were told that they would have to write one more confession, this one to include everything from the time of capture until the present. They were told they wouldn't get another chance, and Charlie Law, laboring through his confession, had the feeling that it was no joke and that he was writing for his life. It wasn't the first time the crewmen had been threatened, but after all that had just happened they believed the Koreans were serious. Law wrote fifty-three pages and went to bed about midnight. The light was still burning.

On Friday, December 20, all was quiet. Hell Week was over. The men ate in the mess hall as previously and were able to relax in their chairs. There was only isolated harassment, and during the afternoon duty officers went from room to room to check on injuries. The worst-beaten men were put in one room and the Korean doctor and Baldridge worked on them. The Koreans were concerned mostly with the black eyes and used hot wax, raw eggs, hot pads, and some kind of salve to get rid of the blackness and the many swellings and bruises. Nonetheless, the men were dismayed in the mess hall at the sight of others, unshaven, black and blue, and swollen.

The feeling was growing, however, that something was up. On December 21 the general called a mass meeting. He was in a good mood but still anxious to lecture the crew.

"It appears that everyone is sincere and repentant," he said once the crew had settled down in The Club.

"The United States is going to kneel down and admit its crimes.

"Since you have admitted your crimes as well, The Democratic People's Republic of Korea has decided to deal leniently with you."

"You are going home."

Even though they had suspected the truth, the men sat silently in disbelief. Finally there was a scattering of applause, then a murmuring arose in the room, hesitant and subdued.

One by one, the men were told to stand up. Each had to express his gratitude to the Koreans and repeat his repentance of his sins. The Koreans were consistent to the last.

The Koreans didn't say, but the crewmen were pretty certain they were going to leave the following day, and there was little sleep for them the night of December 21. It was still like a dream, but the men had to be awake to appreciate that after nearly eleven months to the day they were about to become free men again. Almost as important to them was the fact that the food improved as the hour of repatriation neared.

Charlie Law was helping to clean up the mess hall after dinner that night when Fetch came in. "Well, you going home soon," Fetch said, his hands in his pockets. "You see family. They be happy to see you."

Law said, "Yeah, Fetch, we're going to miss you."

Fetch turned away. "No, no, you just say that."

Law thought that the Americans were the only friends that Fetch had ever had.

On the night of Sunday, December 22, the haggard men of the *Pueblo* filed from their "home" and onto buses, which took them to the train station in Pyongyang. All the Korean junior officers who had been their custodians for so long, and their tormentors, accompanied them. The general was nowhere to be seen, but his final warning still rang in the crew's ears.

"Do not make signs as you cross the bridge. Do not look back."

While the train carrying the crew from Pyongyang moved slowly through the night to Kaesong, about eighty miles southeast of Pyongyang, a phone rang in the home of Robert Ayling in Staunton, Virginia. The caller was Winthrop G. Brown of the State Department. "You will be interested to know," Brown said, "that the release has been perfected. I congratulate you on your efforts."

On the train to Kaesong, Specs sat next to Chuck Ayling and said, "Did you know your father has been to Moscow and East

Berlin?" Ayling was surprised and said he didn't know. "He wanted to come to North Korea," Specs said, "but we wouldn't let him."

The crewmen, still marching as prisoners of the Democratic People's Republic of Korea, filed off the train in Kaesong under the watchful eyes of the junior officers, and onto buses. The windows were covered and the buses were cold. Don McClarren, huddled in his blue padded jacket, noted the eerie similarity between their arrival eleven months ago, and their departure.

As the buses bumped slowly over the road to the bridge that would lead them to freedom, several men began to sob, and even the obdurate Charlie Law felt emotion swelling in his throat. Not a religious man, Law was nonetheless groping for something that he remembered vaguely from his Sunday School days. The phrases kept slipping in and out of his mind and he kept blinking and trying to grasp and hold the words together in one piece.

Tim Harris, fighting back tears, thought about his wife. He had been away from her much longer than he had been with her in their short marriage, and the memory of her swirled in a golden fog in his mind.

Steve Woelk, his body aching from the long ride, wanted a shower and something to eat. But mostly he wanted to go home to Kansas.

Angelo Strano wanted a good cup of coffee, but mostly he wanted to shake the hand of a free American. He wondered what kind of reception they would get on the other side of the bridge.

Charlie Law's reverie was interrupted by someone who said, "Well, maybe we'll all get medals when we get back."

"No," Law said wearily, "you get medals for charging machine-gun nests. You don't get medals for this." Then he settled back into his seat, still seeking the elusive phrases as the buses began to slow down, their gears grinding. The crew had arrived at the bridge.

At Panmunjom, promptly at 9 A.M., General Woodward signed the apology that the North Koreans had waited eleven months for, then just as promptly read his repudiation of the document. General Pak ignored the repudiation but chattered angrily about what he called the "premature announcement" by the United States of the crew's release. While the crewmen sat silently in their cold buses no more than two hundred yards from freedom, Woodward and Pak argued the matter. The release had been timed for 11 A.M., but the negotiators finally agreed to make it 11:30 A.M., apparently as "punishment."

The men had been told the timing of the release, and as 11 A.M. came and went they began to look around nervously. Finally, at 11:30 A.M., the door of the bus carrying Commander Bucher opened and a junior officer called his name. Bucher, great circles under his eyes and his face gaunt and pale, limped to the front, and stepped down into the bitter air. A light snow was falling, and Bucher glanced at the gray, barren hills, then walked toward the bridge to freedom, barely twenty-five feet from the door of the bus and guarded at both ends by North Korean soldiers. Freedom began six feet past the end of the bridge.

Odd Job was waiting for Bucher at the bridge, his arm outstretched to restrain him. Someone called Bucher's name, and Odd Job raised his arm and grunted. As Bucher started across, loudspeakers began to play a recording and Bucher heard his own voice echoing hollowly behind him. "I am Commander Lloyd Bucher, captain of the USS *Pueblo* . . . who was captured while carrying out espionage activities. . . ."

One by one the men were called from their buses, the lowest ranking first, and brought to the bridge, where they were to follow at twenty-foot intervals.

North Korean guards stood along the low hills, rifles in their hands. "Do not look back . . . do not make signs . . . you will be shot."

Their heads down, their hands at their sides, the crewmen started across, but the Koreans still had not relinquished them.

" . . . the whole crew of my ship and particularly myself would be honored . . . our act was a criminal act . . . that we will be forgiven leniently . . ."

Charlie Law vaguely heard his name called and he walked to the front of the bus, as though in a dream. The phrases were coming back to him finally. As he stepped off the bus, a hand grabbed him and swung him around. He had started in the wrong direction, but once righted he walked to the bridge, paused and answered when his name was called, and then began walking slowly across.

The loudspeaker behind him blared a closing phrase: "I do humbly confess . . ."

But Charlie Law hardly noticed. The words tumbled through his mind and formed on his lips as the tears rolled down his cheeks.

"Yea, though I walk through the valley of the shadow of death . . . I will fear no evil . . . for Thou art with me."

Epilogue

THE UNITED STATES MOVED QUICKLY once the last member of the *Pueblo* crew, Lieutenant Edward R. Murphy, Jr., stepped across the line to freedom in South Korea. The men were flown to Ascom City, ten miles west of Seoul, for a brief stay in an Army hospital. From there they were flown to Midway Island and then to San Diego, where their families awaited them. The Navy had brought the families there for a Christmas reunion.

The crewmen received thorough medical treatment, and then began endless hours of interrogation as the United States attempted to find out what had really happened on that bitterly cold day in the Sea of Japan nearly a year before. Intelligence units were also anxious to determine as closely as possible just what had been surrendered to North Korea.

On Monday, January 20, 1969, a Navy court of inquiry convened at the Naval Amphibious Base in Coronado, California, adjacent to San Diego, to inquire into the circumstances of the seizure of the *Pueblo,* and the detention of its captain, Commander Lloyd M. Bucher, and crew.

The court of five admirals, presided over by Vice Admiral Harold G. Bowen, Jr., heard testimony for nearly two months, much of it in secret, from every member of the crew. All the admirals of the court had seen action off the port of Wonsan during the Korean War. Their questioning was sharp and to the point, and not always sympathetic. Commander Bucher had violated one of the basic tenets of Navy tradition: he had given up the ship. Among senior officers, it was an unforgivable sin regardless of the circumstances. Bucher had broken the code; he had surrendered without a fight. "We could excuse it," a senior officer said, "if he had fired just a couple of shots," and maybe put a little more blood on the decks.

On the third afternoon of the hearing, Captain William R. Newsome, counsel for the admirals of the court, advised Bucher that he was suspected of violating Naval Regulation 0730: "The Commanding Officer shall not permit his command to be searched by any person representing a foreign state nor permit any of the personnel under his command to be removed from the command so long as he has the power to resist."

Under attack, the crewmen for the most part closed ranks around Bucher and gave him their allegiance. They also closed ranks on themselves, and no man emerged as a failure. They didn't tell the court everything because, fortunately, the court didn't ask, and some of the lesser men escaped censure.

And, while the court droned on, life went on. Stuart Russell, Charlie Law, and Don McClarren got married.

After two months, the court ended its proceedings and retired to deliberate and deliver its findings. On May 6 the findings were made public. They were harsh.

The court recommended trial by court-martial for Bucher on five counts: permitting his ship to be searched while he had the power to resist; failing to take immediate and aggressive protective measures when his ship was attacked by North Korean forces; complying with orders of the North Korean forces to follow them into port; negligent failure to ensure, before departure for sea, that his officers and crew were properly organized, stationed, and trained for emergency destruction of classified material; and negligently failing to complete destruction of classified material aboard the *Pueblo* and permitting the material to fall into the hands of the North Koreans.

The court also recommended trial by court-martial for Lieutenant Stephen B. Harris for derelictions before and during the capture of the *Pueblo*, and a letter of admonition for Lieutenant Murphy for dereliction in failing to organize and lead the crew on to day of the seizure.

It recommended a letter of reprimand for Rear Admiral Frank L. Johnson, commander of naval forces in Japan, whose responsibility it was to ensure that the *Pueblo* was properly prepared and protected, and a letter of reprimand for Captain Everett B. Gladding, director of the Pacific Naval Security Group, for failing to ensure the readiness of the intelligence section aboard the *Pueblo*.

A letter of reprimand, the Navy's most severe nonjudicial censure, could affect an officer's chances for advancement. A letter of admonition is a warning.

But, on the day that the board's recommendations were released, Secretary of the Navy John B. Chafee overturned them. "They have suffered enough," he said of the *Pueblo* crew.

Chafee said he was making "no judgment regarding the guilt or innocence of any of the officers." He was deciding only that they shouldn't be punished or tried.

"The major factor," Chafee went on, "which led to the *Pueblo*'s lonely confrontation by bold and hostile forces was sudden collapse of a premise which had been assumed at every level of responsibility and upon which every other aspect of the mission had been based—freedom of the high seas.

"The consequences must, in fairness, be borne by all rather than by one or two individuals whom circumstances had placed closer to the crucial event."

If justice was served by Secretary Chafee, so was the Navy, which could now retire from the fray and leave further probings to the writers, the historians, and Congress.

On May 7 it was announced that Commander Bucher had been assigned to the Navy's graduate school at Monterey, California, for a year's study toward a master's degree in management. Of the seventy-nine remaining members of the Pueblo crew, seventy-eight were assigned shore duty. Signalman Wendell G. Leach was assigned to the destroyer *Haynsworth*.

Several, meanwhile, indicated that they were leaving the Navy, and Lieutenant Murphy resigned shortly after the board's announcement, saying his Navy career was ruined regardless of Chafee's decision.

The board of inquiry released a summary of praise it had for ten *Pueblo* crewmen. The summary lauded Lieutenant Frederick C. Schumacher for creating methods "to confuse and harass the Koreans"; Charlie Law, for displaying leadership "which was acclaimed by almost all of his fellow crewmen"; Sergeant Hammond, "as the salient example of resistance demonstrated by the members of the *Pueblo*'s crew"; Chief Goldman, for being "always insistent that naval discipline be maintained"; Don Bailey, Charles Sterling, and Gerald Hagenson, for "excellent leadership"; Sergeant Chicca and Earl Kisler, for "their resistence to the demands of the Koreans"; and Dale Rigby, for his "youthful compassion and devoted attention" in caring for three wounded roommates.

Even this didn't tell the whole story.

Nothing ever will.

The Crew of the Pueblo

Their rank is of the day of capture

Commander Lloyd M. Bucher,
  Pocatello, Idaho

Lieutenant Stephen R. Harris,
  Melrose, Massachusetts

Lieutenant Edward R. Murphy,
  San Diego, California

Lieutenant (j.g.) Carl F. Schumacher,
  St. Louis, Missouri

Ensign Timothy L. Harris,
  Jacksonville, Florida

Chief Warrant Officer Gene H.
  Lacy, *Seattle, Washington*

Steward's Mate Rogelio P. Abelon,
  Ambabaay, Philippines

Communications Technician Michael
  W. Alexander, *Richland, Washington*

Steward's Mate Rizalino L. Aluague,
  Subic City, Philippines

Communications Technician Wayne
  D. Anderson, *Waycross, Georgia*

Fireman Richard E. Arnold,
  Santa Rosa, California

Communications Technician Charles
  W. Ayling, *Staunton, Virgina*

Communications Technician Don E.
  Bailey, *Portland, Indiana*

Hospital Corpsman Herman P.
  Baldridge, *Carthage, Missouri*

Fireman Richard I. Bame,
  Maybee, Michigan

Fireman Peter M. Bandera,
  Carson City, Nevada

Communications Technician Michael
  T. Barrett, *Kalamazoo, Michigan*

Boatswain's Mate Ronald L. Berens,
  Russell, Kansas

Fireman Howard E. Bland,
  Leggett, California

Engineman Rushel J. Blansett,
  Orange, California

Communications Technician Ralph
  D. Bouden, *Nampa, Idaho*

Communications Technician Paul D.
  Brusnahan, *Trenton, N.J.*

Boatswain's Mate Willie C. Bussell,
  Hopkinsville, Kentucky

Yeoman Armando M. Canales,
  Fresno, California

Marine Sergeant Robert J. Chicca,
  Hyattsville, Maryland

Radioman Charles H. Crandell,
  El Reno, Oklahoma

Communications Technician Bradley
  R. Crowe, *Island Pond, Vermont*

Communications Technician Rodney
  H. Duke, *Fayette, Mississippi*

Seaman Stephen P. Ellis,
  Los Angeles, California

Communications Specialist Victor
  D. Escamilla, *Amarillo, Texas*

Storekeeper Policarpo P. Garcia,
  Point Mugu, California

Communications Technician Francis
  J. Ginther, *Pottsville, Pennsylvania*

Chief Engineman Monroe O.
  Goldman, *Lakewood, California*

Communications Technician John
  W. Grant, *Jay, Maine*

Electrician's Mate Gerald Hagensor
  Bremerton, Washington

Marine Sergeant Robert J. Hammond, *Claremont, New Hampshire*

Radioman Lee R. Hayes, *Columbus, Ohio*

Fireman John C. Higgins, Jr., *St. Joseph, Missouri*

Seaman Robert W. Hill, *Ellwood City, Tennessee*

Fireman Duane Hodges, *Cresswell, Oregon*

Communications Technician Jerry Karnes, *Havana, Arkansas*

Communications Technician James F. Kell, *Culver City, California*

Communications Technician Earl M. Kisler, *St. Louis, Missouri*

Boatswain's Mate Norbert J. Klepac, *San Diego, California*

Communications Technician Anthony A. Lamantia, *Toronto, Ohio*

Communications Technician Peter M. Langenberg, *Clayton, Missouri*

Quartermaster Charles B. Law, *Chehalis, Washington*

Communications Technician James D. Layton, *Binghamton, New York*

Signalman Wendell G. Leach, *Houston, Texas*

Commissaryman Harry Lewis, *Springfield Gardens, New York*

Photographer's Mate Lawrence W. Mack, *San Diego, California*

Seaman Roy J. Maggard, *Olivehurst, California*

Seaman Larry J. Marshall, *Austin, Indiana*

Fireman Thomas W. Massie, *Roscoe, Illinois*

Communications Technician Donald R. McClarren, *Johnstown, Pennsylvania*

Communications Technician Ralph McClintock, *Milton, Massachusetts*

Fireman John A. Mitchell, *Dixon, California*

Electronics Technician Clifford C. Nolte, *Menlo, Iowa*

Fireman Michael A. O'Bannon, *Beaverton, Oregon*

Communications Technician Donald R. Peppard, *Phoenix, Arizona*

Seaman Earl R. Phares, *Ontario, California*

Quartermaster Alvin H. Plucker, *Trenton, Nebraska*

Commissaryman Ralph E. Reed, *Perdix, Pennsylvania*

Seaman Dale E. Rigby, *Ogden, Utah*

Communications Technician David L. Ritter, *Union City, California*

Communications Technician Steven J. Robin, *Silver Spring, Maryland*

Seaman Richard J. Rogala, *Niles, Illinois*

Seaman Ramon Rosales, *El Paso, Texas*

Seaman Edward S. Russell, *Glendale, California*

Engineman William W. Scarborough, *Anderson, South Carolina*

Communications Technician James A. Shephard, *Williamstown, Massachusetts*

Communications Technician John A. Shilling, *Mantua, Ohio*

Seaman John R. Shingleton, *Atoka, Oklahoma*

Fireman Norman W. Spear, *Portland, Maine*

Communications Technician Charles R. Sterling, *Omaha, Nebraska*

Communications Technician Angelo S. Strano, *Hartford, Connecticut*

Fireman Larry E. Strickland,
Grand Rapids, Michigan

Gunner's Mate Kenneth R. Wadley,
Beaverton, Oregon

Fireman Steven E. Woelk,
Alta Vista, Kansas

Communications Technician Elton
A. Wood, *Spokane, Washington*

Engineman Darrel D. Wright,
Alma, West Virginia

Harry Iredale, III (Civilian),
Holmes, Pennsylvania

Dunnie Tuck (Civilian),
Richmond, Virginia

Index